THE IRISH THROUGH BRITISH EYES

THE IRISH THROUGH BRITISH EYES

Perceptions of Ireland in the Famine Era

Edward G. Lengel

PRAEGER

Westport, Connecticut
London

Library of Congress Cataloging-in-Publication Data

Lengel, Edward G.
   The Irish through British Eyes : Perceptions of Ireland in the Famine era / Edward G. Lengel.
      p.   cm.
   Includes bibliographical references and index.
   ISBN 0–275–97634–3 (alk. paper)
   1. Ireland—History—Famine, 1845–1852.   2. Ireland—Foreign public opinion, British—History—19th century.   3. Public opinion—Great Britain—History—19th century.   4. Famines—Public opinion—Great Britain.   5. Ireland—Relations—Great Britain.   6. Great Britain—Relations—Ireland.   7. Ireland—History—1837–1901.
I. Title.
DA950.7.L46   2002
941.5081—dc21   2001058049

British Library Cataloguing in Publication Data is available.

Library of Congress Catalog Card Number: 2001058049
ISBN: 0–275–97634–3

First published in 2002

Praeger Publishers, 88 Post Road West, Westport, CT 06881
An imprint of Greenwood Publishing Group, Inc.
www.praeger.com

Printed in the United States of America

The paper used in this book complies with the
Permanent Paper Standard issued by the National
Information Standards Organization (Z39.48–1984).

10 9 8 7 6 5 4 3 2 1

To Andrew Curtis Lengel

In Memory

Contents

Preface

This book had its origins in a seminar paper I prepared for a graduate British history class in the spring of 1994. At that time little of note had been published about the potato famine save Cecil Woodham-Smith's *The Great Hunger*, dating from 1962; an important book that was nevertheless deficient in its treatment of many aspects of the crisis. My original intention had been to examine the policies of the Peel and Russell governments in relation to the commonly held assumption that doctrinaire adherence to laissez-faire policies had hindered a prompt and meaningful response to the famine. Within a short time after the completion of my paper, however, a number of fine works had appeared on that very subject, and in the next few years book after book appeared in timely commemoration of the famine's 150th anniversary.

Every aspect of the famine, with one notable exception, seemed to be once more under the microscope. The exception was the question of how the English public perceived the crisis. In my view this was no small omission, since even a cursory reading of the primary source material indicates that the English view of the Irish and the famine was quite complex. Most historians, however, seemed to have been content with the simple assertion (based on an uncritical reading of L.P. Curtis and others) that the English considered the Irish inferior and molded their policies accordingly. It was in an attempt to bring out some of the subtleties of this difficult subject that I undertook to study English perceptions of the Irish in the mid-nineteenth century. It quickly became apparent that English opinion on Ireland was highly volatile rather than stable. It also appeared that the famine was a turning point not just in the generally recognized sense of physical suffering, but in its impact on how the English thought about Ireland, England, the empire and even the nature of humanity itself.

The decision to write on this subject led me into two treacherous minefields, for if Irish history is by definition a controversial, complex and sensitive subject, so is modern social/cultural history. I was relatively unfazed when some readers accused me of being pro-English while others condemned my supposed bias in favor of the Irish. More serious, in my view, has been the (thankfully rare) criticism that I dared to write about language without grounding myself in the theories of postmodernism or one of its variants or successors. Few recent works in social or cultural history lack a solid theoretical framework for their arguments, and who was I to presume to do otherwise?

A plea of unfamiliarity with theory would certainly earn me little credit among historians concerned with such things; it would also be false. On the other hand, to plead deliberate omission might be to present myself as that increasingly rare beast, the traditionalist social historian, and thus doom myself to academic oblivion. Yet omission is the plea I must make. I consider many of the newer modes of historical interpretation, such as gender history, to be of real value up to a point; some others I must confess to think completely pointless. In any case, attempting to force my subject into a theoretical framework would distract from my central arguments, and to no real purpose. My humble objective is to learn what the English thought of the Irish, why, and what it meant in terms of practical policy. I will leave presenting the theoretical implications to those scholars who are better suited to it by knowledge and inclination.

This is not to say, however, that I draw no broad conclusions from this study, even if they may appear prosaic in comparison to the lofty aspirations of the historical theorists. In my view, the study of English perceptions of the Irish during the period of the potato famine reveals some of the most unattractive facets of human nature. The potential power of the media to work evil is readily apparent in the thoroughly reprehensible conduct of the editors of the *London Times*, whose impact on hardening English attitudes, thus exacerbating the famine, has not been sufficiently recognized. Perhaps equally contemptible was the willingness of the English public, with some notable exceptions, to accept such hateful language despite their own initial instinct to react to the famine in a more charitable manner. The process by which the English first blinded themselves to the horrors of the famine and then blamed the victims is all the more troubling because it cannot be reduced to a simplistic charge of "racism," from which we might try to insulate ourselves. Failings like national pride, greed, and moral and intellectual cowardice played their part along with racial hatred, and all are alive and well in the twenty-first century.

It is difficult to know where to begin offering my acknowledgments for the completion of this study, as so many people have helped me along the way. Among the faculty of the Corcoran Department of History at the University of Virginia, thanks are due particularly to professors Nicholas Edsall and Lenard Berlanstein. Both of them provided intellectual inspiration and not a little understanding at those times when graduate student life proved a bit much for my nerves. The distinguished staff of the Papers of George Washington, including but not limited to W.W. Abbot, Philander Chase and Frank Grizzard, lent their support and encouragement to this project in its initial form as a dissertation and in its final form as a book. I would also like to thank the Thomas Jefferson Memorial Foundation at the University of Virginia for providing in the form of a Dumas Malone Traveling Fellowship the financial resources that made possible the completion of my dissertation, and ultimately of this book. I would also like to offer my particular thanks to Heather R. Staines and all of the editors at Greenwood Press who have contributed to the completion of this book.

I cannot adequately express my gratitude to my wife Laima and my parents Alan and Shelbia. The support and inspiration they gave buoyed me throughout my years in graduate school and subsequent career as a documentary editor. My brother Eric provided just the right combination of love and mockery, routing (I hope) any incipient smugness or self-importance. Finally, my children Mykolas, Laura and Tomas with their love and smiles kept the tempests of academic teapots, and the concerns of real life, in their proper perspective.

1

Race, Gender, Class and the Historiography of English Perceptions of the Irish

One of the most promising recent developments in historical scholarship has been the increasing attention devoted to the study of language. Although the overenthusiastic and even careless manner in which some historians have written about language understandably detracts from the quality of some otherwise interesting work, it remains an important avenue of historical inquiry that well merits further exploration. Research in this field has proven illuminating in a number of areas, particularly in the history of nationalism and imperialism, where it has significantly altered our perception of the ways in which people of different ethnic origins interact with and conceptualize each other.

It is now widely accepted that nationalism in its popular aspect necessitates the creation of an "other" against which the nation and its people define themselves. Much the same is true of imperialism, where a set of definitions are created to justify distinctions between the colonizer and the colonized. The process by which these definitions are formed, however, is difficult to pin down, for the identity and relative importance of the factors that contribute to the definition of what Homi Bhaba has dubbed "the other" are by no means agreed on.[1] Race, gender and class have each been identified as crucial elements in the process, but the sense of their relative importance varies from scholar to scholar.

The resolution of this issue is complicated by the inability, or unwillingness, of some cultural historians to place their subjects in a specific historical context. By looking at centuries rather than decades, and constructing generalized theses of power and oppression, these historians lose sight of the processes by which popular attitudes were formed in the heat of political contention. Instead, the language of nationalism and imperialism appears monolithic and unchanging, or perhaps the only constant element amid the turmoil of social and political change. The nuances and variety of popular attitudes that might have become apparent through close attention to the social and political stresses of one or two decades are thereby largely obscured.

More specific attention to particular, important periods of time would better reveal the dynamic of "discourse" or popular thought as a constantly evolving entity, dependent to a large extent on social, economic and political events and popular attitudes toward them. Careful study of a limited time period would enable the historian to better sympathize, if not empathize with his subjects, realizing the specific circumstances of their world and thereby better understanding why they thought and acted as they did. Trite as it might be to insist on this principle, its absence cripples some recent studies that take the present as a starting point for the definition of grand trends in the history of centuries.

Nowhere is the potential value of the study of language more evident than in the history of English relations with Ireland. This subject has been a popular testing ground for many new ideas about the development of popular thought. Recent work has revealed a great deal about the nature of English rule in Ireland, and informed some very beneficial new avenues of research.

Unfortunately, however, some of the pitfalls that plague cultural historians particularly abound in the history of English-Irish relations. Excessively broad studies, often basing their conclusions on modern definitions of certain words and concepts, have created a stereotyped picture of English rule comprehensible in light of current social and political problems but sometimes bearing little relation to historical reality. Most notable in this respect are the efforts beginning in the 1960s and 1970s of historians who explored how language that would now be considered racist determined both English perceptions of, and policy in, Ireland. These studies, usually covering periods of several centuries, sought to establish a grand trend in English perceptions and treatment of the Irish, a trend characterized by language that was racist in nature even when not based on a biological system of racial difference. In this view everything from the atrocities of Cromwell to the mismanagement of the potato famine could be laid at the door of a monolithic, substantially unchanging English belief in innate Irish inferiority. Some of these historians used the word "racist" to describe English attitudes toward the Irish in whatever period of history. Others admitted the occasional absence of racial terminology (as in the early nineteenth century) but insisted that the essence of the English view at such times was no different from that of any other period when the Celtic race was loudly condemned as innately perverse and inferior.

The two most important scholars to take this approach were L.P. Curtis, Jr. and R.N. Lebow, writing respectively in 1968 and 1976.[2] Curtis, in his extremely influential book *Anglo-Saxons and Celts: A Study of Anti-Irish Prejudice in Victorian England*, argues for a fundamental continuity in English perceptions of the Irish throughout the nineteenth century. The assumption that the "'native Irish' were alien in race and inferior in culture to the Anglo-Saxons" persisted, claims Curtis, as the principle on which English understanding of the Irish was based throughout the nineteenth century.[3] Thus the Irish almost always appeared in English minds as wildly temperamental and even schizophrenic, "childish, emotionally unstable, ignorant, indolent, superstitious, primitive or semi-civilized, dirty, vengeful, and violent." In other words, they were moral and physical opposites of the Saxon English.[4]

Curtis admits that it was not until the 1860s that the English based their explanation of Irish difference on arguments from science and biology, but argues that this was only one phase in an essentially unchanging conviction of innate Irish inferiority dating back to the sixteenth century.[5] English attitudes always involved varying elements of religion, class, and race, Curtis claims, but the result in terms of contempt for the Irish people was the same, and the predominance of biological arguments for Irish inferiority after 1860 did not actually involve any significant change in overall attitude.[6]

Lebow, in his book *White Britain and Black Ireland*, devotes much attention to British perceptions of the Irish in the first half of the century. Lebow describes in fair detail the complexities of the liberal view and its emphasis on the moral and economic reform of the Irish.[7] He also recognizes and traces to some extent the emergence of a more avowedly racist view of the Irish that began to take hold on the English imagination in the middle of the century. He argues, however, that the same prejudices and stereotypes of Irish character underlay both philosophies, and that in essence these were the same that had informed British opinion for centuries:

Anti-Irish sentiment was widespread among almost all segments of the British population [writes Lebow] . . . widespread and virulent expressions of anti-Irish prejudice predate the industrial revolution. They had been part of the British scene for centuries. The only novelty in Victorian times was the fact that the prejudice was increasingly articulated in the terminology of racial differentiation. Racist expressions were merely the age-old anti-Irish prejudice couched in the jargon of the day. In this author's opinion the Victorian attitude was in no way qualitatively distinct from the derision and fear of the Irish which preceded it.[8]

Although not asserting that biological arguments of racial difference lay behind English policies in Ireland throughout history, Lebow nevertheless claims that popular stereotypes and a belief in innate Irish inferiority did not fundamentally change over time. Liberal and racist interpretations of the Irish question therefore amounted to substantially the same attitudes being expressed in different terminology, and the results for the Irish, he implies, were much the same.

This school of historical thought has had a profound effect on the study of the history of English-Irish relations. In the recent avalanche of new literature on the history of the potato famine of 1846–1852, for example, the idea of English racism is dominant. The result has been a tendency to generalize about the nature of English policy in Ireland throughout history. The English, most scholars seem to conclude, allowed the Irish to starve (or, in some extreme arguments, engineered their starvation) out of a persistent, historic conviction in Irish inferiority. The famine therefore appears as an entirely characteristic and even unexceptional episode in the history of English perceptions of the Irish. Conflicts and variations in the English view of Ireland are treated as aberrations rather than evidence of profound changes in thought.

If Curtis and Lebow are right, however, it is difficult to understand why, in the mid-nineteenth century, English liberals and racialists (the latter defining Irish difference in racial terminology) should have disagreed as bitterly over Ireland as they did. If their views were in fact fundamentally similar, Ireland would never have become the divisive issue in England that it became and remained for decades to come. In fact, Curtis and Lebow profoundly underestimate the significance of the changing English perceptions of Ireland in the nineteenth century, missing the very important distinctions between, for example, the attitudes of Lord John Russell and the editors of the *Times*. These attitudes were not only substantively distinct in nature, but had important consequences in the formulation of English policy toward Ireland. An English aristocrat and a middle-class industrialist in the 1840s or 1850s might agree that the Irish were lazy, but they would violently disagree about why it was so, and the impact of the ascendancy of one or the other theory on English policies in Ireland could be profound indeed.[9]

Other historians have taken a different angle on the subject, though generally arriving at much the same conclusions as Curtis and Lebow. While not denying the importance of historical English racism, these more recent scholars attribute it to a tendency of the human mind to view the world in binary, or gendered, terms. In this line of reasoning the English were imperialists because they were racists, but they were racists because their thinking was gendered.[10] Evidence for this, in the form of sexual terminology in English descriptions of the Irish, is not lacking. The tendency of both English and Irish writers to attribute "feminine" characteristics to the Irish persists throughout the nineteenth century, as does the assumption of English "masculinity." The implications of the use of this sort of language changed markedly, however, in the course of two decades between 1840 and 1860. In the prefamine years, gendered language appeared in the form of a rhetoric of marriage that justified assimilation and complementarity. After the famine, it was more often a means of enforcing separation and a more overtly colonial relationship between the two islands.

The assumption that race is—like gender—a binary category is itself problematical. The language of race was used by the English to describe a wide scale of difference, from Asians and Africans to Spaniards, French, Irish and English. Perceptions of the degree of superiority of one race over another and the permeability of boundaries between races could change markedly in a short period of time. The differences between the English and the Irish were in the 1840s supposed to be far fewer, and much easier to overcome, than those separating English and Africans. In the 1860s, by contrast, the Irish were considered not only very different but were more strictly separated from the English. Racial difference did not always entail polarity.

As the period 1840–1860 shows, race and gender were shifting categories of thought. There was no "nineteenth-century English view of the Irish race," nor was there any "nineteenth-century English means of conceptualizing Ireland through gender"; each depended on the political and social priorities of particular years or decades. As this indicates, cause and effect where race and gender are concerned are by no means straightforward. English views of race and gender did not themselves determine how the English thought about the Irish. These categories did, however, provide a vocabulary for the expression of opinions that depended on social, economic and political circumstances.

Where does class fit into all of this? For some historians, class was *the* defining element in English perceptions of the Irish.[11] These scholars argue that the English attitude toward the Irish was not substantially different from English perceptions of their own working poor. Methods for reforming the one were, therefore, supposedly seen as equally efficacious in uplifting the other. There is undoubtedly some truth in this concept, just as there is in some of the arguments about the significance of race and gender. Evidence for this may be found in the period 1840–1860, but only up to a point. In the first half of the 1840s, it is true, English plans for reforming the Irish were similar (although not identical) to those held in relation to the English poor. As we shall see, however, the famine brought a reevaluation of the principles of political economy, but only as they related to the Irish, and not the English poor. The two were demonstrably not the same in the English mind-set.

Race, gender and class are each discernable in English perceptions of the Irish, but none can be said to have been the element that determined the course of popular thought. Anne McClintock similarly argues that it would be incorrect to privilege "one category over the others as the organizing trope."[12] Each category, she notes correctly, underwent shifts in definition over time. At the same time, race, gender and class were not distinct modes of thought, but interacted with and influenced each other.[13]

THE IMPERIAL CONTEXT

Many of these issues relate also to the role of Ireland as a part of the British empire. This was not as clear-cut as some have made it out to be. Next to India, in the 1840s Ireland was believed to be the most important imperial possession. Unlike India, however, Ireland was also considered before the famine to be an integral, though estranged, member of the British family of nations. As spouse or "sister island," Ireland's relationship with England was much closer than India's could ever be. The full realization of Ireland's integration into the family was the goal of liberal legislation.[14]

This view of Ireland's place persisted until the famine forced theoreticians to face the fact that the civilizing mission there had failed. As in India after the Sepoy mutiny, the evident failure of the Whig-utilitarian model of empire did not cause most Englishmen to seriously question whether the empire as it stood should be retained or was morally justifiable. The guilt for the failure of the old ideals was laid at the door of the colonized rather than the colonizers, and the theories of empire were modified to accommodate the revelation of native perversity. In the process, Ireland was moved much more clearly into the role of a colony, while its status as a member of the British family was downplayed.

These parallels between the Irish and Indian experiences of imperial rule have led many historians to generalize further and assume that for all intents and purposes the Irish were treated and indeed perceived by the English as no different from Africans or Asians. This interpretation is aided by the simplistic understanding of English attitudes discussed above. Few scholars have been willing to address this problem of the imperial role of Ireland directly,[15] and while there is no space here for a comparative study of the African, Asian and Irish experiences of English colonial rule, some of the points raised by this book may contribute to a better understanding of the issue. In any event, it is clear that the English were much more willing to perceive the Irish as being of a type with non-European peoples after the famine than they had been before, when the Whig-utilitarian model of empire still held sway.

The language of imperialism as it relates to perceptions of native peoples has been the subject of a substantial amount of scholarly attention. One of the most significant works in this field is Edward Said's *Culture and Imperialism*, which deserves consideration here for the points it makes on the formation of imperial language and culture. Briefly stated, Said's argument is that imperial relationships are far more complex than a clash of opposites. Instead, imperialism is a process that involves a great deal of interaction between the cultures of the ruling and subject peoples. Even so, the ruling people will always attempt to deny this interaction and construct an image of the subject people as something immutably separate, the "other."

The English perception of Ireland since the twelfth century, which Said sees as representative of imperial attitudes in general, boils down in his view to the assumption that "they are inferior, we are superior."[16] He argues further that one "centrally important truth needs constantly to be insisted upon. The one relationship that does not change is the hierarchical one between the metropole and overseas generally, between European-Western-white-Christian-male and those peoples who geographically and morally inhabit the realm beyond Europe (Africa, Asia, plus Ireland and Australia in the British case)." He repeatedly assumes that creation of the "other" involves in all cases an effort to create a strict division between colonizer and colonized. Thus, in his view, the colonizer always attempts to create an absolute dichotomy of superior/inferior, strong/weak, intelligent/foolish, male/female and so on, between ruler and subject. The rise of ethnography and racialism, in Said's view, leads to a "codification of difference" but does not change the essentially hierarchical nature of the imperial relationship.[17] Even in liberal imperial discourse, he claims, the native "figures as someone whose natural depravity and loose character necessitate a European overlord."[18] As he argues in the Irish case:

Irish people can never be English any more than Cambodians or Algerians can be French. This it seems to me was always the case in every colonial relationship, because it is the first principle that a clear-cut and absolute hierarchical distinction should remain constant between ruler and ruled, whether or not the latter is white.[19]

The relevance of Said's arguments to the broader field of imperial history cannot be addressed here. The applicability of many of his assumptions to the Irish example is, however, problematic. The evidence does bear out Said's central assertion that a hierarchical relationship between the two islands was fundamental whatever theories may have been used to justify it. His placement of Ireland in a fully imperial context, however, is for the 1840s difficult to sustain. In addition, the rhetoric of marriage used to describe the English-Irish relationship in the years before the famine did not involve a rigid distinction between colonizer and colonized, nor did it involve denial of compatibility and even the potential admixture of peoples. Imperial rule was not regarded simply as the rule of the strong over the weak or the masculine over the feminine, but as a partnership of different natures. Consummation of the marriage did not erase distinction, but did involve a sharing of qualities toward the goal of making each partner whole. Said's generalizations are correct for Ireland in two major respects: that the hierarchy of England as ruler and Ireland as ruled would always be maintained, and that the Irish could never be believed capable of becoming the same as the English. At the same time, however, before the famine and to a limited extent after it, Ireland did not appear in English eyes as an incompatible inferior and polar opposite of the English.

Historically, Said sees little change in the image of Ireland in English thought. From the twelfth century, he argues, the Irish were seen as a "barbarian and degenerate race," while "since Spenser's 1596 tract on Ireland, a whole tradition of British and European thought has considered the Irish to be a separate and inferior race, usually unregenerately barbarian, often delinquent and primitive."[20] He is correct in the sense that the debate over the question of whether the Irish could be redeemed persisted on fairly constant terms over the hundreds of years following the conquest. The arguments by which differing points of view on Ireland were advanced changed considerably, however, as did the degree to which either attitude was accepted by educated English opinion.

Andrew Hadfield and John McVeagh's survey of English writings on Ireland demonstrates the extent to which imperial discourse did and did not change. Ample evidence exists to illustrate the tenacity over the centuries of a strand in English thought that portrayed the Irish as bestial, inferior and even subhuman. Giraldus Cambrensis, writing in 1189, contributed to this attitude, as did Edmund Spenser in 1599.[21] Others, such as Sir John Davies in 1612, saw much hope for improvement in Ireland and blamed the country's troubles on social and economic causes rather than any innate perversity of her people.[22] Some writers went so far as to openly express the hope that the "Irish will turn English."[23]

Although there is no space here to trace the various trends in English thought on Ireland since the twelfth century, it is worth noting that the debate over Irish improvability was not unique to the nineteenth century, but was present from the time of the conquest. The means by which the "improvers" hoped to redeem the Irish did change, however. Whereas pre-eighteenth century writers were much more likely to stress religious reformation as the primary means of improvement, religion played very little part in the arguments of improvers in the 1840s. The degree to which the improvers' arguments were popularly accepted varied widely, and it is worth emphasizing that the popular rejection of Whig ideals concerning Ireland in the 1850s was nothing new in the long-term view of English-Irish relations.

THE GREAT FAMINE

The absence of a suitable explanatory schema for English treatment of Ireland also appears in the failure of scholars to adequately explain the reasons for the English government's poor handling of the potato famine of 1846–1852. Traditionally, historians have argued that the apparent callousness of Lord John Russell's Whig government in refusing to countenance massive government aid to prevent starvation was a product of dogmatic adherence to laissez-faire economic principles. Recent scholarship by Boyd Hilton, Peter Mandler, Peter Gray and others has rightfully challenged the traditional interpretation by demonstrating the extent to which the Whig government was critical of laissez-faire attitudes and willing to transgress them.

Unfortunately the destruction (despite the continuing resistance of some historians) of the arguments for the laissez-faire explanation for government policy has done little more than leave a vacuum in its place. Peter Mandler hints that the Whig government was held hostage to "ethnic and national prejudice" that viewed the Irish as inferior and their suffering as a just punishment from God.[24] Boyd Hilton and Peter Gray expand on this, suggesting that religious evangelicalism was behind the insistence of some officials that extensive efforts to alleviate suffering from the famine would deny the benefits that the suffering could bring through atonement.[25] These arguments contain elements of truth but do not fully explain English attitudes.

To an extent, these historians fall into the trap of pointing to prejudice without examining the nature of it. Whig officials were constrained by popular opinion, but only to a limited degree, and not because popular attitudes were based on prejudice while those of the ministers were not. The absence of any extensive survey of public discourse on Ireland has hindered scholarship in this respect. The widespread assumption that English public opinion on Ireland was almost invariably racist has led in some works to the creation of a false dichotomy between Whig policy and public opinion that did not in fact exist. Government policy from 1841 to 1852 was usually in line with popular discourse on Ireland, but the nature of this discourse was neither racist in the commonly understood sense of the term, nor dominated by the ideals of evangelical Protestantism.

THE "DAMNABLE QUESTION"

The "condition of Ireland question" was a matter of heated public debate in Britain in the years before, during and after the famine. Daniel O'Connell's Repeal movement, the potato famine, and Irish emigration to England and Scotland caused widespread consternation and curiosity among the British as to the reasons for Irish poverty and the nature of the Irish people. Official thought on these issues thus formed in the context of a complex and emotional public discourse.

Before the famine, mainstream middle-class perceptions of the Irish rejected race in its biological sense as a term of analysis. Observers and theorists, encouraged by the classical liberal belief in the capacity of all men for improvement, insisted that English and Irish were naturally equal if not identical in character. Irish backwardness was assumed to be the product of economic circumstances fostered by the ethnic and religious discrimination practiced by the Anglo-Irish ascendancy and the English government. This fashionably "progressive" view dominated thought among both Whigs and Peelites, although a minority, including Tory protectionists like Lord George Bentinck, were more inclined to defend the Anglo-Irish establishment and advocate a paternalistic system for relieving Irish distress.

The mainstream "progressive" view itself aimed to further justify and strengthen British rule in Ireland. Irish moral improvement was possible, the argument went, but only after generations of tutorship under English law and the English middle class. The object at hand was therefore to enforce a uniform system of law throughout the British Isles and to encourage English and Scottish entrepreneurs to settle temporarily in Ireland, hiring and improving Irish laborers. The potential for Irish improvement was affirmed, but was held to be possible only in union with Great Britain.

The civilizing mission was, however, inadequate as a justification for union. For one thing, it begged the question of what was in it for the English. For another, it failed to address the issue of what would happen once the expressed purpose of union, namely Irish civilization, was achieved. To argue that the Irish would simply never be able to take care of themselves and must always require English guidance, would appear to negate the purported goal of union, to civilize the Irish to European standards and teach them to care for themselves. The idea of the civilizing mission was thus supplemented by the idea of English-Irish union as marriage, by which, as we shall see, union became a natural, symbiotic partnership and an end in itself.

The idea of union as marriage denied the possibility that the Irish might one day become so fully improved as to wish to exist independently. The civilizing mission retained its goal of moral uplift, education and the eventual realization of natural equality through social and legal reform. To this was added the hope that civilization would lead the Irish to realize what were assumed to be their innately feminine characteristics. Through patience and kindness, not coercion, the English could encourage the development in the Irish of their innate virtues of creativity, tenderness, sensitivity, chastity, submissiveness and predilection for poetry and music. The Irish partner would thus complement English strength, thrift and levelheadedness, and to some extent make up for the English lack of feminine qualities. The assertion that the union was natural did not preclude Irish consent, which it was assumed would be forthcoming once the advantages of the bond were made plain.

The private papers and public sayings of Whig leaders are very much in accord with middle class attitudes. Ministers rejected race as a term of analysis and indicated their hopes of improving the Irish people under a benevolent and noncoercive English regime and English law, with the ultimate goal of strengthening the Anglo-Irish marital union. Whig economists and officials hailed Irish economic potential and encouraged English investment. This faith in English law and the English middle class as a means of educating (or domesticating) the Irish was central to the reaction of the Whigs when faced with the potato famine. Thus the government emphasized the need for the mercantile middle class to take matters in hand, utilizing English law in the form of the Poor Law and their own natural thrift and sobriety to help the Irish through the crisis. It was hoped that in the long run this would inspire the Irish to gratefully accept the English middle class as their natural teachers and rulers. Russell also hoped that a measure of government intervention to supply food to the Irish would endear English rule to Irish hearts. In this, however, he collided with an emerging new strand in British public opinion that rejected what had until then been the prevalent assumptions about the nature of the Irish people.

The primary purpose of rhetoric and theory was to justify the political priority of maintaining the union. When the events of 1845–1852 belied the idea of the civilizing mission and a happy marriage, political priorities did not change; the union was still to be maintained at all costs. Theories, however, had to and did change, and very rapidly. As the famine progressed, Irish starvation and poverty demonstrated the failure of English rule to civilize, while the Young Ireland rebellion of 1848 appeared to leave idealistic notions of a happy marriage in ruins. Public opinion therefore began to adopt the stridently held conviction of what had until then been a small minority of scientists and intellectuals, that the Irish were not only immutably different but also racially inferior, and should be treated as such.

Many protectionist Tories and English aristocrats who owned land in Ireland had long held the belief that Ireland was an entirely distinct nation, with a people utterly different from the English. Though admitting that the Irish had some good qualities (the same feminine traits admired by the Whigs), they insisted that the Irish were also a naturally rebellious, unintelligent and dirty people who stood no chance of moral improvement. English law and English liberties were unsuited to such a people; instead, they needed to be ruled by a combination of coercion and paternalistic benevolence. The proper goal of the government, therefore, was not to further integrate the Anglo-Irish "marriage," but to foster a stronger English military, bureaucratic and aristocratic presence in Ireland.

Although the influence of those who held this view of the Irish was small in the years before 1846, during the famine years they found a number of important allies with whom they sought to redefine popular thought on Ireland. Frustrated by the apparent failure of English law, middle-class settlement and famine relief to work a noticeable improvement in the Irish character, and stung by the "ingratitude" supposedly demonstrated by the 1848 rebellion, a few ethnologists, newspapers such as the *Times* of London, and others joined the Tories in arguing that there was something wrong with the Irish after all. The Scottish ethnologist Robert Knox, writing in the *Medical Times* in the early 1840s, was the first of many scientists and academics to argue that the Celts were a genetically inferior race that needed to be treated accordingly. The private papers of John Thadeus Delane, editor of the *Times*, reveal how this powerful organ grasped Knox's ideas wholeheartedly and, especially beginning in the famine years, preached the gospel of innate Irish inferiority. Although the *Times*, Knox and the Tories still represented only a minority opinion by 1850, they were loud enough to frighten the Whigs into accepting their prescriptions of more coercion and less British "charity" for the Irish. Thus Russell had to abandon his plans to spend "English money" on Ireland, privately bemoaning the anti-Irish prejudice that he believed to be prevalent among the British public.

Liberals and racialists carried on a running battle through the 1850s over the question of the Irish race. Liberals saw the growth of middle class tourism in Ireland during the 1850s as a new means for perfecting the marriage of the

two countries. Racialists, however, continued to insist on Irish incompatibility, and supported a series of measures restricting Irish emigration to Britain.
Protestant evangelicals, who saw the famine as a blow to Irish Catholic pres-
tige, thought they saw an opportunity to effect a final reformation of Ireland,
and launched an aggressive campaign of proselytization in both Britain and
Ireland. British workers, faced with postfamine Irish immigration and an apparent threat of competition for jobs, reacted violently at times, but frightened
their social superiors further by showing signs of imitating Irish rebelliousness
and cooperating with them in class warfare. Finally, Irish nationalists entered
the fray by violently condemning the smug assumptions of the liberals and
agreeing with the racialists that the Irish were racially distinct, but also racially
superior to the "mongrelized" Anglo-Saxons. At the same time, however, they
embraced English notions of the feminine nature of the Celt, insisting that it
was just these values that made them "truly Irish."

METHODOLOGY AND THEORY

The purpose of this book is to contribute to a more comprehensive, detailed
knowledge of English perceptions of the Irish in the critical middle years of the
nineteenth century. This knowledge will hopefully help to explain some of the
most troublesome aspects of English policy in Ireland during this period. In
addition, it should illuminate certain points of mid-nineteenth century liberal
thought relating to the nature and ultimate purpose of humanity. More
broadly, I hope to challenge some commonly held assumptions concerning the
history of prejudice and racism, and suggest a more critical approach to this
central problem in the history of human relations.

The methodology of this book is simply put. My technique is to survey, as
comprehensively as possible, printed material on Irish subjects published in
England or Scotland from 1840 to 1860. The material includes fictional literature, political and economic tracts, travel accounts, historical and "scientific"
monographs and periodical literature. One of the most intriguing aspects of
my research has been the sheer volume of source material. This is so not only
for the famine years, for which source material may be expected to be prolific,
but also for the years 1841–1845 and 1852–1860. For the whole of these two
decades, Ireland bordered on being a preoccupation for the English, even when
there were apparently no outstanding events to attract attention.

The questions on this subject that interested English writers quite naturally
preoccupied the Irish. The quantity of literature written on the "condition of
Ireland question" by Irish authors in the 1840s and 1850s is enormous.[26] Some
of this material is discussed in the course of this book, particularly that pro-

duced by Anglo-Irish writers. Said's notion of popular perceptions as "contra-puntal ensembles," if accepted, certainly necessitates an approach to popular literature that is not one-sided. Limitations of time and space, however, make it impossible to adequately explore Irish perceptions here, and this potentially fruitful avenue of inquiry must be left for future research.

Another major source has been the unpublished papers of British politicians and ministers. The amount of material relating to Ireland here is also very great. Attention to this source is natural given that one of the purposes of this study is to relate public opinion to official policy in early Victorian England. One weakness of many purely cultural or political historical studies is their ten-dency to consider their source material in near isolation, by either wholly aban-doning or clinging to traditional source material, as the case may be. The structure of this book, in which chapters on public opinion and official policy alternate until 1852, reflects my desire to achieve some sort of synthesis be-tween political and cultural history.

The exception to this is the final chapter on the period from 1852 to 1860, which focuses almost entirely on cultural issues. My decision to do so was purely pragmatic. To end the book with the subsiding of the famine and the downfall of Lord John Russell's government in 1852 would be to neglect one of the central points of my thesis: that racialism became in the decade after the famine a dominant factor in English thought on Ireland. At the same time, however, to add another chapter on the politics of 1852–1860 would be diffi-cult, given the complexities of coalition politics and the legislative inertia of the Palmerston years. I have therefore limited my discussion of official policy to the legislation enacted locally and nationally relative to Irish immigration, which was in any case the most pressing Irish concern for the British govern-ment in those years.

Another point is in order about my use of terminology. Historians too often use the word "race" to denote impermeable boundaries and strictly graded scales of inferior and superior. I prefer when using the word to specify whether it was used in the sense of a loosely or firmly defined category. At the same time, I use the word "racialist" to denote a set of opinions that tended to see race as an immutable category that was a primary element in the formation of national characteristics. Finally, the term "public opinion" is used in this study to de-scribe the attitudes of the educated, or roughly middle- and upper-class, Eng-lish population. While I have not avoided the subject of working-class English opinion, I have admittedly not treated it as fully as it merits. It is impossible, however, to undertake further research on this subject at this time without cre-ating a more bloated and unwieldy book than this one is already.

Finally, I do not presume to present here a work that is informed by a specific theory of the structure, dynamics and function of language. While a refusal to engage with many of the currently popular theories on language and the "creation" of reality might seem atavistic to some, in my view it is only common sense. The enthusiasm of some modern scholars who seek to emphasize the importance of language by boasting of "the absence of a stable, empirical reality"[27] results in a perspective that inevitably becomes dated, and seems to me neither useful nor very compelling. Although some historians write as if the precise role and meaning of language in human society were commonly understood, even specialists have yet to reach anything approaching consensus on the subject.

I have instead chosen to approach my subject with the tentative understanding that language is both a means of explaining "what is really out there" and a method by which people choose what of that reality they will see. Reality is itself created only in the sense that opinions help to determine the ways in which people manipulate their environment and each other. The galling circumstances of Irish life in the mid-nineteenth century were thus in part the product of English misrule. The English misinterpreted the causes of these realities, and instead of justly criticizing themselves, blamed the Irish, adopted a more backward policy toward them, and reinforced the wretchedness of the Irish people. Yet another vicious circle was, therefore, added to the sad story of English rule in Ireland.

NOTES

1. Homi Bhaba, "The Other Question," *Screen* 24, 6 (1983), 18–36.
2. They had many imitators, such as Liz Curtis, *Nothing but the Same Old Story: the Roots of Anti-Irish Racism* (London: Information on Ireland, 1984), and David Cairns and Shaun Richards, *Writing Ireland: Colonialism, Nationalism and Culture* (Manchester: Manchester University Press, 1988). In the latter work the authors, inspired by the contemplation of luminaries such as Michel Foucault and Hayden White, attempt (unsuccessfully in my view) to explain the historical problem of English-Irish relations.
3. L.P. Curtis, Jr., *Anglo-Saxons and Celts: A Study of Anti-Irish Prejudice in Victorian England* (Bridgeport, CT: Conference of British Studies, 1968), 5.
4. Ibid., 53.
5. Ibid., 18.
6. Ibid., 19.
7. Richard Ned Lebow, *White Britain and Black Ireland: The Influence of Stereotypes on Colonial Policy* (Philadelphia: Institute for the Study of Human Issues, 1976), 30–32.

8. Ibid., 15.

9. Sheridan Gilley is one of the few historians to seriously challenge the arguments of Curtis and Lebow. They were, Gilley claimed, unduly inclined to see the Irish question in light of the experiences of blacks in the United States. In Gilley's view no comparison between the two is legitimate, since the English generally acknowledged the Irish as a European people not easily distinguishable as a race apart. Instead, Gilley contends that a "mixed stereotype" operated where English perceptions of the Irish were concerned. The stereotypical Irishman was by this understanding a mixture of good and bad points, with the relative emphasis on one or the other depending on the English mood. Thus one writer might represent Paddy as both indolent and industrious, stupid and bright, violent and peaceful. More generally, in times of crisis the English would be more likely to express harsh opinions of the Irish, while in times of relative tranquility opinion tended to be more understanding and tolerant. Sheridan Gilley, "English Attitudes to the Irish in England, 1780–1900," in Colin Holmes, ed., *Immigrants and Minorities in British Society* (London: George Allen & Unwin, 1978), 89–90.

10. See especially Thomas A. Boylan and Timothy P. Foley, *Political Economy and Colonial Ireland: the Propagation and Ideological Function of Economic Discourse in the Nineteenth Century* (London: Routledge, 1992); see also Cairns and Richards, *Writing Ireland*, ch. 3, "An Essentially Feminine Race" (Manchester: Manchester University Press, 1988). Elements of this argument appear elsewhere, as in John P. Harrington, ed., *The English Traveller in Ireland: Accounts of Ireland and the Irish through Five Centuries* (Dublin: Wolfhound Press, 1991), 265.

11. Sheridan Gilley and R.F. Foster are the most notable advocates of this concept.

12. Anne McClintock, *Imperial Leather: Race, Gender and Sexuality in the Colonial Contest* (New York: Routledge, 1995), 8.

13. McClintock's fundamental points on the structure (but not necessarily the function) of imperial language are generally on target. She weakens her general arguments, however, by basing them with respect to Ireland on questionable source material, as for example in her generalization (based on an uncritical reading of Curtis and Lebow) about "the English stereotype of the Irish as a simianized and degenerate race" (ibid., 52). In addition, though she admits "the historical instability of discourse on race," she goes on to fudge the distinction between differing conceptions of race in the nineteenth century, assuming their "shared racism" (ibid., 8, 49). In fact, the practical implications of differing outlooks on race were substantial with respect to English policy in Ireland.

14. Tempting as it may be to make the argument that Ireland's place in the empire was fully "domestic," there is some evidence to the contrary. The Irish were, for example, often considered ideal soldiers for imperial expeditions (for example, W.H. Maxwell, *History of the Irish Rebellion in 1798; with Memoirs of the Union, and Emmett's Insurrection in 1803*, 3rd ed. [London: H.G. Bohn, 1852], 316). Nor were educated Irish excluded from positions of influence in the English press or govern-

ment (Sheridan Gilley, "English Attitudes to the Irish in England, 1780–1900," in *Immigrants and Minorities in British Society*, Colen Holmes, ed. [London: Allen & Unwin, 1978], 88–93; R.F. Foster, *Paddy and Mr. Punch: Connections in Irish and English History* [London: Penguin, 1993], 287–289).

It is worth noting that as late as 1911, English Liberals were attempting to propagate the notion of Britain as a "family of nations," along much the same lines as those advocated in the 1840s (John S. Ellis, "Remaking the Celt: British National Identity, Empire, and the 1911 Investiture of the Prince of Wales," *Journal of British Studies* 37 [October 1998], 391–418).

15. See Michael Hechter, *Internal Colonialism: The Celtic Fringe in British National Development, 1536–1966* (Berkeley: University of California Press, 1975).

16. Edward W. Said, *Culture and Imperialism* (London: Chatto & Windus, 1993), 127.

17. Ibid., 127–128.

18. Ibid., 202.

19. Ibid., 275.

20. Ibid., 266, 284–285. Said, like many other historians, no doubt relies for these statements on the works of L.P. Curtis and R.N. Lebow.

21. Andrew Hadfield and John McVeagh, eds., *Strangers to That Land: British Perceptions of Ireland from the Reformation to the Famine* (Gerrards Cross, Buckinghamshire: Colin Smythe, 1994), 26–27, 75–76.

22. Ibid., 80–83.

23. Ibid., 126.

24. Peter Mandler, *Aristocratic Government in the Age of Reform* (Oxford: Clarendon Press, 1990), 252.

25. See Boyd Hilton, *The Age of Atonement: The Influence of Evangelicalism on Social and Economic Thought, 1795–1865* (Oxford: Clarendon Press, 1988), and Peter Gray, *Famine, Land and Politics: British Government and Irish Society, 1843–50* (Dublin: Irish Academic Press, 1999).

26. It is worth noting that much of this material was published in London and wound up in the collections of the British Library. Transcripts of popular meetings and discussions in Ireland, such as those of the Repeal Association, were assiduously reproduced by the English press, albeit often with acid commentaries.

27. Christopher Morash, *Writing the Irish Famine* (Oxford: Clarendon Press,1995), 4. Morash also argues that "Like all past events the Famine is primarily a retrospective, textual creation. The starvation, the emigration, and the disease epidemics of the late 1840s have become 'the Famine' because it was possible to inscribe those disparate, but interrelated events in a relatively cohesive narrative" (ibid., 3). His purpose in making this unprovable assertion is difficult to determine.

2

Public Perceptions of the Irish Question, 1840–1845

Irish affairs preoccupied the British public in the years preceding the famine. Parliament and successive governments found it difficult to escape what George Dangerfield was later to call the "damnable question"; but ministers were not the only ones enduring headaches over Ireland and Irish issues. In the first half of the 1840s, the "condition of Ireland question" gripped the popular imagination as never before.

Discussion of Ireland was likely to conjure up a strange mixture of emotions in an English audience. On one level Ireland—wild, fertile, dotted with remnants of a mysterious past and an ancient race of noble savages—stirred the romantic elements in the English imagination. Ireland was for many a nearly irresistible temptation for imaginative fancy, travel and often settlement. It could also be an object of fear[1] and even anguish, however. In its rebelliousness Ireland appeared to threaten the material foundations of British prosperity, while in its poverty and moral degradation it seemed a standing reproach to the principles on which the so-called civilizing mission of the British empire was based. A leader-writer of the *Times* asked shortly before the beginning of the famine, "What is to be done with Ireland? What can be done with it?" and lamented:

We conquer in vain, we rule in vain, whilst the native jewel of our imperial diadem is thus tarnished. Our boast of foreign subjugation is turned
to mockery by the present contrast of domestic serfdom. Our vaunted
mission of civilization becomes a laughing-stock to nations who look at
the barbarism which festers on our shores.[2]

As this passage indicates, Ireland was both an imperial and a domestic problem. Her people would, it was hoped, ultimately "amalgamate" with those of
England,[3] but they would also always remain the "other." In this sense Ireland
posed problems to the English psyche that India did not, for though utilitari-
ans hoped to civilize India, they did not moot the possibility of merging the Indian and English peoples to the point where they would become
indistinguishable. India was a distinctly imperial problem. Ireland was not so
easy to categorize. The public balked at recognizing as colonial a relationship
between two white European peoples, but also had difficulty contemplating
the idea that Irish and English could ever be one. The English were challenged
to conceptualize union with Ireland without admitting equality of power between the two. Attempts to resolve this intellectual quandary lay at that heart
of the changes in English perceptions of Ireland throughout the nineteenth
century.

Printed material relating to the Irish question in the years before the famine
reflects the strong interest of the English in the affairs of the country. Pamphlets expressing one or another view of political and economic problems appeared every year in large numbers, especially as Daniel O'Connell's Irish
movement for the repeal of the Act of Union, and the findings of the 1843
Devon Commission on the Irish land system, came up for debate in the House
of Commons. Historical monographs and textbooks often devoted space to
comparative expositions on English and Irish history, while ethnographers
searched in the history of Ireland for the origins of the Irish people, their culture and their language. Travel guides and diaries began to gain popularity with
the public, while the "Irish novel" came into its own as a fashionable literary
genre. Together these printed works contributed to a new popular conception
of Ireland that had been emerging since the beginning of the century.

Political and economic tracts on Ireland were printed in such numbers that
it is difficult to do more than select a representative sample for analysis.[4] Pamphlets in the British Library for the period of 1840 to 1845, though representing a multitude of viewpoints on the problems with and cures for Irish poverty,
do contain a number of features in common. Whatever their differences about
the ultimate causes of poverty, the authors of these works were alike in their
confidence that a cure ultimately could be found.

The arguments advanced in these pamphlets generally fall within two broad categories, which for the sake of convenience shall be called Whig and Tory.[5] The former based their arguments on the conviction that English rights and laws should be made to apply equally to both islands in the confidence that the Irish might eventually profit from them as much as the English were supposed to have already done. Advocates of a Tory philosophy argued that Ireland was not yet ready for equal treatment, because of a set of "special conditions" in the country that were vaguely and variously defined by the authors. The preponderance of the pre-1845 pamphlets studied here advanced Whig viewpoints, although as we shall see the Tories shared, or were at least unwilling to openly contravene, certain Whig assumptions about the nature of the Irish themselves.

Whig analysts of Irish problems laid special emphasis on Irish history in their arguments for the application of more equitable laws in both islands. The anonymous author of *Ireland and Irish Questions Considered* (1842) drew conclusions from Irish history that were typical of most Whigs. The problem, it was said, was not that the English had conquered Ireland, but that the conquerors failed to extend their own rights and privileges to those they had conquered. English oppression and denial of education to the Irish, who were "denied the benefit of English laws," had resulted in the their being "step by step, degraded to a state inferior to that of the wandering Arab."[6] The Irish, never truly civilized, had been made wholly barbaric by ungenerous English behavior.

If the English would extend their own laws and civil liberties to Ireland, however, there was every hope for redress. The ideal of progress itself demanded it, for "this state of society, in the nineteenth century, cannot long continue."[7] As James Grant put it, "There is one way, and one way only, of crushing repeal. That is by rendering Ireland in reality what it is nominally— an integral part of the British empire," instead of ruling it as "a conquered province."[8] In terms of legislation, this meant the extension of the Poor Law to Ireland in the same form as it existed in England. It also meant that legislation tending to treat the Irish poor differently from the English, either through greater generosity or the restriction of civil liberties, should if possible be avoided.

Confidence that equal treatment would bring equal results for the two countries was closely interconnected with the tenets of political economy. The ideals of this philosophy were necessarily applicable to all peoples. James Johnson in advocating the extension to Ireland of a poor law on the English model made this point in insisting that the same principles of moral regeneration were applicable to the poor of both nations, even if the Irish were degraded to a "double degree."[9] The possibility that the effectiveness of these principles might vary according to the racial makeup of the people to whom they were applied was, as yet, an idea that few were willing to entertain openly. As we shall see, however, Irish humanity and "natural" equality did not imply sameness, or equality of power, of Irish and English.

The anonymous author of *The South of Ireland and Her Poor* (1843) characterized the opinions of a typical English Whig as follows: "He thinks that all that is to be done for the lower classes, to make them English peasants, is to legislate for them as he would for his own countrymen, forgetting their totally different origin, the traces and effects of which exist as forcibly now as they ever did."[10]

Ireland was, for this and other authors of what I have dubbed the Tory school, unable to digest the benefits of English liberties under its present conditions. Irish humanity and the eventual potential for Irish integration into the union was not rejected by the Tories. It appeared to them, however, that the kind of solutions that had apparently proved efficacious in England for moral and economic improvement were not equally applicable in Ireland. Instead, extraordinary measures for Ireland were deemed necessary, and ranged from suggestions for a wider and more generous application of the Poor Law to coercion for both landlords (forcing them to employ the poor) and peasants. Coercion would entail denying the Irish many rights and liberties available to Englishmen, but while Whigs[11] tended to argue that this would only further degrade Ireland and divide her from England, their opponents insisted that coercion was absolutely indispensable until the Irish earned English liberties for themselves.

Exactly what the sources of Irish difference were was a question that Tory authors generally preferred to dodge, leaving it instead an open question whether the peculiarities of the peasantry resulted "from the air, as some deduce the habit of making bulls; whether from the origin of the natives (Punica), or whether it be the result of non-education."[12] Although many Tory authors hinted that Irish peculiarities were due at least in part to their Celtic origin, this did not necessarily imply that they considered racial characteristics immutable.[13] Nor were these differences, whose characteristics were agreed on by almost all shades of English opinion, considered indicative of Irish racial inferiority. Difference could even appear as something to be respected, as the anti-Whig and antirepeal author Daniel Owen-Madden argued:

> There is a class of Imperialists who propose to govern Ireland without the slightest regard to local feelings, or to Irish prejudices. They would wish to obliterate Ireland in the map of the Empire, and to substitute West

Britain. They would first deride all Irish instincts, malign all Irish character, and then proceed to treat a concursive and semi-celtic population, as if it inherited the individualism and characteristic phlegm of English nature. This school of Imperialists is one made up of Whigs, Whig-Radicals, and Economists, steeped to the lips in the chilling philosophy of Benthamism. Many of them as individuals reject the tenets of the Benthamite creed, but when they deal as politicians with the interests of Ireland, they overlook all the acquired and natural distinctions between the countries, and require the Irish to grovel down in abject and slavish subserviency to England. They would not leave to Ireland a memory, a proud recollection, a generous native impulse, or a single national character of any kind. They would try and reduce it into being the tame and commonplace copyist of England.[14]

Daniel O'Connell's repeal movement was, quite naturally, a central topic of discussion in political and economic tracts on Ireland. In the first years of the 1840s the Liberator, as O'Connell was commonly known, organized a series of large, peaceful demonstrations in Ireland calling for the repeal of the Act of Union and the restoration of the Irish parliament, which had been defunct for half a century. This was an issue on which almost all English writers, whether Whig or Tory, were agreed, for the issue had ramifications far beyond English-Irish relations. The end of the union appeared to many to be, materially speaking, a grave threat to the stability of both the empire and England itself. As Owen-Madden argued, if the union was repealed "England would cease to be a great substantive Power, and Europe would be left at the mercy of Russia, France, Austria, and Prussia," while the British empire "would be gone for EVER!"[15] Repeal was also a moral and intellectual challenge, for the denial of the English right to rule the Irish struck at the very root of the British imperial system. To justify English rule in Ireland, conversely, was to justify the empire.

As threatening as repeal appeared to the empire and even the survival of England itself, the English antirepeal response was surprisingly subtle. O'Connell was rarely demonized in mainstream English literature, though Irish Protestants did their best to represent him as a monster. Most accounts of him expressed respect for his evident preference for legal methods of reform, but portrayed him as a misguided and even hypocritical politician. The fear was not so much that he would lead his followers into an uprising, but that he was losing control of the movement he had started, which might end in a conflagration against his wishes. James Johnson, writing in 1844, expressed his fear that "his unruly steeds (the priests and the people) were on the point of running wild over the earth." He continued by recounting a bizarre, paranoid dream in which the "popular phrenzy" of a repeal mob, backed by "columns of soldiers with the tri-coloured flag," overwhelmed the "bewildered and irresolute" O'Connell and led the country into a catastrophic war in which the victor remained uncertain.[16]

The Irish repealer masses, though objects of fear, do not necessarily appear as objects of derision. Witnesses of the "monster meetings" staged by O'Connell frequently commented on the sober and nonviolent character of the crowd. They admitted with honesty that the Irish treated English observers in a friendly and polite manner. Father Mathew, an Irish priest whose temperance movement of the 1840s was very successful while he lived, was given the credit for much of the apparently reformed character of the Irish. Ironically, however, this sobriety appeared ominous to many English, for it suggested a firmness and determination in the national mood that might eventually sweep O'Connell aside and lead to open rebellion.

Reassurance on this subject was provided, at least in part, by confidence that separation was ultimately impossible. Although some based this assumption on the simple statement that England was stronger, the assertion was more often justified by a faith that repeal contradicted the laws of nature. The *Times* reiterated in 1847 its long-standing position on the continuing issue of repeal, explaining that

> The condition of Ireland is, directly, the condition of the British empire. No legislative union can tighten—no Utopian separation could dissolve—that intimate and close connexion between the two islands which has been formed by the hand of nature, and consolidated by the operations of time . . . . Each year cements by closer fusion the twain branches of the Saxon and the Celtic stocks. . . . Whilst our passions are the most excited, and our jealousy the most vigilant, terror and passion are found equally unavailing to keep those apart whom a higher Power than man's has joined by the contiguity of position and the bond of mutual dependence.[17]

The "childish" plan of repealing the union "humanly speaking, is unattainable," argued the Reverend M.P. Perceval. "As to her physical power[s]," he claimed, "I see no reason from her history at any period to estimate them very highly"; indeed, the country if independent would be a sure prey to the larger states. Ireland appeared as naturally weak, feminine and safe only within a tight union with the strong English partner. If Ireland would participate fully in the union with England, however, she would take "her full share in its influence, glory, and renown," while at the same time "the moral benefits she might confer on the British Empire are incalculable."[18]

Exactly what sort of ideals the marriage might be based upon was another issue altogether. Here there was some difference between Whig and Tory, for although both were agreed on the need for a closer union, the means of securing
Irish affection for and loyalty to that bond was a matter for debate. For Samuel
Smiles, quoting an unknown author, gentleness and equality was the surest
means of winning the heart of Hibernia: "the Irish are indeed a tractable nation, and though they have resisted chains of iron, they may easily be con-
ducted by a kindly hand with a silken thread."[19] Owen-Madden, who scorned
"the cuckoo cry 'assimilate! assimilate! assimilate!' " and declared coercion to
be "absolutely necessary," was of a different opinion, and argued for a firm pa-
ternal hand.[20] Some writers reasoned the impossibility of repeal of the union
from natural law. For Owen-Madden and others "the utter impossibility of
'Repeal' " was because "England is stronger and will never consent to it."[21]

There was little doubting the fact that Ireland was a fertile land brimming
with potential, given the necessary injection of English capital. Writers of economic tracts laid much emphasis on the suitability of Irish bays and waterways
for penetration by English commerce; the land itself was considered to be ex-
ceptionally good but poorly managed.[22] Even as Ireland was potentially very
fruitful, however, she was also considered vulnerable to exploitation by others.
The case for rapid English development of Ireland was justified not only on
moral grounds, but also out of an often expressed fear that Ireland might elope
with America, France or even Russia.

One weapon commonly used against the dangers of repeal and the concomitant threat of foreign intervention in Ireland, was history. The repealers, of
course, considered the history of English-Irish relations as a vindication of
their view that the union was pernicious. Antirepealers were therefore quite
naturally forced to fight on this ground, but it was a battlefield on which they
were confident of victory. The study of history was, after all, considered by
Whigs and others to be central to an understanding of human progress, and
opponents of repeal considered the history of English-Irish relations to be by
no means unfavorable to their own point of view.

Samuel Smiles's 1844 work, the *History of Ireland and the Irish People, under
the Government of England*, is typical, in terms of its interpretation and conclusions, of many of the histories of Ireland appearing in England at this time.
Smiles's own approach to the subject was avowedly utilitarian, based on the assumption that history was

a general accumulation of experiments, successful and unsuccessful, all
tending towards the solution of the grand problem— how mankind can
be governed so as to secure for the mass the largest possible amount of

happiness and liberty, [therefore] a careful perusal of the history of Ireland cannot fail to teach a most impressive and instructive lesson.[23]

His narrative, of course based on "a strict and impartial view of facts," is a detailed statement of the Whig interpretation of Irish history.[24]

Little disagreement existed among antirepeal historians of Ireland about the state of the country before the English conquest. Ireland was, by all these accounts, "a frightful scene of anarchy and savage warfare, and . . . the people were degraded by uncouth manners, and barbarous customs and laws."[25] Smiles did not challenge this interpretation, agreeing that the factionalism and political backwardness of preconquest Ireland had had "the most injurious and debasing effects on the character of the Irish people . . . obliterating all distinctions between right and wrong, and producing that state of moral degradation which both disposes and fits men to be slaves."[26]

The conquest, insofar as it created the grounds for a possible transferral to Ireland of English liberties, had the potential to carry Ireland to as auspicious a prosperity as that enjoyed by nineteenth-century Englishmen. Had the conquerors chosen to treat the Irish as partners rather than slaves, and extended English law in its fullness to the conquered lands, "a community of interests would thus have sprung up; both invaders and natives would ere long have merged into one people." This had obviously not happened; but the reason had nothing to do with any alleged defects in the Irish themselves. Tragically, the English had chosen to install in Ireland an aristocratic, reactionary elite, "invariably the most inveterate enemies of public liberty," to rule the country and resist liberal reforms. "All the cruel acts," added Smiles, "which we have referred to, together with a great many more of kindred spirit, emanated from this body" and the Irish Parliament they eventually formed.[27]

The history of Ireland under the rule of her English-backed aristocratic ascendancy was one long tale of coercion, religious bigotry, and woe to the people. While the English secured victories for the "people's liberties" in the Civil War and the Glorious Revolution, the Irish remained foolishly "devoted in their attachment to the infamous house of Stuart, and the readiest to shed their blood in defense of their hereditary right and privilege to oppress."[28] This of course gave the English a reason to continue to oppress them, and the Irish were "imbruted" as a result. This was perpetuated throughout the eighteenth century by the "monster values" of the "protestant ascendancy party of Ireland," as a result

dulling the understanding, blighting the morals, and often causing slavish submission to oppression, alternated with fierce outbreak and revolt, with daylight drunkeness, and riot, and midnight outrage, incendiarism, and murder—until at length the mischiefs, long working in the heart of the people, had reduced them to the lowest stage of civilized beings, and their existence became actually pleaded by the wrong-doers as a defense of their own abominable cruelty, and a sufficient reason why they should be perpetuated for ever![29]

Hope for redress appeared only with the social changes of the late eighteenth century, "in a body of men who now came into notice . . . the MERCHANTS and TRADESMEN of Ireland were laying the foundations of future fortune, prosperity, and liberty." The Irish "government had reduced the great mass of the people to beggary, want, and utter destitution"; but as the Irish Parliament weakened in the last decades before the Union, "the people began to 'help themselves,' and 'heaven helped them,' ere long, to a share of its choicest blessings." These hopeful trends appeared to culminate in the Union: "The union of the two countries might, and ought to have been, a great step in the history of civilization. Union is one of the greatest ideas of modern times."[30]

Unfortunately, however, the promises of union, including religious freedom and, more importantly, the opening up of Ireland to the gentle tutorship of the English middle class, had not come to pass. This was largely because the union "left the corrupt interests—chief among which were the church and the aristocracy—untouched."[31] The realization of Irish potential could only come through the true consummation of the union, in which the old feudal interests and the established Church could be overcome, and English laws and liberties extended fully to Ireland.

Smiles's history of Ireland is worthy of careful study because it was, to a great extent, representative of the sort of historical works on Ireland appearing in England at this time. To be sure, Smiles's radical and nonconformist propensities were not shared by many of his countrymen, especially in his criticism of the established Church. His central point, however, that Ireland could have been like England if England had not failed to treat her as an equal through the extension of equal laws and rights, was a conclusion shared by almost every historian of Ireland writing in the 1840s. The publisher William Chambers went even further, pointing to Irish history as proof that "Ireland is to England what Greece was to Rome—the spot whence it derived not a little of its civilisation, and which it afterwards maltreated in requital," and adding that Irish moral debasement had parallels in "fifty different regions of the globe," including many parts of Europe.[32] The problem, *contra* the Repealers, was not that England had brought Ireland into too close a union, but that the English had allowed the union to remain unconsummated by not bringing Ireland close enough, and had thus not shared fully with her the fruits of English liberties. The possibility that the Irish could generate their own liberties, or a middle class substantial enough to rule the country, was not considered by Smiles or any of his fellow historians.

W.H. Maxwell stands out as a significant exception to the rule in this seeming consensus on the meaning of Irish history. This Protestant Irishman was popular in England as a writer of fiction in the 1820s and 1830s, but by the 1840s his star had waned and he was living in penury.[33] Unlike William Carleton, another Irish Protestant author, he was unwilling in his writings to conceal his violent anti-Catholicism and contempt for the Irish Catholics as a people, factors that may possibly have had something to do with his unpopularity in England, where by the 1840s "Orangeism" was seen as an enemy to peace in Ireland.

Maxwell's only major work of history, the *History of the Irish Rebellion in 1798* (1845) is in many respects the antithesis of the historical narrative portrayed by the Whigs. The preface to this work, with its protestations of "strict impartiality" and professed appeal to an audience of "the moderates of both sides," includes the sort of language favored by the liberal interpretation of Irish history. The story itself, however, is a strident anti-Catholic diatribe that harps on the "atrocities" of the Irish nationalist rising against British rule in 1798 in the true Orange tradition. There is little here to justify the idea that English misrule was the cause of Irish degradation; in Maxwell's mind the peasants, or "savages," were themselves entirely to blame. The illustrations by George Cruikshank portray the rebels as savage and vaguely subhuman. Whatever the Whigs may have said, Maxwell did not give much hope that the "savages" could be redeemed. In one passage indicative of Irish Protestant suspicions of efforts at moral reform in Ireland, Maxwell wrote:

It was a very singular fact, that the outbreak of the Irish rebellion was preceded by a moral reformation in the peasantry—a strange preliminary to be followed by such consequences. For months before the explosion took place, intoxication was rarely observed, and men who had been habitually drunken, suddenly became reclaimed. The temper of the peasantry, naturally pugnacious, underwent a change; the fairs and markets were undisturbed by quarreling; and factions, who had been at feud for a century, smoked the pipe of peace together, and met at dance and wake without the customary interchange of broken heads . . . the deferential manner, with which they generally addressed their superiors, was no longer visible in their bearing; and occasionally, in inebriety or unguarded anger, they darkly hinted that a change in property and government was at hand.[34]

In 1845, Maxwell's interpretation was a lonely cry for intolerance, but by 1852, amid rapidly changing perceptions of the nature of Irish troubles, it had gone into a third edition.

Maxwell's work is indicative of another aspect of the debate on Ireland before the famine: it was a debate in which the Irish fully and vocally participated. The frequency with which English readers read, and English writers referred to Irish contributions to the debate is evidence for Edward Said's contention that discourses of imperialism were constructed by both colonizer and colonized. As Thomas Boylan and Timothy Foley have argued, before the famine Ireland was the subject of a protracted campaign by Irish political economists seeking moral and economic reform on the same terms sought by the English. Ascendancy figures such as Archbishop Whately were leading figures in the movement, but so also were the small numbers of middle-class Irish merchants and some intellectuals. In their scheme, "stern English logic was to replace Irish rhetoric and the manly ethic of strenuous competition was to replace a morally admirable (in traditional terms) but economically unproductive ethic of self-abnegation and altruism."[35] As we shall see, Irish writers of fiction, such as Anna Maria Hall and William Carleton, were also significant contributors to the debate. Their support of the liberal outlook on Ireland was especially important because of the air of authority and knowledge of Ireland that they brought to the discussion.[36]

After the famine, Irish disillusionment with the rhetoric of political economy and English-Irish marriage would be manifested in Celticism, or Irish insistence on their own racial distinctiveness. In the first half of the 1840s, however, most images of the Irish people, by both English and Irish authors, contained none of the racist imagery to which L.P. Curtis has devoted so much attention. Indeed, although disgust at Irish moral habits was commonplace, the Irish were often complimented for their physical attributes. And while writers often reviled Irishmen for their poor moral habits, they just as frequently expressed admiration for their physical strength and proportions.

What many English men and women most admired in Ireland, however, was Irish women. According to William Makepeace Thackeray,

> The charming gaiety and frankness of the Irish ladies have been noted and admired by every foreigner who has had the good fortune to mingle in their society; and I hope it is not detracting from the merit of the upper classes, to say that the lower are not a whit less pleasing. I never saw in any

country such a general grace and manner of *ladyhood*. In the midst of their gaiety, too, it must be remembered that they are the chastest of women, and that no country in Europe can boast of such a general purity.[37]

Portrayals of Irish women emphasized their manners, physical attractiveness, and even superior (to Irishmen) understanding of economy. Their prime attribute, however, was said to be their chastity. This view was undoubtedly, at least in part, the product of honest observation, but it also conveniently suited a rhetoric that represented Hibernia as an excellent marriage partner for John Bull.

The dominant philosophy of race for the first half of the century was "monogenism," a traditional Christian-based belief in the essential brotherhood of man as one species.[38] James Cowles Prichard, a radical abolitionist who was most active in the first decades of the century but whose works were continually reprinted through the 1850s, was the doyen of this school of thought. His misleadingly titled 1831 work, *The Eastern Origin of the Celtic Nations*, was intended to demonstrate the uses of philology for proving the "affinity of nations."[39] As Nancy Stepan has argued, "Prichard's monogenism stood firm as the basic assumption of racial studies in Britain until well into the 1840s, forming a strong bulwark against the growing tide of facile racism."[40]

The characteristics of peoples, according to Prichard and other monogenists, were products of environment. Changes in the characteristics could be worked by changing the environment, by improving living standards, education, and so on. This was, however, the work of generations, since the assumption of the monogenists was that national attributes were mutable but also inherited in the Lamarckian sense.[41] Owen-Madden's assessment of the racial characteristics of Irish Protestants, for example, though appearing straightforwardly racist to modern readers, is on close inspection based on a monogenist concept of national difference:

The Anglo-Irish race preserves characteristics distinct from the great mass of the Celtic population. But the Protestants of Ireland also differ essentially from their English brethren in Britain. They form a new kind of Irish people. They are rich in Saxon self-reliance, and they are also endowed with Celtic sensibility and ardour. Their character was formed in the eighteenth century, when Ireland possessed an Aristocracy, partly resident, and a Legislature. Their blood is nearly as hot as that of the Catholics. The Anglo-Irish have imbibed far more of the national character of Ireland, than they have imparted of their hereditary English qualities.

For matters purely intellectual they are as Celtic as if they had not a drop of British blood. Exclusive institutions have alone preserved them from being completely merged in the national character of Ireland.[42]

This interpretation of racial difference was used by both Whigs and Tories to justify such "facts" as the tendency of English migrants to Ireland to acquire the habits of the Irish after two or three generations, the futility of teaching older Irish peasants new habits and the need to concentrate on reforming the younger ones instead, and the importance of English tutorship for many generations before major changes could be worked in the Irish people.

Polygenism, the idea that God had created the races of the world separately, "was an old heresy, going back to the Renaissance."[43] It had been reinforced by the eighteenth-century notion of the Great Chain of Being. By the first decades of the nineteenth century, however, its advocates were a tiny minority who had almost no voice in the scientific community.[44] Robert Knox, who had been attempting to publicize this approach with respect to the Irish in the early 1840s through a variety of articles, did not by his own admission receive widespread approbation until after the first years of the famine.[45]

Travel accounts by Englishmen in Ireland exist from the twelfth century. It was not until the eighteenth century, however, and especially from the 1770s, that this sort of literature appeared very frequently.[46] Even so, before the 1840s tourism in Ireland was not an industry but a concern of a relatively small number of people, most of whom were interested in the country for social or economic reasons. The factors inhibiting large-scale leisure travel to Ireland before the early 1840s were largely physical. Cheap steamship service from Liverpool or Holyhead to Dublin became available in the early 1820s, but even so travel beyond Dublin to the scenic west was a matter of great hardship before the first rail links to the west appeared at the end of the 1830s.[47] Improved transportation coincided with increased interest in the "condition of Ireland question" to induce a surge in travel to Ireland in the beginning of the 1840s.

The most popular and widely read travel guide to Ireland in the 1840s was *Ireland: Its Scenery, Character, etc.*, a three-volume work written by Anna Maria Hall and her husband Samuel Carter Hall, both respected novelists. The work was published from 1841–1843 in monthly installments and, as noted in the preface to the first volume, sales "far exceeded our most sanguine hopes, having more than doubled the calculation of the Publishers. By the Press of England and Scotland—we believe universally—we have been greatly encouraged; and also by Ireland, with very few exceptions."[48] This was no idle boast. Through the 1850s other writers on Ireland continued to refer to it as the standard work, James Johnson calling it "the best that ever appeared on Ireland."[49]

A central theme in the work of the Halls on Ireland was the confident belief that the British Isles were in the process of consummating a marriage that would lead to mutual prosperity and happiness. Attempts to move Ireland in the direction of autonomy were thus as unnatural and immoral as trying to encourage a man's wife to greater independence:

> A union, based on mutual interests, is rapidly cementing. The insane attempts to procure "Repeal" may retard, for a time, a consummation for which every upright British subject must devoutly wish; but a growing intelligence and increasing intimacy are barriers which the advocates of the measure will vainly endeavour to break down.[50]

James Johnson, the author of another travel account, developed this theme further by showing the impossibility of divorce:

> A repeal of the Union would eventually divorce Hibernia from John Bull "*a mensa et thoro*—and that without alimony of maintenance. It is true that she might, perhaps, be at liberty to form another matrimonial connexion—but with whom would this new *liaison* be? Johnny Crapaud—or Cousin Jonathan?[51] Hibernia is not of the constitution to live in blessed singleness during the remainder of her life.[52]

William Thackeray's *Irish Sketch-Book* (1843) was probably the most popular Irish travel book in England after the Hall's. It was the first of Thackeray's books to reach a second edition, and was probably one of his most personal works. It originated in his attempt to find relief abroad from the encroaching mental illness of his Irish wife and their collapsed marriage. Though this tragedy is only alluded to in the book, the tone of writing is remarkably intimate and candid. The journey itself, lasting from the summer to the autumn of 1842, was extensive, constituting a practical circuit from Dublin through the south of the island to the wilds of the west, on to the comparative "civilization" of the north, and back to Dublin again.

The *Irish Sketch-Book* helped to earn for Thackeray, both among his contemporaries and modern scholars, a reputation as a racist and religious bigot. Actually Thackeray's view of Ireland was if anything moderate by the standards of his contemporaries, though in fundamental aspects his attitude was wholly within the mainstream of the liberal consensus on the country. Phyllis Weinroth Bernt's dissertation on Thackeray and the Irish in this sense draws the wrong conclusions from the right observations. Though it is true that the *Irish Sketch-Book* is permeated with Thackeray's disgust at, in Bernt's words,

Irish "filth, laziness, superstition and improvidence," this does not necessarily entail that the novelist saw these conditions as inevitable or the fault of the Irish themselves.[53]

Thackeray's tendency to tease his reader makes the *Irish Sketch-Book* somewhat difficult to evaluate, but it is also representative for showing the odd combination of apparently contradictory opinions that characterized English perceptions of Ireland. On the one hand, he frequently lambasts the Irish peasantry for their "ragged lazy contentment" and unwillingness to learn to care for themselves.[54] At the same time, however, he protests his "hearty sympathy and goodwill" toward the Irish poor, adding that "no people are more eager for learning, more apt to receive it, or more grateful for kindness, than the Irish."[55] He also frequently contrasts English arrogance and vulgarity with Irish kindness and simplicity.

In his journey from southern to northern Ireland, Thackeray notes a strong contrast in the attitudes and prosperity of the people. "What is the cause of this improvement?" he asks:

> *Protestantism* is, more than one Church-of-England man said to me; but, for Protestantism, would it not be as well to read Scotchism?—meaning thrift, prudence, perseverance, boldness, and common sense, with which qualities any body of men, any Christian denomination, would no doubt prosper.[56]

It is in the light of such statements that Thackeray's supposed racism needs to be considered. Thus at first a sentence like the following, contrasting northern Irish with southern, may seem to uphold Bernt's thesis: "The people's faces are sharp and neat, not broad, lazy, knowing-looking, like that of many a shambling Diogenes who may be seen lounging before his cabin in Cork or Kerry."[57] As Thackeray makes clear in the preceding quotation, however, and as he argues elsewhere in the *Irish Sketch-Book*, differences of physiognomy and character were not immutable. They were, rather, evidence of environmental conditions, and as the mainstream scientific view of the day held, change of environment could wholly transform a "race" of men. Thackeray was thus able to "hope that the middle class, which this increase of prosperity must generate . . . will exercise the greatest and most beneficial influence over the country."[58]

Prefamine travel accounts largely uphold the liberal image of Ireland as a land of tremendous economic potential groaning under archaic feudal rule. Ireland appears in early travel literature as a premodern land on the verge of facing the inevitable march of progress, for which the Act of Union and the British middle classes were to form the wedge. Although no one questioned the ultimately beneficent nature of this progress for Ireland, the characteristic liberal ambivalence concerning the past expressed itself through romantic portrayals of Irish antiquity and the doomed peasant way of life. The Rev. Caesar Otway, an Irishman whose works were popular in England, helped to create this vision of Ireland as

> the land of ruins and memorials—of powers and people that have succes-sively passed away. The ruined fortress—the devastated abbey—the lonely *dun*—the fairy-footed rath—the round tower that sends its slen-der shaft on high to assert that the almost imperishable simplicity of its form can survive human record, and even outlast man's tradition—these are what render Ireland a land interesting to the traveller.[59]

This romantic fascination with the Irish past is typified in the near-obsessive interest with which English travelers sought out Irish "Round Towers." The origin of these structures, now known to have been early Christian, appeared to many early Victorian tourists to be somehow linked with the mysterious events of Irish prehistory. The most common explanation early in the nine-teenth century was that the towers were built by an extinct race who preceded the Celtic incursion into the island, and some Victorian tourists who com-pared the workmanship of the towers with the crude peasant huts frequently clustered nearby were often tempted to believe a Celtic origin of the towers im-possible.[60] Otway speculated that these and other ancient monuments were built by "an energetic and intelligent race" of ancients "whose intellectuality was . . . much superior to the battling barbarians called MILESIANS" who suc-ceeded the ancient race.[61]

Another popular speculation, drawn from the works of Thomas Moore, was that the towers "proved" the Asian origins of their builders, be they Celts or pre-Celts, given the supposed similarity of architecture between the Irish tow-ers and Indian temples of "fire-worship."[62] For the most part, however, English tourists used the round towers to support their own version of Irish history by representing them as evidence of the civilization to which the Irish once aspired and to which they might again return with English help. The contrast of towers and huts came to symbolize the extent to which illiberal government had pre-vented the regeneration of a once noble people.

These sentimental feelings for certain elements of traditional Irish life were mixed, however, with disgust at other symptoms of Irish backwardness which, it was hoped, would be eliminated by the progress of commercialism. Beggary in particular appeared as an abomination, as Thackeray noted with disgust:

I confess with regard to the beggars, that I have never yet had the slightest sentiment of compassion for the very oldest or dirtiest of them, or been inclined to give them a penny; they come crawling round you with lying prayers and loathsome compliments, that make the stomach turn; they do not even disguise that they are lies; for, refuse them, and the wretches turn off with a laugh and a joke, a miserable grinning cynicism that creates distrust and indifference, and must be, one would think, the very best way to close the purse, not to open it, for objects so unworthy.[63]

Thackeray qualified this hatred of beggars by expressing, as did most other travel writers, his "hearty sympathy and goodwill" for the deserving poor.[64] He also contributed to a growing literary genre, the Irish novel, in which the possibilities in and obstacles to the regeneration of the Irish peasantry were being explored.

No complete understanding of English perceptions of the relationship with Ireland would be complete without study of popular fiction. As Edward Said has argued, "the novel, as a cultural artefact of bourgeois society, and imperialism are unthinkable without each other."[65] It is therefore somewhat surprising that few historians have yet undertaken to study the literature of this period as a means of understanding the Anglo-Irish relationship. A brief survey of the very rich popular literature on Ireland in the 1840s is indispensable. Indeed, the British reading public in the 1840s appears to have had a nearly insatiable desire for novels and poems about Ireland by both English and Irish writers. This offers a useful opportunity to practice what Said has called "comparative literature," the purpose of which "is to move beyond insularity and provincialism and to see several cultures and literatures together, contrapuntally."[66]

Novels of Irish life had been popular in England ever since Maria Edgeworth's *Castle Rackrent* (1800), a classic indictment of landlordism in Ireland that would inspire many early Victorian writers. Not until the end of the 1830s, however, did Irish novels break into the English mass market.[67] William Carleton, Anna Maria Hall, Joseph Sheridan Le Fanu, Charles James Lever, Samuel Lover, William Hamilton Maxwell, William Thackeray and Anthony Trollope, along with many lesser authors, produced a wide variety of fictional representations of Irish life. Ireland and the Irish were at the same time popular topics for theatrical treatment. The popular works of "Anglo-Irish" authors cannot have failed to contribute significantly to the formation of English perceptions of Ireland. Indeed, an English man or woman interested in reading about Ireland was probably more likely to read something by an author of Irish ancestry like Edgeworth, Carleton, Lover or Lever than by Thackeray or Trollope.

Charles James Lever, considered "the best-known Irish novelist of the century" by the *Dictionary of National Biography*, was born in Dublin, though his father was a building contractor from Lancashire. He spent his youth studying medicine and traveling in Canada and the Continent before entering the Dublin literary scene through contributions to the *Dublin University Magazine* in the 1830s. *The Confessions of Harry Lorrequer* (1839), his first novel, was a great success on both sides of the Irish Sea and established his reputation as a popular novelist of Ireland. Subsequent novels such as *Charles O'Malley, the Irish Dragoon* (1841) and *Jack Hinton, the Guardsman* (1842) increased his public following, though, as the *Dictionary of National Biography* notes, this was "largely with the English reading public; the Irish frequently suspected Lever of perpetrating objectionable national caricatures."[68] Throughout the early 1840s he continued to travel to London and the Continent, before finally settling on the latter in 1845, never to return to Ireland.[69]

Harry Lorrequer is unexceptional as literature. The plot centers on the adventures, loves and humiliations of the title character, an English officer stationed in Ireland in the 1820s. Lorrequer is not himself Irish, but spends a great deal of time there and meets a number of amusing Irish characters who recount to him many stories of Irish peasant life, which Lever treats in separate chapters. Lever's Irish are, though light-hearted and inclined to get into trouble, not the bumbling clowns common on the stage or in the work of Samuel Lover.

Most novels of the genre contained heavy doses of moralizing. Lever's work is no exception, but his preaching is more subtle than that of Carleton, Edgeworth or Hall. The remarks concerning the poverty and degradation of the peasantry are, however, no less remarkable for being mild in tone and hidden within the nominally humorous anecdotes of Lorrequer's Irish acquaintances. Lever's method in four of these stories is to draw attention to the sad plight of the Irish peasants by the ease with which they pass for savages from America, Asia or Africa.

In one of these stories, a theater manager who has been touring Dublin with a show featuring native American "savages" finds, when the latter choose to return home, perfect replacements in some "wild Irish" peasants preparing to sail to England for the harvest:

> Their uncouth appearance, their wild looks, their violent gestures, and, above all, their strange and guttural language, for they were all speaking Irish, attracted the attention of the manager . . . It was scarcely necessary to alter anything about them, they were ready made to his hand, and in many respects better savages than their prototypes.[70]

In another story, an Irish landlord on seeing a "savage" in a London road show is shocked to discover that it is in reality one of his poor tenants who is obliged to masquerade as an "African Irishman" in order to pay the rent. The landlord on seeing this is immediately converted to become "a great friend to the introduction of poor laws."[71] Irishmen in two other stories impersonate respectively a Turk and a Delaware Indian chief.[72]

The Irish do not, however, appear in these tales to possess an innately barbaric nature. Their ability to pass as uncivilized emanates from the degradation to which poverty or drunkenness (in the case of the Delaware "chief") has reduced them. The Irish language likewise lends to their appearance of savagery. In no instance, however, does Lever portray physiognomy or innate mental character as making the Irish into savages. Quite pointedly he ascribes their degradation to moral causes, which remedial measures such as a poor law might be expected to correct. The same comparisons of the Irish to American Indians, Turks or Africans would reappear in the postfamine period, but the conclusions drawn would be very different from those of the 1830s and 1840s.

Samuel Lover was born in Dublin into a Protestant mercantile family. An accomplished artist and musician, he helped to found the *Dublin University Magazine* in 1833 before relocating to London in 1835. He finished his first novel, *Rory O'More*, in 1837, and collaborated in the same year with Charles Dickens in founding the literary journal *Bentley's Miscellany*. *Handy Andy* (1842), his most popular novel, established him on the London literary scene. He sustained his popularity through the end of the 1850s with a series of one-man performances in London and America dubbed "Irish Evenings," involving the performance of traditional songs and reading of fables.[73]

Handy Andy first appeared in *Bentley's Miscellany* in 1837 and was published as a book in 1842. The title character exemplified an age-worn literary and dramatic tradition that represented the Irish peasant as an *omadhawn*, or "rustic clown."[74] Andy's slapstick bumbles and oxymoronic "Irish bulls" are central to this comic novel and representative of "the Genius of farce, who presides so particularly over all Irish affairs."[75] At the same time, however, Andy's antics are intended to inspire the reader's affection, not disgust, nor is he representative of the average Irishman or even the average Irish peasant. Andy's family, though naive and superstitious, are not fools. Edward O'Connor, a Protestant landlord of native Irish stock, is a handsome, romantic hero as well as an Irish "patriot."

The villains of the tale are not the simple Irish peasantry or the enlightened proprietors. This honor is reserved instead for Squire O'Grady, a profligate and cruel landlord whose disordered household reflects his moral corruption, and Mr. Furlong, a middle-class Irishman who strives to become "ginteel" by adopting an English accent and mannerisms. O'Grady's malignancy is expressed through his desire to misguide Englishmen into believing that the Irish peasantry must be bullied and coerced. Furlong, meanwhile, is condemned as one of "the mongrel breed of Irishmen, who speak ill of their own country."[76] His attempts to gain an English accent result only in his acquiring a strange manner of speaking foreign to both countries.[77]

Furlong's failure to become an Englishman reflects Lover's apparent rejection of the possibility that the Irish could become English. The Irish were, as Lover reiterated again and again, a unique people with a peculiar national character. Their distinctiveness, Lover argued, was exemplified in the difference between Northern and Southern Irish. "The Northerns retain much of the cold formality and unbending hardness of the stranger-settlers from whom they are descended, while the Southern exhibits that warm-hearted, lively, and poetical temperament for which the country is celebrated."[78] Edward O'Connor, an Irish patriot and one of the heroes of *Handy Andy*, argues from his knowledge of history "a strong connecting link between the people of Carthage and Ireland."[79]

At the same time, however, he reminded his English readers not to heed

the impertinent self-conceit of presuming and shallow strangers, who fancied their hackneyed and cut-and-dry knowledge of the common places of the world gave them a mental elevation above an intelligent people of primitive habits, whose simplicity of life is so often set down to stupidity, whose contentment under privation is frequently attributed to laziness, and whose poverty is constantly coupled with the epithet "ignorant."[80]

Difference in no way implies inferiority or even incompatibility. Instead, Lover argues through his novel for a peaceful union of English and Irish not unlike that espoused by English liberals through the rhetoric of marriage. English characters in *Handy Andy* are well-meaning but distrustful of the Irish and thus too apt to coerce them. English authority is, however, never challenged, nor is there any appeal for Irish equality within the Union. Instead, Lover appeals to Ireland's rulers to civilize "Paddy" through kindness: "Oh! rulers of Ireland, why have you not sooner learned to *lead* that people by love, whom all your severity has been unable to *drive?*"[81] Lover's goal was to represent the Irish as objects for English affection, not fear. The Irish would always, with their feminine character traits, be different from the English; but they could also, if treated with love and kindness, become civilized and amiable partners in the Union.

William Carleton attained a substantial measure of popularity in both England and Ireland during the 1830s and 1840s. He was born the youngest of fourteen children in a Catholic peasant family from County Tyrone in Ulster. Though originally intended for the priesthood, Carleton converted to Protestantism as a young man and from the beginning of his writing career in 1828 nursed a deep and abiding anti-Catholicism.[82]

Traits and Stories of the Irish Peasantry, Carleton's most famous and enduring work, originally appeared in two volumes in 1832 and 1833, though some of this collection of short stories had appeared in 1829. The first editions were published in Dublin to general acclaim. It was the revised edition of 1843–1844, however, that achieved the widest popularity on both sides of the Irish Sea, reaching "an enormously wide market."[83] The purportedly realistic stories, sometimes humorous and often overbearingly sentimental, were in their Irish editions often violently anti-Catholic. In the later English edition the stories, besides being adorned with attractive illustrations by "Phiz," were also extensively edited for an English audience by ridding them of openly anti-Catholic passages. Carleton was unafraid to place these before an Irish readership but apparently deemed them unsuitable for the more cultivated members of the English middle class.

The unwillingness of most educated English to attribute Irish backwardness to the Catholic religion is in some respects surprising. Indeed, overt anti-Catholicism is rare in the mainstream literature. What one finds instead, especially among authors with Whig predilections, is a sense that religious intolerance in a broad sense was a factor in the troubles of Ireland. Nor was blame laid at the door of Catholic zealots alone. Orange Protestant fanatics were regarded with if anything greater disgust than were their Catholic counterparts.

C.C.F. Greville was typical of Whig writers in his argument that anti-Catholicism, "the genuine spirit of modern Toryism," must be extirpated and that "Catholics must be satisfied."[84] Protestant proselytism in Ireland appeared to Greville and those of like mind as not a potential cure but a pointless provocation. Advocates of a Tory interpretation of Irish troubles were more willing to be critical of Catholicism and to hold out the possibility of the conversion of Ireland to Protestantism in the distant future. Even so, they were unwilling to call openly for anti-Catholic legislation or vigorous proselytism, nor did they even argue that Catholicism was a major source of Irish degradation. The Tory Daniel Owen-Madden, who railed at "the disgusting arrogance of very many Priests" and insisted that "Catholicism is favourable to every species of *absolutism*," qualified these assertions by remarking that "the priests are effects rather than causes" of Irish degradation, and that "to drive Catholicity from the minds of the Irish may be pronounced impossible."[85]

Irish novels of the prefamine period advanced two typical constructions of the Irish priest. A "good" priest was unthreatening because he did not take Catholicism or his personal morals too seriously. Charles Lever's Father Malachi in *Harry Lorrequer* and Anthony Trollope's Father McGrath in *The MacDermots of Ballycloran* are typical of this stereotype. Intelligent and educated in France, they waste little breath on theology or preaching. Instead, they mix freely with the common people, Father Malachi to the extent of heavy drinking, overeating and ribald conversation. Maynooth-educated priests such as Trollope's Father Cullen or Lever's Mr. Donavan are by contrast portrayed as intractable fanatics whose devotion to their faith leads them almost inevitably into puritanical zeal and violent political agitation.[86]

Religious conflict, rather than Catholicism or Protestantism per se, therefore appeared in the English understanding as a source of Irish suffering. It was all very well for an Irishman to be religious, but for him to proselytize his fellows was almost inevitably to antagonize them and thus sow the seeds of conflict. In the Whig world view, religion was ideally a matter of personal conscience, with of course the limitation that it must be Christian, and the paradox that Anglicanism was best suited to the realization of a private, comfortable and peaceful faith. The Irish, perhaps as a factor of their intrinsically feminine natures, made the mistakes of holding their religious convictions too passionately and not keeping them to themselves.

William Carleton therefore avoided the subject of religion in the 1840s, preferring to dwell on the customs and manners of the peasantry that were reasonably distinct from their faith. Much more than Edgeworth, Lover or Lever, Carleton's subject was the Irish peasant. His peasant background inspired within him a deep affinity for the poor Irish and anger at how this class had been represented in literature. Carleton hated Lever, publicly accusing him of perpetrating "disgusting caricatures of Irish men and women," and attacked Mrs. Hall for misunderstanding the peasantry.[87] Though Carleton maintained a close friendship with Lover, he had little respect for an *omadhawn* like Handy Andy. Carleton's introduction to *Traits and Stories* is worth quoting at length for the light it sheds on the author's appreciation of the role played by the peasant in the Irish literary genre:

It is well known that the character of an Irishman has been hitherto uniformly associated with the idea of something unusually ridiculous, and that scarcely anything in the shape of language was supposed to proceed from his lips but an absurd *congeries* of brogue and blunder. The habit of looking upon him in a ludicrous light has been so strongly impressed upon the English mind, that no opportunity has ever been omitted of throwing him into an attitude of gross and overcharged caricature, from which you might as correctly estimate his intellectual strength and moral proportions, as you would the size of a man from his evening shadow. From the immortal bard of Avon down to the writers of the present day, neither play nor farce has ever been presented to Englishmen, in which, when an Irishman *is* introduced, he is not drawn as a broad grotesque blunderer, every sentence he speaks involving a bull, and every act the result of headlong folly, or cool but unstudied effrontery. . . . It passed from the stage into the recesses of private life, wrought itself into the feelings until it became a prejudice, and the Irishman was consequently looked upon, and treated, as a being made up of absurdity and cunning—a compound of knave and fool, fit only to be punished for his knavery or laughed at for his folly . . . unconsciously creating an unfriendly feeling between the two countries—a feeling which, I am happy to say, is fast disappearing, and which only requires that we should have a full and fair acquaintance with each other in order to be removed forever.[88]

Carleton aligned himself with many English liberals in endeavoring to present a picture of the Irish peasantry based on reason, not "prejudice," insisting on the "objectivity" of his approach and reassuring his readers that his stories "may be relied on as truthful and authentic."[89] In this spirit the *Traits and Stories* was advertised and presented "as a scholarly work, no mere collection of stories."[90]

For all the wonderful variety of characters in Carleton's short stories, they do share certain traits in common. They are passionate, prone to drunkenness and fighting, but also very willing to be led by enlightened authority. Naturally intelligent, they are woefully uneducated and have an attraction to superstition, which along with a love of authority contributes to the power of the Catholic church. When treated well, their emotional nature finds expression in poetry and music; when oppressed, they become violent to the point of savagery. Interestingly, the tendency of Irishmen toward improvidence is frequently offset by the sobriety and good sense of Irish women.

The tendency to represent the Irish with idealized feminine characteristics such as impulsiveness, sensitivity and aptitude for poetry and music is common in Carleton's work. In the introduction to the *Traits and Stories*, he states that

the Irish . . . are a naturally refined people; but by this I mean the refinement which appreciates and cherishes whatever there is in nature, as manifested through the influence of the softer arts of music and poetry. The effect of music upon the Irish heart I ought to know well, and no man need tell me that a barbarous or cruel people ever possessed national music that was beautiful and pathetic . . . It is no wonder, then, that the domestic feelings of the Irish should be so singularly affectionate and strong, when we consider that they have been, in spite of every obstruction, kept under the softening influence of music and poetry.[91]

In *The Black Prophet* (1847), Carleton uses the feminine character of Sarah M'Gowan to represent Ireland's needs and potential:

It is impossible to say to what a height of moral grandeur and true greatness culture and education might have elevated her, or to say with what brilliancy her virtues might have shown, had her heart and affections been properly cultivated. Like some beautiful and luxuriant flower, however, she was permitted to run into wildness and disorder for want of a guiding hand; but no want, no absence of training, could ever destroy its natural delicacy, nor prevent its fragrance from smelling sweet, even in the neglected situation where it was left to pine and die.[92]

Government mismanagement and tendency to coerce rather than uplift the Irish contributes to Sarah's tragic but noble end. The lesson for Hibernia and John Bull is obvious; she cannot live on her own but may be uplifted through a gentle matrimonial embrace.

Lover, Lever and Carleton were the most popular Anglo-Irish novelists of this period, but they were not without competition. Anna Maria Hall's stories, though not nearly as well-known as her travel writings, were not insignificant. The stories she published in *Stories of the Irish Peasantry* (1840) were much in keeping with her middle-class background and English education, however, being characterized by a simplistic preachiness less conspicuous in Carleton.[93] Joseph Sheridan Le Fanu's *The Cock and Anchor: A Chronicle of Old Dublin City*, a dark story of the decline of the Anglo-Irish gentry, appeared in 1845, though it failed to attract the readership of his later gothic horror stories.

Anglo-Irish literature of the early 1840s is representative of the two-way street of discourse on Ireland. It is clear that novels by Irish authors had a profound impact on English perceptions of Ireland. At the same time, the opinions of the novelists themselves were influenced by English attitudes. "Irish writers during this period . . . were inordinately sensitive to English opinion, and not only because their earnings depended on it."[94] In some instances, no doubt, Irish novelists consciously pandered to their English reading public, Carleton's revision of *Traits and Stories* being one example. The Anglo-Irish culture within which these novelists lived was itself heavily influenced by English beliefs, and the tendency of Anglo-Irish writers to reflect English opinions was therefore also a product of personal conviction.

A number of English authors attempted to capitalize on the flourishing Irish literary genre, with limited success. William Thackeray and Anthony Trollope made the most notable attempts, but failed to substantially impress English readers, though ironically these works are better known today than those of the Anglo-Irish authors whom they often imitated. In the world of fictional literature in the 1830s and 1840s, Irishness was a concept defined by Anglo-Irish, and imitated by English, authors.[95] The perceptions and assumptions one finds in fiction produced on both sides of the Irish Sea are therefore remarkably similar.

The Luck of Barry Lyndon, William Thackeray's first novel, was written partly in mockery of Harry Lorrequer and other rogue heroes of Charles Lever, whose detestation of Thackeray was warmly reciprocated.[96] The hero of the tale, Barry Redmond, is an initially sympathetic Irishman whose violence and impulsiveness are calculated to eventually provoke distaste in the reader. His European adventures appear to culminate in his marriage to a wealthy English-woman, an event that would likely conclude a Lever novel. In this marriage, however, the roles of Hibernia and John Bull are reversed, with an Irish husband and an English wife. Instead of a chaste and devoted Irish wife married to a thrifty and stable English husband, this marriage unites an unchaste and decadent Englishwoman with a spendthrift and erratic Irishman. The disastrous end of the marriage in such circumstances is a foregone conclusion.

Like Thackeray, Anthony Trollope was deeply influenced by the works of Carleton, Lever, Edgeworth, Maxwell and others in his own literary depictions of Ireland. Trollope was, however, more familiar than Thackeray with Irish life, having served as a postal clerk in what is now County Offaly from 1841 to 1851. He not unnaturally drew on this knowledge in his first two novels, *The MacDermots of Ballycloran* (1847) and *The Kellys and the O'Kellys* (1848). Critics praised the novels, but they were generally unpopular in England.[97]

The MacDermots of Ballycloran, which Trollope finished in July 1845 but could not get published until March 1847, is in many ways a typical prefamine English portrait of Ireland. Though in form a straightforward story of the tragic downfall of a once noble family, it is also a moral tale in the time-honored tradition of the genre. Trollope, like Edgeworth, Carleton and others, was obsessed with the classic tale of "an extravagant landlord, reckless tenants, debt, embarrassment, despair, and ruin."[98]

The novel is particularly interesting, however, for its overtly gendered representations of the relations within the British family of nations. Feemy MacDermot symbolizes her family's disgrace through her seduction and ultimate destruction at the hands of Myles Ussher, a zealous Anglo-Irish Protestant and revenue policeman. Ussher in turn meets death at the hands of Feemy's brother Thady, who suffers the ultimate penalty under the auspices of the legal authorities. Robert Tracy in his introduction to a recent edition of the novel argues that Trollope chose Feemy to represent Hibernia degraded at the hands of English rapacity.[99]

Trollope does go to great lengths to establish the fully Irish nature of the MacDermots and of Feemy herself. The family had, over the generations, been careful to intermarry only with others of fully "Milesian" stock. Significantly, however, this preoccupation with race only sped the family on the road to ruin by subverting pecuniary considerations in the formation of marriage alliances. The MacDermots' insistence on retaining their Irish character and "feudal" Irish ways only exposes their inability to live independently.[100]

Ussher does not, however, represent the English, but the Anglo-Irish seducer who degrades Hibernia in the absence of an effective English competitor, and who the British government has in its ignorance placed in a position of power. Indeed the only manifestation of English authority in the novel appears near the end, when a distant Lord Lieutenant attempts to overturn Thady's conviction but backs down in the face of opposition from his Anglo-Irish underlings. Ussher rather represents the Anglo-Irish, who understand seduction and coercion in relation to Hibernia but little else.[101] His own behavior towards Feemy reflects this as he first seduces and then carries her off by force, while toward the Irish peasantry he practices only violence, trickery and coercion. Thus Feemy, though portrayed by Trollope as strong-willed and full of potential, is ultimately destroyed by enforced proximity to and dependence on an Anglo-Irish rake, while her brother, representing the old Irish ascendancy, falls victim to a passionate nature and a coercive political establishment and is ultimately incapable of rescuing her.

Another facet of the Irish literary genre was the theater. The "stage Irishman" had been a fixture in English theater since the sixteenth century. Until the middle of the eighteenth century, Paddy on the stage was not always portrayed in an unflattering manner. In the decades leading up to and immediately following the Act of Union, however, the stage Irishman increasingly appeared as a purely comic figure worthy only of amused contempt.[102] The Englishman who allowed these plays to shape his conception of the Irish would probably have arrived at conclusions similar to those expressed by one of Maria Edgeworth's fictional Englishmen:

I did not expect to see twenty trees in the whole island. I imagined that I should have nothing to drink but whiskey, that I should have nothing to eat but potatoes, that I should sleep in mud-walled cabins, and that I should hear nothing but the Irish howl, the Irish brogue, Irish answers, and Irish bulls.[103]

Edgeworth, in her *Essay on Irish Bulls* (1802), was one of the first to make an effort to counter the image of Paddy as a droll imbecile. "Irish bulls" (oxymoronic phrases) and the ludicrous Irish accents common on the stage were targeted by Edgeworth and later Carleton as obstacles to understanding for which more "realistic" dialogues should be substituted. Samuel Lover's popular "Irish evenings" appear also to have had this goal in mind with their emphasis on Irish culture, folklore and music. On the whole, however, the typical Irish stage plays seem to have resisted reform, quite unlike the Irish genre in prose fiction. Lover himself was guilty of producing theatrical heroes similar to Handy Andy: fun-loving, hard-drinking, hard-fighting buffoons, often with pretensions to aristocracy or business.[104] The most significant exception to this was a type also popularized by Lover, the devil-may-care rogue, such as the title character of his 1837 play, *Rory O'More*. Plots alternated from violent slapstick to gushingly sentimental portrayals of Irish culture and rural life.[105]

The lack of sophistication of most plays in this genre, it may be speculated, may have made them unpopular with the English middle class and thus shielded them from middle class pressure for revision in favor of greater realism. Not until Dion Boucicault published *The Colleen Bawn* in 1860 did an Irish play appear that might have appealed to the educated middle class. Popular drama with Irish themes appears before then to have been comparatively unpretentious and of uniformly low quality.[106] The persistence of the late eighteenth-century model of the stage Irishman in these works therefore likely contributed to the concomitant low esteem that Englishmen outside the educated middle classes held for Irish immigrants in the 1840s and 1850s.

A leading element in the formation of English middle-class public opinion on Irish issues was the popular press. *Punch*, with a circulation of about 30,000 at the beginning of the famine,[107] has been singled out by historians such as L.P. Curtis as representative of the sort of anti-Irish racism that is supposed to have prevailed throughout the nineteenth century. As R.F. Foster has recently demonstrated, however, before the mid-1840s cartoons and articles in *Punch* did not represent the Irish as physically or mentally inferior.[108] Henry Mayhew and Douglas Jerrold, the radical founders of the magazine, instead worked through writers such as William M. Thackeray to espouse a moralistic and philanthropic stance on human affairs. Thus cartoons and jokes poked fun at supposed Irish character flaws but did not represent Irish characteristics as any more or less immutable than those of other peoples.[109]

The *Times* had a particularly powerful voice, though oddly enough modern historians have paid little attention to its statements on Ireland. The newspaper consistently devoted a great deal of attention to the "condition of Ireland question," but was no friend of the Irish people; indeed, abuse of the Irish was a regular feature of its columns. Leader articles disparaged the peasantry as an "ignorant and fiery multitude" easily deluded by the promises of rabble-rousers such as O'Connell.[110]

At the same time, however, the *Times*, like the majority of the British public, had by the beginning of 1845 not yet come to explain Irish difference on the basis of racial inferiority. Editorial suspicions that Irish degradation might be attributable to a perverse national character remained submerged under a veneer of liberal rhetoric, in which national characteristics were thought to be malleable in the long run and the moral improvement of the Irish was considered possible with effort. In an 1845 article about increasing poverty in Ireland before the potato blight, the *Times* argued that

> it is a fatal assumption to ascribe these calamities exclusively to the errors and infirmities of the Irish character; and set about alternately coercing and cajoling, as if it were a child or a maniac we had to deal with. No empire has ever yet treated a whole section of its subjects as inferior in heart and mind without incurring the condemnation of posterity.[111]

Other articles advanced the standard argument that the Irish were morally degraded but not wholly irredeemable.

In the autumn of 1845, however, the newspaper began to adopt a new stance simultaneously with the advance of the potato blight in Ireland. On August 21, 1845, the *Times* introduced to its readers the "Irish Commissioner" charged with an enquiry into the "Condition of the People of Ireland." The leader article declared that Englishmen had learned too little about Ireland from "irregular travels and tales" and "formal reports" like those of the Devon Commission. "Presumptuous as it may be called, we anticipate more effectual results from the more simple and personal agency of our correspondent. His efficiency will be proved by objectors." John Thadeus Delane, the editor, no doubt relished the prospect of wounded outcries of "landlord or Molly Maguire," in response to the devastating revelations of his commissioner.[112]

His choice for commissioner was a young barrister named Thomas Campbell Foster, whose skills in argumentation might be expected to stand the newspaper in good stead. Foster is an obscure figure, a native of Leeds who wrote a number of legal tracts and failed in an attempt to enter Parliament as a "liberal-conservative" in 1867.[113] In his first article he described himself as "a stranger to Ireland, and wholly devoid of Irish prejudices, with no motive whatsoever save an earnest desire to ascertain the truth, and to state it with strict impartiality."[114]

Foster's explanations of the causes of Irish poverty appeared at first to be unexceptional. Shortly after he arrived in the island he declared that "the source of all mischief in Ireland . . . is the *want of employment*."[115] He too saw hope in "a perfect assimilation of the two nations, for an extension of English sense and liberality to the Irish landlord, and English industry and obedience to the Irish tenant," which did not at present exist because "the union has not been consummated."[116] Though admitting the importance of race in, for example, explaining the difference between Ulster and Connemara, he insisted on the prospect of social remedies to erase the effects of racial difference.

Within a couple of weeks, however, Foster began to temper his continuing hope in social remedies with the conviction that the problem of racial difference would always remain. "There they are," he declared, "and we must make the best of them."[117] He did not delay long in elucidating his attitude further, though he was wary of offending Whig sensibilities of both the Irish and English varieties. His racial explanation of Irish trouble carried disturbing implications for proponents of self-help in Ireland:

Now, I know right well that I write on tender ground, and that I lay myself open to the charge of "national prejudice." . . . But I do not come to bandy compliments, but to ascertain facts, and to state them. It is the *nature* of the men on the east coast of Ireland [by which Foster means Ulster], by their activity, their enterprise, their intelligence, and their industry, to rise to wealth and to prosperity—to push themselves to accomplish greatness. . . . It is the *nature* of the men on the west coast to cling with strong affection and prejudice to old habits, to their land, to their kindred. Enterprise is forced upon them; they do not seek it as one of the pleasures of existence. . . . I am far from praising one race of people or blaming the other for that which is their *nature* and which they cannot help. This is not the part either of honesty or wisdom. Knowing the qualities of the men on the east, we may safely leave them to take care of themselves; they can run alone. It is the men on the west who . . . will require our aid, our instruction, our guidance, our example—who will require to be urged on, praised on, shamed on, led on, and, if necessary, forced on. Unfortunately for them, and for the country, the very opposite course has been taken—they have been oppressed, kept back, and *left to themselves*, and they starve.[118]

Foster's ideas, it needs to be emphasized, were very much against the mainstream of popular thought. The sources of his convictions can only be speculated at, and probably included members of the Anglo-Irish ascendancy with whom he came into contact. It is not unlikely, however, that he had also read the works of Robert Knox, who had gathered a small number of disciples to spread the news of his racial "discoveries" to the masses. Knox himself was frustrated that he was not credited for making known the "fact" of the centrality of race in explaining Irish troubles. As he sneered sarcastically in his 1850 work *The Races of Men*, "The proprietors [of the *Times*] sent a reporter to Ireland who made out this fact: nothing additional that I am aware of, unless it be that he ascertained that the middlemen and landlords were mostly Celtic also! Profound observer! Why did he pass St. Giles's? Marylebone? Whitechapel?"[119] Knox was perhaps ungrateful considering that the *Times* was responsible, in the famine years, for presenting a despairing English public with racial theory as an alternative to a liberal policy that seemed to have failed, and thus popularizing Knox's theories.

SUMMARY

Race in the biological sense played only a minor role in the British understanding of Irish difference before 1845. Writers who spoke of "race" in reference to Ireland almost always used the word in a social or class-based sense. The word had in 1845 not yet become a foundation for English justification for Irish submission. British writers did, it is true, maintain a deep suspicion of innate Irish difference. Though racial characteristics were popularly believed to be impermanent, the Irish even while becoming equals remained different, and subordinate.

In this sense an apparent self-contradiction lay at the heart of mainstream English attitudes toward Ireland. Although the assumptions of the age did not allow for the possibility that the Irish (or, indeed any people) were unimprovable, few English questioned the tradition of British dominion in Ireland as consisting of English rule and Irish subservience. The desire to fully assimilate Ireland into the British family of nations was commonly expressed,[120] but so was the determination to maintain the unequal relationship of the two islands. Were the Irish ever improved to the extent of being admitted as full moral and physical equals of the English, their desire for independence could no longer be denied, but to justify their subservience on the basis of inherent racial inferiority would have been to reject the dogma of the improvability of all men.

As we have seen in this chapter, the rhetoric of marriage provided a conceptual framework for reconciling these contradictions. Although the idea of the

Celtic as feminine and the English as masculine was a tradition of long standing on both sides of the Irish Sea, it was not until the second quarter of the nineteenth century that these assumptions were enmeshed within a rhetoric of the union as marriage.[121] In the Anglo-Irish union, the partners were said to be not unequal, but different. The English would realize themselves through the practice of a public and masculine role within the marriage, while the Irish would find their destiny in a feminine and domestic role. Integration of the two through "consummation" of the marriage would result in each making the other whole, bringing English values to the Irish and Irish values to the English. Marriage between a man and a woman was, as Lynda Nead has shown, conceptualized in much the same manner in Victorian England:

> The underlying principle of gender division in the nineteenth century was that the two sexes were different and complementary. Woman was never described as inferior to man; rather, she was different, and her differences were to be valued since they entirely complemented male attributes.[122]

In the English-Irish union, as in marriages of men and women, reality and rhetoric were of course not identical. Most English writers in the first half of the 1840s would have (and often did) angrily deny any accusations of Irish "inferiority." In reality, their professions of belief in Irish equality were belied by the fact that in almost every respect they treated the Irish as inferiors. Whether this hypocrisy was conscious or unconscious is not for the historian to say, but it is worth emphasizing again that the metaphor of marriage was a rhetorical device aimed at reconciling, at least on the surface, liberal ideals of human equality and the English determination to perpetuate their domination of Ireland.

The subordinate role of Ireland in the Anglo-Irish marriage was always clear—Hibernia could not survive independently. Once domesticated, however, the Irish would prove happy and congenial partners in the Union. The English therefore maintained an optimistic belief that Irish moral and social improvement would follow on their domestication through the spread of English law. Reconciled in the marital bliss of the Union, the two peoples would become friends and allies. Though the rhetoric of marriage remained a central element in the liberal attitude toward Ireland through the 1850s, the famine would for many Englishmen challenge the notion that the English and Irish could ever achieve marital bliss.

NOTES

1. Thomas Carlyle became convinced in the 1840s that Ireland was the center of the European "suppuration." Kenneth J. Fielding, introduction to *The Collected Letters of Thomas and Jane Welsh Carlyle*, Clyde De L. Ryals and Kenneth J. Fielding eds. 24 vols. (Durham: Duke University Press, 1995), 22:xii.

2. *Times* (London), April 14, 1846.

3. Usually this expressed goal of the Anglo-Irish union was combined with references to the earlier amalgamation of Saxon and Norman and sometimes Scottish and English.

4. This study does not take into consideration pamphlets published outside of England and Scotland, or unavailable at the British Library. Though very many pamphlets were published in Dublin they appear to have been largely intended for Irish, and often Irish nationalist, audiences.

5. In no sense are these categories clear-cut, though they do in general coincide with the expressed opinions of the leaders of the respective parties with regard to Irish policy, as we shall see in subsequent chapters.

6. "A Fellow of the Dublin Law Institute," *Ireland and Irish Questions Considered* (London: J. Hatchard and Son, 1842), 36–37, 44.

7. Ibid., 72.

8. James Grant, *Impressions of Ireland and the Irish*. 2 volumes (London: Hugh Cunningham, 1844), 2:189–190.

9. James Johnson, *A Tour in Ireland; with Meditations and Reflections* (London: S. Highley, 1844), 162–165.

10. Anonymous, *The South of Ireland and Her Poor* (London: Saunders and Otley, 1843), 9.

11. Including, as we shall see, Lord John Russell.

12. Anonymous, *The South of Ireland*, 11.

13. See below, in this chapter, for a further discussion of racial theory in England at this time. Racial characteristics were in the 1840s not yet widely considered to be either sharply defined or permanent.

14. Daniel Owen-Madden, *Ireland and Its Rulers; since 1829*. 3 vols. (London: T.C. Newby, 1843–1844), 3:238. The author exaggerated Whig principles, of course, which were based upon the idea that while morals and habits could be changed, the ultimately feminine aspects of Irish nature could not.

15. Ibid., 1:43–46.

16. Johnson, *A Tour in Ireland*, 79–83.

17. *Times* (London), January 25, 1847.

18. Rev. M.P. Perceval, *The Amelioration of Ireland Contemplated, in a Series of Papers* (London: W.J. Cleaver, 1844), 5–12.

19. Samuel Smiles, *History of Ireland and the Irish People, Under the Government of England* (London: William Strange, 1844), x.

20. Owen-Madden, *Ireland and Its Rulers*, 1:127–128, 154.

21. Ibid., 1:46.

22. The multitude of plans advanced for the development of Ireland in this period are closely interlinked with the course of English politics, and will be discussed in the next chapter.

23. Smiles, *History of Ireland and the Irish People*, ix.

24. Ibid., x.

25. C.C.F. Greville, *Past and Present Policy of England towards Ireland* (London: Edward Moxon, 1845), 1.

26. Smiles, *History of Ireland and the Irish People*, 20.

27. Ibid., 26, 42.

28. Ibid., 168.

29. Ibid., 258–259.

30. Ibid., 470.

31. Ibid., 471.

32. *Chambers' Edinburgh Journal*, new series 7, 160 (23 January 1847), 49.

33. Sir Leslie Stephen and Sir Sidney Lee, eds., *The Dictionary of National Biography*, 21 volumes (Oxford: Oxford University Press, 1917–), 13:137–138.

34. W.H. Maxwell, *History of the Irish Rebellion in 1798; with Memoirs of the Union, and Emmett's Insurrection in 1803*, 3rd ed. (London: H.G. Bohn, 1852), 84.

35. Boylan and Foley, *Political Economy and Colonial Ireland*, 126.

36. Some Irish writers, most significantly the poet and historian Thomas Moore, maintained a romanticized concept of Celtic history and character. These works were popular in England and contributed to the English belief in the poetic and romantic qualities of the Irish character.

37. William Makepeace Thackeray, *The Irish Sketch Book, 1842* (Oxford: Oxford University Press, 1908), 66.

38. Nancy Stepan, *The Idea of Race in Science: Great Britain 1800–1960* (Hamden, CT: Archon Books, 1982), 1.

39. James Cowles Prichard, *The Eastern Origin of the Celtic Nations, Proved by a Comparison of Their Dialects with the Sanskrit, Greek, Latin, and Teutonic Languages: Forming a Supplement to Researches into the Physical History of Mankind*, 2nd ed. (London: Houlston and Wright, 1857), 3–9.

40. Stepan, *The Idea of Race in Science*, 3.

41. Ibid., 36. Prichard denied that learned behavior could be inherited, but in this he was running against a majority of scientists who continued to advance the Lamarckian model. See Michael Banton, *Racial Theories* (Cambridge: Cambridge University Press, 1987), 7–23.

42. Owen-Madden, *Ireland and Its Rulers*, 1:1–2.

43. Stepan, *The Idea of Race in Science*, 29.

44. Nancy Stepan has little to say about the reasons for the subversion of polygenism by monogenism at the beginning of the century, and little other research has been done on the subject. It would appear, however, that this intellectual shift was connected in some manner to the rise of the doctrines of social and economic liberalism, which assumed that its laws were applicable to all people equally.

45. Robert Knox, *The Races of Men: A Philosophical Inquiry into the Influence of Race over the Destinies of Nations.* 2nd ed. (London: Henry Renshaw, 1862), 14–15, 565.

46. Arthur Young's *A Tour in Ireland* (1780) was the most widely read and influential travel account to appear in this period. Most travel books written in the mid-nineteenth century refer back to it as a standard.

47. John Heuston, "Kilkee—the Origins and Development of a West Coast Resort," in Barbara O'Connor and Michael Cronin, eds., *Tourism in Ireland: A Critical Analysis* (Cork: Cork University Press, 1993), 20.

48. [Mr. & Mrs. S.C. Hall], *Ireland: Its Scenery, Character, etc.*, 3 vols. (London: Howard Parsons, 1841–1843), 1:vii.

49. Johnson, *A Tour in Ireland*, 38–39.

50. [Mr. & Mrs. S.C. Hall], *Ireland*, 1:2.

51. That is, France or America.

52. Johnson, *A Tour in Ireland*, 144.

53. Phyllis Weinroth Bernt, "William Makepeace Thackeray and the Irish: A Study in Victorian Prejudice" (University of Nebraska Ph.D. 1979), 12.

54. Thackeray, *Irish Sketch-Book*, 102.

55. Ibid., 91, 61.

56. Ibid., 303.

57. Ibid., 302.

58. Ibid., 364.

59. Rev. Caesar Otway, *A Tour in Connaught: Comprising Sketches of Clonmacnoise, Joyce Country, and Achill* (Dublin: William Curry, Jun. and Company, 1839), 4–5.

60. The similarity of this attitude to that of Americans of European origin who attributed native American burial mounds to an ancient "superior race" is striking.

61. Otway, *A Tour in Connaught*, 262.

62. Catherine M. O'Connell, *Excursions in Ireland during 1844 and 1850* (London: Richard Bentley, 1852), 52–55. Though prefamine visitors to Ireland often noted this idea of Moore's, it appears not to have received much attention in England until after the famine.

63. Thackeray, *Irish Sketch-Book*, 42–43.

64. Ibid., 91.

65. Said, *Culture and Imperialism*, 84.

66. Ibid., 49. Cultures in Said's understanding are "contrapuntal ensembles" formed by the interaction of both dominating and dominated discourses (Ibid., 59–60).

67. Barbara Hayley, "'The Eerishers are marchin' in leeterature': British Critical Reception of Nineteenth-Century Anglo-Irish Fiction" in Wolfgang Zach and Heinz Kosok, eds., *Literary Interrelations: Ireland, England and the World*, vol. 3, *National Images and Stereotypes* (Tübingen: Gunter Narr Verlag, 1987), 40–41.

68. In England he maintained a reputation as the best Irish novelist well into the 1870s (Barry Sloan, *The Pioneers of Anglo-Irish Fiction 1800–1850* [Gerrards Cross, Bucks: Colin Smythe, 1986], 191).

69. *Dictionary of National Biography*, 11:1017–1019.

70. Charles James Lever, *The Confessions of Harry Lorrequer* (New York: The Century Co., 1905), 220.

71. Ibid., 362.

72. Ibid., 393, 405.

73. *Dictionary of National Biography*, 12:176–178.

74. Maureen Waters, *The Comic Irishman* (Albany: State University of New York Press, 1984), 4–5.

75. Samuel Lover, *Handy Andy* (London: J.M. Dent, 1907), 99.

76. Ibid., 207.

77. Ibid., 111.

78. Ibid., 298.

79. Ibid., 407. This argument for the North African heritage of the Irish was not unpopular in the 1840s.

80. Ibid., 116.

81. Ibid., 310.

82. Robert Lee Wolff, *William Carleton, Irish Peasant Novelist: A Preface to His Fiction* (New York: Garland Publishing, 1980), 4.

83. Barbara Hayley, *Carleton's "Traits and Stories" and the 19th Century Anglo-Irish Tradition* (Totowa, N.J.: Barnes & Noble, 1983), 274.

84. Greville, *Past and Present Policy of England towards Ireland*, 107, vii.

85. Owen-Madden, *Ireland and Its Rulers*, 1:255–266.

86. The policy of supporting the Catholic church as an instrument of social control in Ireland, of which government support for Maynooth was one aspect, will be discussed fully in the next chapter.

87. Eileen A. Sullivan, *William Carleton* (Boston: Twayne, 1983), 20, 109.

88. William Carleton, *Traits and Stories of the Irish Peasantry*, 2 vols. (London: William S. Orr and Dublin: William Curry, Jun. & Co., 1843–1844), 1:i–iii.

89. Ibid., 1:viii.

90. Hayley, *Carleton's "Traits and Stories,"* 275.

91. Carleton, *Traits and Stories*, 1:xxii–xxiii.

92. William Carleton, *The Black Prophet: A Tale of Irish Famine* (London: Simms and M'Intyre, 1847), 452.

93. Sloan, *The Pioneers of Anglo-Irish Fiction 1800–1850*, 138–144.

94. Waters, *The Comic Irishman*, 10.

95. Although as mentioned above, the Anglo-Irish authors felt themselves constrained not to blatantly transgress what they believed to be the assumptions of the English reading public. Likewise, it is certainly true to say that the Anglo-Irish authors borrowed much of their definition of Irishness from what English writers presented in travel writings and other nonfictional literature.

96. The two had originally been close friends before a falling out, following which Lever attempted to ruin Thackeray's reputation in Ireland by publicly characterizing the *Irish Sketch-Book* as anti-Irish. Bernt, *William Makepeace Thackeray*, 234.

97. Robert Tracy, introduction to Anthony Trollope, *The MacDermots of Ballycloran* (Oxford: Oxford University Press, 1989), ix-xi.

98. Trollope, *The MacDermots of Ballycloran*, 3.

99. Robert Tracy introduction to ibid., xv-xvi.

100. Trollope, *The MacDermots of Ballycloran*, 9–10.

101. Ibid., 64.

102. G.C. Duggan, *The Stage Irishman: A History of the Irish Play and Stage Characters from the Earliest Times* (New York: Benjamin Blom, 1969), 289–290.

103. Ibid., 279.

104. Waters, *The Comic Irishman*, 42–43.

105. James Malcolm Nelson, "From Rory and Paddy to Boucicault's Myles, Shaun and Conn: The Irishman on the London Stage, 1830–1860" *Eire-Ireland* 13 (Fall 1978): 81–92.

106. Duggan, *The Stage Irishman*, 280–281.

107. Peter Gray, "*Punch* and the Great Famine," *History-Ireland* 1 (Summer 1993), 27.

108. Foster, *Paddy and Mr. Punch*, 173–174.

109. Gray, "*Punch* and the Great Famine," 26–27.

110. *Times* (London), April 1, 1845.

111. *Times* (London), June 26, 1845.

112. *Times* (London), August 21, 1845.

113. *Dictionary of National Biography*, 7:503.

114. *Times* (London), August 21, 1845.

115. *Times* (London), August 25, 1845.

116. *Times* (London), August 27, 1845.

117. *Times* (London), September 12, 1845.

118. *Times* (London), September 16, 1845.

119. Knox, *The Races of Men*, 14–15.

120. See for example, John Russell to Lord Auckland, September 23, 1846, PRO 30/22/5C, ff. 255–256, Public Record Office.

121. Of course the increasing Irish political dependance on England resulting from the Act of Union made it much easier to conceptualize the English-Irish relationship as matrimonial.

122. Lynda Nead, *Myths of Sexuality: Representations of Women in Victorian Britain* (Oxford: Basil Blackwell, 1988), 34.

3

Official Britain and the Condition of the Ireland Question, 1841–1852

Mid-nineteenth century Irish history is a relatively popular subject, but the tendency of political and social-cultural historians to move in separate orbits has limited the usefulness of many studies of the period. Political biographies of Peel and Russell and analyses of their administrations have generally neglected to give attention to popular opinion, both in terms of its constraining influence on legislation and its tendency to shape the attitudes of the politicians themselves. Many social and cultural studies, meanwhile, neglect to place public thought in the context of political events, and at the same time fail to trace the diffusion of popular attitudes among the politically influential.

This chapter cannot pretend to remedy this deficiency in the historical literature. Its purpose is rather to suggest some trends in the interaction of politics and culture as it related to the Irish question during the Peel (1841–1846) and Russell (1846–1852) administrations, and to evaluate the historical literature in the light of these trends. That popular ideas and divisions on the Irish issue were reflected in the attitudes of the governing elites is unsurprising. The degree to which rapidly changing popular attitudes first outstripped and then constrained the policies of Whig politicians in the famine years is, however, noteworthy, and tends to contradict historical studies that either ignore or misinterpret the impact of public opinion on policy-making.

In addition, the famine years are revealing for the light they shed on the manner by which popular attitudes evolved in conjunction with changes in the political sphere. The profound transformation in British perceptions of the Irish that marked the decade from 1845 to 1855 was to a large extent in response to shifting perceptions of political ways and means in Ireland. As political and economic factors appeared to limit the options available to the rulers of Ireland, a new definition of the Irish people and their role in the empire emerged in adaptation to the new political circumstances. As will become evident in this and the following chapter, this process really began at the popular level. The Whig political leaders clung for quite some time to prefamine conceptions of the Irish problem, but they were forced, often unwillingly, to respond to trends working on the minds of the English public at large.

THE PEEL ADMINISTRATION

When the Conservative Sir Robert Peel took office in 1841, there was little cause for optimism that he would be either able or willing to work much change in Ireland. The preceding Whig administrations had devoted a relatively large amount of attention to the affairs of the island, but the Conservatives hoped to keep Irish affairs firmly in the background. In 1841 conditions seemed appropriate for this purpose. The Irish party in parliament had been considerably weakened by recent elections, the Irish countryside was more or less at peace, and Daniel O'Connell seemed reasonably quiet after having secured a series of minor reforms in partnership with the Whigs in the 1830s. Repealers and other Irish radicals who would not remain silent were studiously ignored by the government. As Peel wrote to his Home Secretary Sir James Graham, "when a country is tolerably quiet, it is better for a Government to be *hard of hearing* in respect to seditious language than to be very agile in prosecuting."[1]

Even in quiet times, Ireland was for Peel primarily a security issue. As such, he worked in his typically pragmatic manner to keep the island stable. Peel intended to accomplish this end ideally by binding Irishmen more fully to the state, not through widespread social reform, but by bringing Irish Catholics into government offices, supporting multidenominational and Catholic educational establishments, and promoting state endowment of the Irish clergy. A letter of August 1843 to the Lord Lieutenant of Ireland, Earl de Grey, laid out Peel's ideas on the first principle in some detail:

What is the advantage to the Roman Catholics of having removed their legal disabilities if some how or other they are constantly met by a preferable claim on the part of Protestants and if they do not practically reap the advantage of their nominal Equality as to Civil Privilege? . . . Why has the Protestant a preferable Claim? Because he has had for a long series of years the advantage of monopoly—of privilege secured to him by law. . . . Surely there must be many Roman Catholics of intelligence—tired of Excitement & Agitation, on whom a Favour of the Crown bestowed on one of their Body would have a beneficial effect.[2]

Graham appended a note to this letter declaring, "I consider the doctrines contained in Sir Robert Peel's letter full of wisdom and truth; and I am prepared to subscribe to every word of it."[3] On education, Graham reflected the prime minster's own attitude in a letter to Peel of November 1841:

The peculiar circumstances of Ireland must never be forgotten: the religion of the great body of the People is without endowment: and if the State is to assist in their Education, it must administer it in the best form, which will be accepted, not in the mode, which a Protestant Government might most desire. You may not at once make Converts; but the tendency of even the partial admission of Truth is to mitigate Error and to dispel the darkness of Superstition.[4]

On provision of the clergy, Graham again echoed Peel's own ideas in a letter to him of October 1843: "Without an adequate Provision for [Ireland's] Clergy of the National Religion, a conciliatory Policy must be incomplete and ineffectual."[5]

Despite Graham's almost constant support, Peel was forced to carry these policies through against a significant amount of opposition from within his own party. The Irish government under de Grey granted offices only under duress. The Anglican establishment successfully (with the exception of the seminary at Maynooth) resisted any movement toward state support for separate religious educational establishments. Finally, the possibility of paying Irish priests withered in the face of Protestant and Catholic opposition. The "Tory" element of the Conservative party is not an easily identifiable group, but even if we associate it loosely with those who would later be known as Protectionists, it is difficult to generalize about their perspectives on the Irish. Bentinck, Stanley and Disraeli, the most prominent Protectionist politicians, generally took little interest in Ireland before 1845. Their response to the famine demonstrates little of the preoccupation with moral improvement of the Irish that characterized Peel and the Whigs.

The political opposition to Peel outside his party, by contrast, lacked both the strength and the will to effectively push the Conservatives toward reform in Ireland. John Bright, for example, expressed more public concern over Irish affairs than any other radical politician. From his entry into Parliament in 1843 he actively campaigned for the stimulation of industry in Ireland, the absence of which he blamed on "the fruits of aristocratic & territorial occupation & privilege."[6] Like Samuel Smiles, Bright believed that the best means of reviving Irish fortunes was to strike at the "feudal fetters" that bound the Irish people. He therefore advocated measures aiming at "free trade in land" and the disestablishment of the Church of Ireland.[7] His presuppositions about the causes of Irish misfortune were, as we saw in the last chapter, to a large extent shared by the British public, but the solutions he proposed were less popular and found little support outside the ranks of fellow radicals like Richard Cobden and religious nonconformists.

Peel's ideas were similar in many respects to those of the "Whig" school, which as we have seen emphasized integration as the ideal goal of Irish policy and treated religion as a divisive issue that needed to be overcome. Peel's concept of integration was for the most part limited to the government and education. His eagerness to minimize the temporal influence of religious ideas in Ireland was, however, very much in line with popular thinking.

Peel's reluctance to translate ideas into action in the area of social reform in Ireland was, however, evident in his response to the proposals of the Devon Commission. This parliamentary commission under the chairmanship of Lord Devon was instituted in November 1843 to inquire into the Irish land system. Its appearance was in part a response to the resurgence of repeal agitation in that year. Under the scrutiny of extensive publicity the commission advocated a number of reforms in the agrarian and political system in Ireland. Although the government carried into law some of Lord Devon's less significant suggestions, such as a reform in the law on charitable bequests and an increased grant to the Maynooth seminary, the most important recommendation of the commission was the institution of a system of tenant compensation for agricultural improvements. This the Peel administration put forward only half-heartedly in June 1845 as a bill that was quickly defeated.

On the question of the pace and extent of social reform, Peel appears to have been substantially out of step with public attitudes. The demand for economic and social reform in Ireland was pressed by English writers in the years before the famine in a wide array of books and pamphlets. At first glance it might appear that the disproportionate influence of Irish ascendancy politicians in Conservative circles severely limited Peel's options, but there is no evidence to indicate that Peel had any inclination for extensively reforming Irish society.

His advancement of Corn Law repeal in 1845–1846 was a matter of political expediency, though he justified it as Irish social reform legislation.

When O'Connell's repeal agitation appeared again as a force in British national affairs in 1843, the prime minister's response was focused on his primary concern of keeping order. Though at times cynical and opportunistic, Peel's policy was, however, surprisingly moderate under the circumstances. Until 1845 Peel remained reasonably confident about the prospects of his own version of the integration of Ireland into the Union. When the Peel administration came to power in 1841, the Irish political presence in Parliament was at its weakest point in over a decade. The government, delighted at this state of affairs, scrupulously avoided the lurking problem of Irish poverty. In 1842 Chartist activity provided a convenient excuse for keeping Ireland in the background. By the spring of 1843, however, the revival of the Repeal Association and the organization by O'Connell of "monster meetings" in favor of repeal throughout Ireland thrust this unwelcome subject back on the British political stage.

Growing fears of rebellion in Ireland, fueled by panicky letters from de Grey and other members of the Irish administration, led the Conservative government to propose in May 1843 an arms bill limiting the sale and purchase of firearms. The protracted Parliamentary debate on this issue in July was the most significant for years, as Whigs and Radicals joined the Irish in opposing it, though the bill was passed into law in August.[8] The resistance to the arms bill nevertheless convinced Peel to postpone any further coercive measures despite pressure from within his party. He feared as well that pressing a coercion bill would only lead to the spread of unrest into England: "We are not well prepared for it at a time when there is much discontent and dissatisfaction in this Country, and many elements of disorder which it would be very easy to combine."[9]

Until 1845 Peel remained firm in standing against those hot-headed members of his cabinet who advocated a more desperate and repressive response to the repeal agitation. Graham, a sober enough politician under quieter conditions, warned Peel in May 1843 that "the banner of Rebellion is unfurled," with the Catholic hierarchy, the "Tea totallers" and the United States ranging themselves behind the Repeal Association, and that if something was not done immediately "none of us can continue to rule the country."[10] As repeal agitation and rural unrest increased through 1844 and into 1845, some members of the cabinet called for fines to be levied on districts in which a murder was committed. The idea was that the notorious tendency of the Irish to avoid informing on each other could be overridden by the prospect of loss of money, but in January 1845 Peel remained adamantly opposed to this measure:

I object to the imposition of penalties to be levied indiscriminately on a District . . . because I believe that no vigilance on the part of the inhabitants of that District, could in the great majority of these Cases prevent the Commission of the Crime. . . . I think that the penalty would be an unjust one.[11]

Peel's continued confidence in the prospects for the further integration of Ireland into Britain was representative of English popular attitudes as described in the last chapter. In part, the continued insistence on integration was a defensive reaction to the arguments of the repealers, but at the same time it was symptomatic of the resiliency of the liberal view of Ireland even in the face of political stress. Though some historians, notably Roy Foster and Sheridan Gilley, have suggested that English perceptions of Ireland became more or less favorable in direct proportion to the amount of trouble that Irish difficulties were causing, the ability of English liberals to remain optimistic about Ireland even in the face of the "monster meetings" would indicate that only profound stress could lead to a commensurate change in attitudes. Even so, though the repeal agitation was not in itself enough to work a change of outlook, it undoubtedly contributed to the English frustration with Ireland that would lead to the rise of racialism after the famine and to the Young Ireland rising in 1848.

The velvet glove with which Peel at times handled the Irish peasantry was shed when it came to dealing with O'Connell, whom the prime minister was under few compunctions to attack directly. Arresting O'Connell, which was done in October of 1843, appeared to Peel and many of his ministers as the simplest means of defeating repeal. A blatantly unfair trial with a stacked jury resulted in the Liberator's conviction in February 1844, and in May he was sentenced to a £2,000 fine and one year's imprisonment.[12] Although O'Connell's verdict was reversed by the Law Lords in September 1844, his trial and imprisonment had for a year dominated English politics and riveted popular attention. While the *Times* used the trial as an occasion to pursue its vendetta against O'Connell, a number of English writers visited O'Connell in prison and published surprisingly favorable portrayals of a man who was often looked to as the only one capable of standing up to the growing influence of the Young Ireland movement. Lord John Russell, meanwhile, had used the occasion of O'Connell's trial and conviction to provoke a nine-day debate on Ireland in the Commons. Lord Broughton's journal records a conversation with the Whig leader on this subject in January 1844:

He spoke in the strongest terms of reprobation against the Government doings in Ireland, and when I said that I feared the people of England would not sympathise with him in that respect, said he was sorry for it, but that would not reconcile him to injustice or silence him; quite the contrary, he would do his duty with more earnestness. If the people were wrong they ought to be put right.[13]

For all of the conflict aroused by O'Connell's trial, however, it would pale in contrast with what was to come.

THE POTATO BLIGHT

The potato disease, a fungal infection that had been carried to Europe by way of South American guano that was used as fertilizer, made its first appearance in Ireland in August 1845. It did not elicit an immediate response from the Peel administration, though ministers were well aware of the potentially catastrophic effects of a failure of the potato crop because of the extreme dependence of the Irish peasantry on this source of food. For months, however, it was difficult to discern just how widespread would be the damage left in the wake of the disease, partly because the rot often became evident in potatoes only weeks after harvest. Peel solicited information on the blight, and read hundreds of letters on the state of the potato crop. These reports varied extremely widely, however, reflecting the uneven progress of the disease.[14] Exacerbating the problem was Peel's suspicion that the Irish could not be trusted to report conditions without inflating their gravity, though at the same time he proved more willing to believe reports of popular unrest. As the prime minister wrote to Graham, "There is such a tendency to exaggeration and inaccuracy in Irish reports that delay in acting on them is always desirable."[15]

The first substantive measure adopted by the cabinet was to order the purchase of £100,000 worth of Indian corn from the United States. This was obviously not enough to make up for the loss of the entire potato crop. Peel hoped, however, to keep prices down by selling small amounts of corn to the Irish at cost through government depots whenever prices threatened to rise. The measure was not without precedent, being similar to one he had adopted as Irish Chief Secretary during a smaller crisis in 1816–1817, and was effective in keeping prices to a manageable level through the spring of 1846.

The measure was not uncontroversial, however. Irish merchants were importunate in their demands that the government cease importing corn, claiming that they were being driven out of business. The prime minister ignored them for a time. He admitted after leaving office, however, that he would before long have had to heed their demands, because abandonment of the Irish food trade by private merchants would have thrown the whole burden of feeding the people upon the British government.[16] Others decried the inadequacy of the measure and demanded that "for God's sake the Government should send out to America for more Indian corn"; but Peel rejected these entreaties in terms that anticipated Russell's later arguments that feeding the peasantry was the business of the Irish landlords, not the English people:

> It is quite impossible for the Government to support four million people. It is utterly impossible for us to adopt means of preventing cases of individual misery in the wilds of Galway or Donegal or Mayo. In such localities the people must look to the local proprietors, resident and non-resident.[17]

Public works were the second major component of Peel's program. A measure accepted by Parliament in March 1846 provided for works that would be financed in equal parts by local taxation and treasury grant. The Irish Board of Works would supervise applications from local authorities seeking government loans to undertake projects such as road building or river drainage. Relief tickets supposedly issued on the basis of need by local relief committees were necessary for anyone seeking employment on the works. In theory, therefore, wages would reach the most needy peasants in the areas hardest hit by the blight, tiding them over and preventing starvation before the next harvest.

Before long, however, a rash of applications for grants swamped the Board of Works. By August 1846, local authorities had made requests worth £1,292,853, of which the Board of Works saw fit to grant £458,143.[18] Accusations of "jobbery" in the distribution of grants almost inevitably arose; indeed, corruption was assumed to attend on most large-scale government operations and to pervade Irish affairs generally. Localities *were* often able to secure grants by lobbying the government when they would not have been able to do so solely on the basis of need.[19] Applications for employment, in addition, far outnumbered the jobs available. By the end of the summer of 1846, it was apparent that the works system was very near to breaking down entirely. The utter ignorance of most British ministers of the true extent of Irish poverty was exposed in the process.

At the same time, the collapse or nonexistence of local relief committees made it impossible to determine which of those seeking employment were in distress solely because of the blight, and which were the "professional poor." Travelers in Ireland had experienced little difficulty in their own minds separating beggars from the "genuinely distressed." It seemed easy enough to give money to a cottier in distress and then to spurn the mendicants of Cork, as Thackeray did. The government's inability to be equally discriminating caused ministers a great deal of anxiety, and contributed in both the Peel and Russell administrations to decisions to limit aid altogether.[20]

One portion of the British political establishment met the crisis by denying that it existed. The Protectionists, Tories like Disraeli and Lord George Bentinck who split with Peel over Corn Law repeal, portrayed the Irish food shortage as a political fabrication.[21] Peel, they argued, was pretending there was a crisis in order to justify his demand for repeal of the Corn Laws. Years later Disraeli continued to insist that "the quantity of food when Parliament met in '46 was much more considerable than the ministry supposed or led Parliament to believe, and in the first five months of that year can scarcely be said to have been deficient."[22]

The current consensus of political historians is that Peel did in fact primarily use the potato blight as an excuse for repeal of the Corn Laws. The weight of evidence supports the contention that he had actually made up his mind on this issue some time before the autumn of 1845. In this sense the potato blight was from 1845 to 1846 little more than a pawn in the battle over Corn Law repeal, with which most politicians were more concerned. Peelites and Whigs played up the significance of the blight as a means of justifying their desire for Corn Law repeal, while Protectionists denied Irish distress in their campaign to maintain the status quo.

It is also true that the scarcity of 1845–1846 was mild compared with the one that followed. There was little or no starvation while Peel was in office, even before the importation of Indian corn began to keep food prices down.[23] There is no evidence, however, to support the contention that Peel did not believe in the reality of the crisis, though no doubt like any skilled politician he knew how to take advantage of it for his own ends. His letters show that he was genuinely alarmed by the blight and feared for the consequences if the tariff on corn were not abolished. Bentinck was by contrast as late as 1847 still calling into question whether there had been any potato disease, let alone a famine, before July 1846.[24]

If politicians were willing to use the crisis for their own ends, they did not extend the same freedom to the Irish peasantry. Fear that the peasants were taking advantage of distress for *their* own ends combined with concern that they would use the blight as justification for violence and outrage. It was during this period of the potato disease that Peel's hitherto optimistic conviction of the prospects for integration, typified by his resistance to calls for coercion, began to crumble. In March of 1845 he wrote Graham that "There is more advantage in repressing outrage by means of the ordinary Laws and above all by the courage and resolution of the owners of property, than by any attempt to supply the place of courage and resolution by extraordinary laws."[25] By December 1845, however, Peel was writing in a memorandum to Graham and other members of the cabinet that in view of reports coming in from Ireland,

> nothing will effect [the pacification of Ireland] but a pecuniary motive . . . the people are so radically corrupt and sanguinary that there is a sympathy with the murderer . . . selfishness and the fear of pecuniary [punishment] must supply the motives to give evidence against an Assassin which the natural and instructive feelings of mankind supply in more favored countries.[26]

Peel, therefore, advocated the district fines that he had rejected earlier and completed his legislation for Ireland in February 1846 with a coercion bill. The fight for this bill would last for months and eventually bring his ministry down, but in the process it also severely, if only temporarily, split the Whigs. Peel's justification of this bill to his own party was highly emotive; in a cabinet memorandum of June 1846, he declared that "the cry in England . . . must be 'Coercion for Ireland,'" and added that the defeat of the bill must signify the victory over the government "not merely of Repealers, but of the disturbers of the public peace and promoters of assassination throughout Ireland," in which event the government must resign.[27]

It is probably not going too far to argue that Peel's rapid change of opinion on the issue of coercion was partially a ploy to draw attention to the severity of Irish troubles and thereby gain support for his effort to repeal the corn laws. Peel's correspondence on the troubles in Ireland nevertheless carries an air of conviction that is difficult to attribute solely to his political opportunism. Examination of his papers reveals the great extent to which the prime minister was snowed under in 1845–1846 by fearful reports from Ireland of the dangers of a full-scale insurrection there. Though far from being a credulous man (before 1845 he was wont to dismiss such reports as "alarmist"), by the spring of 1846 it was evident that the fear of an Irish uprising had taken a strong grip on Peel's mind.

The language of accounts from Ireland in this period makes it easy to understand Peel's fears. Irish landlords first met the potato blight in the fall of 1845 by spreading reports that their tenants were using it as an excuse to refuse payment of rents and stop working in the expectation that the government would eventually support them. Members of the Irish administration such as the chief secretary, Thomas Fremantle, duly passed these fears on to Peel:

> The disposition among the disaffected to make use of their state of alarm for the purpose of preventing the payment of rents is extending—we are

informed from several quarters that a very bad spirit prevails—& two cases are reported this morning of Priests from the altar recommending the people to make no payments—& hinting that, when the famine comes, they may help themselves, the law of nature being superior to the law of man.[28]

Lord Heytesbury, the lord lieutenant of Ireland, at the same time subjected the prime minister to gloomy reports to the effect that "the people begin to show symptoms of discontent which may ripen into something worse."[29] Dr. Lyon Playfair, whom Peel had sent to investigate the causes of the blight, warned him that "political excitement has fevered [the] minds" of the peasantry, to the extent that rebellion was a strong possibility.[30]

Irish landlords, magistrates, merchants and others at the same time harassed Peel with even more alarmist reports. Their letters combined fulminations against the repeal agitation with cries of "cold blooded Murder" and warnings that the future held the probability of "Famine, Disease, and perhaps civil WAR."[31] Local magistrates sent him long and gruesomely detailed reports of atrocities in the provinces.[32] At the same time many of them assured Peel either that the Irish peasants were "horribly indolent" when it came to saving themselves from destitution, or were even "*laughing in their sleeve at the Humbug*" of a potato blight, which they used as an excuse for government aid.[33]

Curiously, few of Peel's English correspondents wrote of the Irish peasantry in anything like the hateful and contemptuous terms typical of letters from Irish men. B.J. Lloyd, a Leeds merchant who had just spent three months in Ireland, assured Peel in January 1846 that "the labouring class of Ireland are disposed to work if work can be found for them," and argued for industrial development and the creation of an Irish middle class.[34] J. Charlton, an English Anglican clergyman visiting the country, spoke confidently of the improvement to be hoped for from education, and ascribed Irish troubles to social causes rather than any innate traits of her people.[35] Other English correspondents saw the advent of civilization in Ireland as achievable through means such as the Poor Law, education, and the replacement of the potato by macaroni as a staple food.[36] Thomas Ensor of London wrote letters in April and May 1846 advocating a liberal and humanitarian policy in Ireland and deploring coercion.

Ireland in her guilty deluded sins demands our pity rather than our vengeance. The crimes we deplore are the natural offspring of the social state in which we have allowed her to remain. . . . Her sons have not lost the principle of improvement. Their very vices show it. There is a natural force of character about the Irish which may be turned to great & noble purposes.[37]

There were a few significant exceptions to the general tendency of Peel's English correspondents to view the Irish situation more charitably than did members of the Irish ascendancy. These were the English doctors Lyon Playfair and Robert Traile, and the geologist and dean of Westminster, William Buckland, sent by the government to investigate the cause and possible cure of the blight. Unfortunately, these men, whose opinions and actions were well-known and influential with the English public and government, almost uniformly blamed the progress and devastation of the blight on the failings of the Irish peasantry. Playfair wrote repeatedly of the peasantry's apparent unwillingness to follow his advice on the preservation of potatoes, complaining of their "reckless" attitude and "complete apathy about the destruction of the crop."[38] Traile sneered at "the miserable apathy, the unmanageable doggedness, of the people, who would not move a hand, but folded their arms to wait, in listlessness & torpid stupidity, the ruin of the food of themselves & their families," and boasted that with fifty men and authority from the government he could "rescue the people from famine" by ventilating potato pits.[39] Buckland wrote in support of Playfair and Traile that "vast mischief is taking place from the inertia of the poor & stupidity of the farmers."[40] All agreed that coercion would be necessary in the face of a rebellion they believed was incipient.

THE RUSSELL GOVERNMENT

Lord John Russell raged in reaction to Peel's coercion bill that the current administration "was the greatest curse to Ireland, and that while they were in office no good was possible there."[41] As he wrote privately, "it is wrong to arrest men and put them in prison on the ground that they *may* be murderers and housebreakers."[42] Significantly, however, he found himself increasingly isolated in this opinion within his own party. Lord Clanricarde, a Whig and an Irish landlord, assured the Whig leader that "the honest peasants—even those not generally fond of the law—are frightened, & very anxious to see order restored."[43] Lord Clarendon, who would later head the Whig administration in Ireland, was more blunt, writing that most of the important Whig leaders were "much annoyed" by Russell's opposition to coercion, and that even "Liberal Irish" Members of Parliament (MPs) who were publicly opposed to the bill privately supported it.[44] Russell maintained his idealism even in the face of such criticism, however, replying to one plea of Bessborough's for coercion that his vision for the future of Ireland included the Irish landlords compelled to act fairly by their tenants,—the national revenue sustained by adequate taxes—crime put down by vigilance & exertion, rather than by shutting up honest people all night—and when measures of severity are necessary taking care to give the soothing as well as the drastic medicine.

The defeat of Peel's coercion bill on June 29 provided Russell and the Whigs with their long-awaited opportunity to do justice to Ireland. At the same time, it gave the Peelites an opportunity to congratulate themselves on their successes in administering the island. Graham, writing to Peel on September 4, flattered him with the assurance, "[Y]ou will think of this and be comforted when friends forsake you, when enemies assail you, and when the tinsel of the vanities of public life becomes tarnished in your estimation . . . In short, your policy has triumphed, and a national calamity has been averted."[45] In fact they should have congratulated themselves on being able to leave office before the real crisis began. As events would demonstrate, in effect there was little difference in the policies of the two governments. Even so, both Russell and Peel showed when out of office that it was easy to be high-minded and idealistic about Ireland when not shouldered with the responsibilities of office.

For most of the duration of the Peel administration, the Whigs in opposition had been eager to portray themselves as the party of justice for Ireland. They prided themselves on what they had done for the country in the 1830s, when Russell in the Home Office had helped to establish a close relationship with Daniel O'Connell, moved toward Irish Church reform, and passed the Irish Poor Law. Fighting opposition from the dogmatically laissez-faire wing of the party, Russell and his supporters had even attempted in 1838 to institute a program of railway building as a public works project. Though Peel managed to defeat this bill and amend others on the grounds of limiting state interference in Ireland, he could not prevent the Whigs from gaining a reputation throughout the British Isles of goodwill to Ireland.[46]

In 1846 Russell continued to command substantial support within his party for a policy of active state involvement in the regeneration of Ireland. The aim was as it had been in the previous Whig administration: to bind the Irish people to the Union through conciliatory legislation, while at the same time reducing the social gulf in Ireland by making Irish landlords responsible for the relief and employment of their own poor.[47] Russell had since his time in the Home Office also developed what was by contemporary standards a radical plan for tenant compensation.[48] At the same time he hoped to continue pushing for Church reform and public works.[49] Bessborough, John Cam

Hobhouse and Lord Morpeth provided an apparently powerful core of support within the Cabinet for Russell's Irish policies.

These principles of governance in Ireland made up one facet of broader principles of administration, which Peter Mandler has labeled "Foxite." Mandler describes the Foxite Whigs in these years as "an unusually tightly knit aristocratic community with a strong inherited political tradition which gives them a heightened sense of political responsibility."[50] Responsiveness to public opinion, or what was perceived as public opinion, was integral to Foxite methods. Attention to the public would, the Foxites believed, help to bind government and people more closely, promoting a sort of vertical integration of the body politic. The "collective welfare" was the aim of enlightened legislation.[51]

Whig-Foxite policy in Ireland must therefore be placed within the context of prefamine English conceptions of the nature of the Irish people. Russell clung fiercely to the liberal understanding of Irish character, though he did not interpret the legislative priorities for their moral and economic reform in the same manner as did the political economists in his party. He resisted racialism well after it had become the vogue in England, writing in the early 1870s that the Irish were not "incurable barbarians," despite the fulminations of "a powerful portion of the press of London."[52] Nor did he, as we shall see, abandon his optimism during the famine, though it was at times subverted by his fears of civil unrest.

Unfortunately for the Foxites, the Prime Minister's personal flaws helped to prevent the realization of their dreams for Ireland. He was both too irritable and too conciliatory, the latter perhaps as a means of making up for the former character trait, but neither worked well in face of the often calm determination of those with whom he had to negotiate. Russell lacked the facility with which effective prime ministers could reconcile diverse cabinets and still get their own way. During the famine years, in addition, Russell's health was poor to the extent that in early 1847 he neared emotional and physical collapse.[53]

In the cabinet assembled in July 1846, therefore, competing interests almost invariably submerged attempts to realize Foxite plans for Ireland. The emergence of factions within the cabinet kept the administration divided over relief policy. In particular, Russell found that Sir Charles Wood at the exchequer, Wood's secretary Charles Trevelyan, and Henry Labouchere, the chief secretary for Ireland, constituted together a formidable contingent of laissez-faire liberals who could be counted on to resist any plans for government intervention in Ireland. In most instances these men were supported by the Marquis of Lansdowne, lord president of the Council and Whig leader in the Lords, and the Earl of Clarendon, president of the Board of Trade, who was to succeed Bessborough in 1847 as lord lieutenant of Ireland. Finally, the fact that several ministers, namely Lansdowne, Palmerston, Cottenham, Clanricarde and Bessborough, were Irish landlords, further limited the political options open to Russell.

The degree of influence that each faction had on the formulation of relief policy is difficult to determine, though the consensus among most scholars appears to be that Sir Charles Trevelyan was the hidden mover behind most ministerial decisions on Ireland.[54] Though recent research by Peter Gray[55] and others has thrown doubt on this estimation, it remains true that Trevelyan worked to create a reputation for himself as the "genius" of Irish relief. His work *The Irish Crisis*, published in 1848 in the *Edinburgh Review* and separately as a pamphlet, was publicized by its author as the official apologia for Irish relief policy—Trevelyan even sent copies of it to Guizot, the King of Prussia, and the Pope.[56] In Great Britain he was successful in acquiring the reputation he desired. One MP, an Irish landlord, declared in Parliament shortly after the publication of *The Irish Crisis* that

> he believed that the Government were not now acting for themselves. He believed that the strings were pulled by some persons in the Treasury—that ministers were acting on the politics—economical theories—of others, and not exerting their own minds on this subject. He had reason, indeed, to believe that they were acting on the theories of Mr. Trevelyan, which were inimical to Irish interests.[57]

Thus, whatever the actual importance of Trevelyan's ideas in the decisions of the Cabinet might have been, he had by the height of the famine come to be regarded by many as the official spokesman on Irish distress.

Given Trevelyan's high profile in the Whig administration of Ireland, it is unsurprising that some historians have chosen to portray him as an inhuman creature, a "Victorian Cromwell." Cecil Woodham-Smith blandly states that Trevelyan "disapproved of the Irish,"[58] though the ideology on which his views were based is left unexplored. Christine Kinealy simply restates Woodham-Smith's evaluation of Trevelyan, portraying him as being insensitive to Irish suffering and contemptuous of the peasantry.[59] For the most part, however, Trevelyan's views were of a piece with those of the English public as a whole. It is true that he often blamed the Irish for their own sufferings, supported emigration, disliked Catholicism, and supported the harshest possible means for making the Irish fend for themselves. Like almost everyone else, however, he believed that the ultimate goal of legislation must be the complete moral reform of the Irish. He considered this end to be very much achievable, albeit with difficulty, and eschewed racialist explanations of Irish troubles.

The Irish landlords were if anything much less sympathetic toward the Irish than was Trevelyan. They did not work together, but had a constraining effect on policy despite the public obloquy to which the popular press exposed them. Russell despised Irish landlords as a group, though he got along well enough with those in his cabinet.[60] The landlords retained the status of "experts" on Ireland that they had enjoyed under Peel, and it was through them that Russell gleaned much of his information on the temper of the Irish people and the effectiveness of government measures in ameliorating starvation and poverty.

As Russell took office, he was subjected to a barrage of advice and entreaties similar to that which his predecessor had been forced to endure. Landlords and Irish government officials continued their abuse of the peasantry and demands for coercion, while constabulary and police provided practically endless accounts of outrages and threats of full-scale rebellion.[61] By the late spring of 1846, however, their cries were being joined by those of ever-increasing numbers of Englishmen and even Irish nationalist politicians like O'Connell. The economist George Poulett Scrope warned Russell in May that Irish distress "may be expected to break out very shortly in some formidable convulsion," while O'Connell wrote a few months later that "there is the greatest danger of outbreaks."[62] Russell took these reports very seriously and wasted no time in reacting, asking his Lord Lieutenant Lord Bessborough, as the latter left for Ireland, "whether a force of 2000 mounted police, in addition to the present force, might not be most useful in putting down outrage, and watching the roads in the disturbed counties."[63]

The first measure of the new administration was to bring an end to the government's importation of food into all except the western counties of Ireland. Russell was not in principle opposed to the interference in private trade that Peel had undertaken. Peel's measure was, said Russell, of enormous benefit to Ireland, but only because "it was very wisely, and likewise with great good fortune for a long time kept a secret both here and in Ireland."[64] Once Peel's order to purchase Indian corn became public knowledge, it spurred cries of discontent among the Irish merchant interests, though very little opposition appeared to it in Parliament. Officials in Ireland were warning the government by April, however, of an incipient rebellion by private traders, who were threatening to cease importing food themselves as long as the government continued to do so.[65]

The food merchants considered themselves to be in a position to coerce the new Whig government into accepting their terms, and did not hesitate to do so. Wood, the new Chancellor of the Exchequer, told Parliament that "many merchants had declared that they would not import food at all if it were the intention of the Government to do so." They reassured the government at the same time that they had the situation well in hand and could meet any crisis so long as there was no state interference in the food trade.[66] At the same time reports came in from Ireland to the effect that large boatloads of corn were waiting in most of the major harbors, but "they were unwilling to unload their cargoes and bring their grain to market as long as the Government supplies lasted, because they were unable to enter into competition."[67]

In the circumstances, it was apparent that continuing Peel's policies would confront the government with nearly insuperable obstacles. Daniel O'Connell believed that the government should continue to import Indian corn, but even he was cognizant of the difficulties inherent in this policy. As he explained through an Irish newspaper,

> the great deficiency is in the supply of food; food is already at a famine-price and the leaving in the hands of the mercantile men the supplying of food as a commercial speculation will necessarily keep it at famine price. The intervention of the government is therefore absolutely necessary; such intervention is surrounded with great difficulties, and will impose an enormous additional burden upon the Government. . . . The Government in keeping down the markets will be very likely to drive the mercantile classes out of the trade, so that the supplying of food will ultimately fall altogether upon the Government.[68]

The Whigs did continue to maintain food depots in the west of Ireland, but a general European food shortage made it impossible to keep them full.[69]

The government hurried to draw up a comprehensive relief program before the end of the summer session of Parliament. The result was the Labour Rate Act, which passed into law on August 28. The new legislation provided for the continuation of public works, but the government would no longer bear the main burden of payment. Instead, landholders in distressed areas would have to repay Treasury loans through local poor rates, at three and one-half per cent interest over the next ten years. The government advanced only £50,000 in the form of a direct grant to the most distressed areas, which could not afford to repay a loan.[70]

On Russell's insistence, public works consisted largely of projects like road building, though some politicians argued that estate improvements should qualify as public works. Opponents of the emphasis on road construction, though primarily Tories and Irish landlords, also included some of the more farsighted Whigs such as Scrope. Road construction, they argued, was of minimal importance to the Irish economy compared to the imperative necessity of agricultural improvements on impoverished estates. Russell countered, successfully, by explaining that his goal was to provide an incentive for Irish land-lords to employ the poor themselves instead of relying on government loans.[71] At the basis of this policy lay the assumption that the Irish landlords had money but were lazy and unwilling to spend it.[72]

Irish landlords were, unsurprisingly, the greatest critics of the measure. Palmerston spoke for many when he grumbled that landlords would soon be residing with their cottiers in the workhouses.[73] Their protests were not strong enough, however, to shake the determination of the government to carry the Labour Rate Act through Parliament. With the exception of the Irish land-lords, there was little disagreement in Parliament with Russell's policies during this session. Russell's intention "to avoid any subject [relating to Ireland] which can give rise to any party division or excite any feeling of animosity" seemed to bear fruit.[74] There was almost no debate on his proposals. The Protectionists would demand more comprehensive relief measures in January but could not do so now, partly because of their previous insistence on the unreality of the po-tato blight.

The Peelites said very little in public about Russell's policies, generally sup-porting the Whigs as a matter of policy. In private, they compared Russell's plans unfavorably with Peel's measures.[75] Even so, their criticism of Russell was mild, and there is little reason to believe that Peel's policies would have been substantially different had he remained in office. At times he even criticized the government for doing too much for Ireland, as in February 1847 when he wrote to the Treasury attacking a proposed measure for furnishing seed corn to Irish landlords. His argument was that the measure would encourage the land-lords to "neglect their duty" and become dependant on state aid and interfer-ence in the economy.[76]

Serious problems with the administration's relief policy arose during the au-tumn. If Russell had hoped that the number of applications for relief would de-cline because of the Labour Rate Act, he was mistaken. As the *Times* observed, local committees allocated large sums for relief "as if there were no such thing as repayment in the memory of the ratepayers."[77] According to Woodham-Smith the landlords believed that the government would not force them to repay the loans once it became apparent that they did not have the money for it.[78] Whether or not this is true, the pressure for relief work became impossibly high as the famine progressed through the autumn. The breakdown of the Board of Works was evident by the end of the year, resulting from a combination of cor-ruption and overburdening of the local administration.[79]

Another, more catastrophic failure of the potato crop made the need for pro-visions desperate not long after Parliament disbanded. Prices rose steadily, though merchants had begun importing food in large quantities.[80] The administration resisted raising wages paid on public works for fear that doing so would divert laborers from working on the land.[81] The prime minister hoped that wages "should not be unreasonable either way."[82] In practice, however, it proved impossible to keep pay proportionate to prices without immense expenditures.[83] The government was unwilling to make these expenditures, and the Irish, lacking money to pay for food, began to starve in large numbers.

The administration was not unaware of the crisis. Labouchere wrote to Russell from Dublin in September, telling him that "it is now plain that unusual efforts of the most extensive kind must be made to save the people from famine."[84] Bessborough warned about "the increasing price and the avarice of the merchants in hoarding their corn" in October.[85] Neither Labouchere nor Bessborough was able to suggest a comprehensive alternative plan for relief, however, and both continued to blame the landlords for much of the distress. There were, therefore, no significant changes in the administration of famine relief until the beginning of 1847. Russell told Bessborough that "provided you can bring Ireland through this crisis, I think Parliament will indemnify us. But if we fail we will have no mercy shown us."[86]

The true dimensions of the starvation in terms of human suffering appears to have escaped Russell and his ministers. The popular press, including the *Times*, were to be sure assiduous in reporting on Irish starvation. First-hand accounts of the intense suffering that characterized the winter of 1846–1847 permeated the press and were distributed in pamphlet form by aid workers and Irish observers. Letters written by ministers in Dublin to London, however, did not ignore popular suffering but tended to show a greater preoccupation with the danger of unrest. Much of this was Russell's fault. Rather than demand accurate and detailed accounts from his ministers in Dublin of the progress of famine, the prime minister bombarded them with questions about the danger of disorder or rebellion in Ireland. At the beginning of December, when the misery of the peasantry was beginning to reach truly awful proportions, Russell submitted to Bessborough three questions that he considered to be most pressing in the circumstances:

I. What is the state of the poor provinces in respect to ploughing & sowing the land—Is the neglect of agricultural operations general or partial?

II. Is there any general purpose in view of the peasantry which induces the extensive arming? Is there a project of refusing rents? or of any insurrectionary movement?

III. What is the force of infantry, cavalry, artillery, & constabulary now in Ireland? Does it fall short of 30,000 men?[87]

POLICY AND PUBLIC OPINION

In August 1846 Harriet Lister, traveling in Ireland, wrote Russell's wife and drew her attention to the question of the "different races" of Ireland. Lister was certain of the strong and enduring differences between native Irish and those descended from English settlers: "It is impossible for the most casual observer not at once, to detect the man of English descent, by the greater neatness and cleanliness of his house and person, and by his superior manner and bearing." Noting the apparent apathy of the native Irish peasantry, she asked in exasperation, "Now what is one to do among such a people?"[88]

John Russell, as noted above, resisted the notes of racialism that were at this time creeping into the public consciousness. His cabinet ministers, though of one mind with Russell in their fears of revolution in Ireland, appear also to have eschewed racial explanations of Irish distress. Though often condemning Irish apathy, their chastisements extended alike to landlords and peasants. Russell wrote in a cabinet memorandum of the Irish landlords that "with some exceptions they are in a state of apathy and dull discontent."[89] The Chancellor of the Exchequer Charles Wood included both peasants and landlords in his complaint, "It seems to me to be the misfortune of Ireland that every man looks to the government for everything. So long as this is the case, I cannot see the prospect of any real improvement in the social condition of the country."[90]

Wood and Trevelyan tended to be most critical of the peasantry, but even so their reports were far from cynical. Wood's all-consuming fear was that relief works were "demoralizing" the peasants. He therefore was most active in demands that the Irish be taught to shift for themselves.[91] The central thrust of the Whig relief measures was to work social reform by making landlords pay for their own poor, but in the autumn of 1846 even the exchequer was confident that this reform could be achieved: "We shall succeed in the end [though] it will not be for many a long month, or many a long year perhaps that we shall get the people in that country to do their duty decently."[92]

The letters of Bessborough and Lansdowne, both Irish landlords, demonstrate their continuing confidence in the government's capability to work real and lasting reforms in the morals and character of the peasantry. Bessborough in his reports to Russell went out of his way to give credit to the peasants for their willingness to work under proper incentives. Lansdowne criticized the stubbornness of the peasantry but looked to education to work a significant change in this respect:

Nothing can be more unreasonable . . . than the expectations of the people, who will seldom do any thing to assist the Govt, yet reckon upon the Govt doing every thing to assist them. Still this is not from stupidity—&

those have much to answer for who have impeded the diffusion of the national schools—& I attribute it as much to the Archbishop [Whately]'s popular lessons in economy having been now taught for some years in those I have seen in the Kerry mountains as to any thing else, than there has been hitherto in that quarter, a comparative state of order in the midst of the greatest privations.[93]

Russell meanwhile played the part of an idealistic dreamer even as he refused to face the reality of Irish starvation. In attempting to convince Lord Auckland of the efficacy of constructing a new harbor and arsenal in Cork, he wrote:

Without looking to any such a prospect as a relief for the present distress, I wish you to consider the proposal as favourably as possible with a view to the establishment of Union feelings in Ireland. We have all sorts of good reasons for concentrating our establishment in England, but the Act of our doing so naturally produces in Ireland an impression, that we consider Ireland as a distant and disaffected dependency. The progress of steam navigation and railroad travelling on the other hand tends to bring all parts of the United Kingdom closer together—I wish Cork county to be considered as Cornwall and there is no less objectionable a mode of doing so than that of establishing a naval arsenal, and forming a naval dock at the Cove of Cork.[94]

By December, Whig ministers were aware of the increasingly hostile mood of the English public toward Ireland. Wood was one of the first to report on this to Russell, and though the chancellor of the exchequer used the changing public mood to justify his own hopes of working moral reform through teaching the Irish self-sufficiency, it was evident that the public did not view withholding aid in an equally "positive" manner as being conducive to moral reform: "From all I hear the English & Scotch all appear in a very anti-Irish mood, & I have seen quite enough to convince me that the feeling is very general against doing much for people who only misuse what they get."[95] Russell was well aware of this, and at the same time was growing increasingly worried about reports of unrest in Ireland. His letters to Bessborough became extremely anxious, demanding reports on the "arming" of the peasantry and expressing the "fear that some bad outbreaks will occur before the Spring."[96] On famine relief he was coming to believe that "any law which encourages apathy, promotes jobbing, & confirms improvidence will clearly be a step in a wrong direction."[97]

In stark contrast to the air of collegiality that had marked parliamentary discussions on Ireland in August, famine conditions in Ireland provoked bitter debate when Parliament opened in January 1847. Irish MPs took the government ment severely to task for its decision to cease food purchases, one of them raging that the government was telling the Irish that "they must die by the rules of political economy."[98] The Protectionists used the debate as an opportunity to seize the role of Opposition Party. Bentinck was true to the powerful landlord contingent in his party by defending the Irish landlords, insisting that the government was unfair in forcing them to pay for public works.[99] His criticism of relief measures was substantially the same as that voiced by Irish MPs, centering on the alleged Whig obsession with laissez-faire principles as the root of the problem.[100]

The Whigs avoided appealing to economic theory in defense of their measures. They argued instead that their Irish policy had been the only one consistent with the welfare of the *English* people. As Russell asked of his accusers, "How could we justify the act that we were affording food to Ireland at a certain low price, while the labouring people in our own country were paying an enormous price for food?"[101] This was not all posturing. The *Times* had been arguing throughout the autumn that England was in no position to safely share its own purportedly scanty food reserves with Ireland. Food was indeed scarce throughout Europe, which was enduring bad wheat harvests in addition to outbreaks of potato blight. Fear of adverse public reaction to further aid for Ireland undoubtedly worked on the minds of the administration. Ministers in any case shared many of the same fears. Russell wrote to Bessborough that "of course the Irish gentry and people are gaping for the money . . . But the English & Scotch must be a little considered. Our food has been greatly raised in price by exportations to Ireland. Our finances are all but deranged by the exertion."[102]

The increasing tendency of the English public to justify its desire to withhold aid to Ireland by accusing the Irish of bringing about their own suffering was most evident in the antics of the *Times*, which drew on the earlier observations of Thomas Campbell Foster to conclude that the Irish were "Asiatics in an European latitude and on a European soil."[103] This language was coming to have an effect on some Whigs. Charles Greville, a junior member of the Whig administration, wrote in his diary on December 12:

The state of Ireland is to the last degree deplorable, and enough to induce despair: such general disorganization and demoralization, a people with rare exceptions besotted with obstinacy and indolence, reckless and savage—all from high to low intent on doing as little and getting as much as they can, unwilling to rouse and exert themselves, looking to this country for succor, and snarling at the succor which they get; the masses brutal, deceitful, and idle, the whole state of things contradictory and paradoxical. While menaced with the continuance of famine next year, they will not cultivate the ground, and it lies unsown and untilled. There is no doubt that the people never were so well off on the whole as they have been this year of famine. Nobody will pay rent, and the savings-banks are overflowing. With the money they get from our relief funds they buy arms instead of food, and then shoot the officers who are sent over to regulate the distribution of relief . . . sturdy beggars calling themselves destitute are apprehended with large sums in their pockets.[104]

He wrote again on March 23, 1847: "But what is still more extraordinary, people have died of starvation with money enough to buy food in their pockets . . . yet they died rather than spend their money in the purchase of food."[105] The *Times* in similar language declared that "men, women, and children are perishing by the hundreds; but they have made up their minds to perish."[106]

Politicians respected the power of this newspaper, even if they did not always agree with it. Irish landlords in the government were especially frustrated at the vicious tone with which the *Times* denounced "that very comfortable, free and easy, life-enjoying, eating and drinking" class.[107] Bessborough's successor Lord Clarendon, though not always happy with the newspaper's influence, concluded realistically that in any case it would have to be dealt with, writing that it "forms, or guides, or reflects—no matter which—the public opinion of England."[108] The shaky political foundations of the Whig administration, most ministers realized, made the support of the *Times* essential.[109] Several members of Russell's government were on friendly terms with the editor John Thadeus Delane; Wood and Trevelyan particularly, but also Clarendon, who exchanged a copious correspondence with Delane throughout his tenure in the Irish administration. The editor of the *Times*, whose leader articles show was swiftly moving to a racialist interpretation of Irish affairs, evidently did his best to lead members of government to the same conclusion. Charles Greville was one of Delane's favorite contacts in the administration.[110] He wrote this reply to a letter from Delane in November 1846:

Thank you very much for a very interesting letter, which exceedingly shakes my previously—but very loosely—formed impressions to the contrary. Without having ever analysed the distribution of races in these Islands, I have been inclined to think that the assumption of the hopeless inferiority of the Celtic, was made a convenient excuse for not employing the most rational & probable means of improving them—what Mr. [Thomas Campbell] Foster says, is certainly very remarkable but admitting the truth of it all, I am not inclined to allow that this inferior race may not be immensely improved by a happy intermixture with the superior, and by judicious appliances moral & legislative.[111]

Charles Wood, who despite his critical view of the peasantry had through 1846 and even 1847 remained hopeful for their ultimate reform and never spoke of them in racial terms, evidently felt comfortable in writing Delane his doubts of the "Celts . . . if it is in them" to be civilized.[112]

Given the growing atmosphere of public hostility to Ireland, it is surprising that Russell's relief measures went as far as they did to placate the Irish landlords and peasantry. First the prime minister proclaimed that the government would forgive half the debt the Irish landlords had incurred on famine relief during the previous year, once they had paid the other half.[113] He did so over the protests of some members of his own party, who demanded that the people of England should not be taxed to bail out the Irish landlords.[114] The landlords found the rest of Russell's relief program so onerous, however, that they had little gratitude to spare for this measure.

George Poulett Scrope called Russell's relief proposals of January 1847 the exact opposite of those enacted the previous August.[115] Certain measures, such as the end of all remaining duties on corn and the repeal of clauses in the Navigation Act that prohibited importation in foreign vessels, met little criticism in the Commons. The rest of the program provoked considerably more debate. Russell characterized the program of public works, on which £4,848,235 had been spent since August,[116] as a failure. Public works would therefore be gradually ended, and replaced by the free distribution of food to the able-bodied through soup kitchens, which charitable organizations had already been running for some time.[117]

Under the Relief Destitute Persons (Ireland) Act, Bessborough would set up local relief committees that would in turn establish soup kitchens. The government would advance the money for this, which the landlords would have to repay over ten years, until a second piece of legislation, the Poor Law Extension Act, could pass in Parliament. This act would classify all distressed people in Ireland as paupers and entitle them to outdoor relief through the Irish Poor Law, which would be modified accordingly. Russell reluctantly included, under pressure from Lansdowne, the qualification that the able-bodied could only receive relief once the workhouses were full.[118] Landholders would bear the burden of relief through the local poor rates. Finally, the government would lend £50,000 to the Irish landlords for the purchase of seed. Direct government loans for soup kitchens would end once the Poor Law Extension Act passed, throwing the entire burden for relief upon the Irish.[119]

The government did not go far enough to satisfy either the Protectionists or the Irish, but Peelite support for the administration guaranteed that any opposition would be ineffective. Throughout the fall and winter of 1846–1847 Peel's followers looked on the attempts of the Whigs to govern Ireland with smug amusement. Lord Lincoln, like Graham, congratulated Peel that in many parts of Ireland "your popularity is much greater than O'Connell's." He contemptuously contrasted Peel's popularity with Whig incompetence:

> As for the executive, I hear the most lamentable accounts of its utter inefficiency. Lord Bessborough is said to be the only man amongst them worth his salt but his indolence is extreme. . . . As for Labouchere his competency is pitiable . . . he has lost his head and is afraid to do anything. . . . As regards the superintendence at home neither the First Lord of the Treasury or Chancellor of the Exchequer has any being and our old incubus Trevelyan lies heavier than ever on this unhappy country [Ireland] of which he knows as much as his Baby if he has one.[120]

Graham concurred, predicting that the Whig administration of Ireland would prove "the most fearful monument of Misgovernment, which History has ever yet recorded."[121] For all their contempt for the Whigs, however, the Peelites advanced no alternative ideas of their own. Peel largely avoided the subject in his own correspondence after leaving office, and in Parliament continued to support Whig measures almost as a matter of course.

In view of Peelite complacency and Irish disorganization, George Bentinck's railway bill of February 4, 1847 appears even more significant as probably the only alternative (really an addition) to Whig policy suggested by an opposition party. The bill advanced railway building as a new form of useful public works, for which the government would provide a £16 million loan that the railways would have to repay at three and one-half percent interest over the next thirty-seven years. Railways, Bentinck argued, were unlike the abandoned system of useless works in that they could be of long-term benefit to the Irish economy.[122]

Historians have made much of the railway bill. Bentinck's motives, according to one historian, were "lofty and pure," while to many others he appears as one of the few politicians of the time unbound by "economic conventions"[123] and truly concerned for the welfare of the Irish people. Bentinck paraded himself as the only political leader with the courage to countenance large expenses for Irish relief. According to Disraeli, when Bentinck introduced the bill to the Commons for the second time he was "loudly cheered by both sides."[124]

Bentinck's private correspondence shows that he was indeed deeply critical of Whig policy. Though he always scoffed at "Peel's Famine" of 1845–1846, he argued that "what should have been done was to have sent seven or eight line of Battle ships in September October November & December [1846] to have brought the Corn to Ireland & *prevented* the people from starving." Unfortunately, as Bentinck saw it,

> Lord John Russell however had pledged himself to the Mercantile Interest that is to the Corn Speculators and Corn Merchants of the City of London "that the supply of the People of Ireland should be left to Private Enterprise and that Private Enterprise and free Trade should not be interfered with."[125]

For the most part, however, Bentinck's decision to challenge the government on Irish relief had little to do with either a desire to challenge economic dogmatism or high-minded moral indignation at the sufferings of the Irish peasantry. Instead, Bentinck wished first to claim for the Protectionists the status of main opposition party. If he wished to keep the Protectionists together as a party and make the Peelites, who openly supported the administration, seem anomalous, moving into opposition was a logical step. Second, once he had taken the first step of moving his party into opposition, Bentinck needed to assert his own position as leader. Introducing a railway bill, and more generally acting as the primary critic of Whig relief policy, was one way of accomplishing this.[126] He was, in fact, making famine relief into a party issue.

Another reason for the introduction of the railway bill was the Protectionist desire to support the interests of its own Irish landlord elements while also providing an issue on which Whig Irish landlords might split with their party. Bentinck was attempting to capitalize on the rage felt by most Irish landlords at the verbal and legislative abuse being meted out to them by the Whigs and the popular press. An attempt to bring all Irish landlords into the Protectionist orbit was made in the House of Lords, where for a time Stanley created an alliance of Irish interests that cut across party lines.[127]

At first, this group rallied behind Bentinck's railway bill as an alternative to Russell's measures.[128] In the Commons Bentinck pushed his bill and attacked Russell's proposal for Poor Law extension, claiming that it put a too heavy burden on Irish landlords.[129] In the Lords most of the Irish landlords returned the favor by expressing support for the railway bill and condemning outdoor relief.[130] Lansdowne was half-hearted in defending the government's measures in the Lords, going out of his way to absolve the landlords of any responsibility for the famine and emphasizing that the measure would be only temporary.[131]

When he learned of Bentinck's proposal, Russell wrote to Wood that "as a question of finance there is some difficulty. But the employment of 110,000 unskilled labourers is a great temptation."[132] The technical difficulties associated with such a bill appeared to be formidable, however, and the potential benefits to the Irish peasants did not seem to justify the expenditure. Also, England was at the time going through a financial crisis involving heavy pressure on the Bank of England.[133] Wood advised Russell that the money market was tight and government securities weakening, which did not bode well for a project as expensive as Bentinck's. Both Russell and Wood feared that a rash of railway speculation, partly responsible for English financial troubles, would follow approval of the bill.[134]

Bentinck's bill was doomed from the start. Russell, perhaps sensing Protectionist wishes to destroy the Whig alliance with the Irish "party" in the Commons and encourage a defection of Whig Irish landlords, threatened these groups with resignation if they allowed the bill to be read a second time.[135] The Irish MPs, who had hitherto supported the measure, gave in and did not support the bill when it came to a vote; neither did the Whig Irish landlords. Peel carried most of his followers with him in voting against Bentinck.[136] The bill went down in the Commons on February 16 by a vote of 332 to 118.

Once Bentinck's scheme was dead, the Irish interests adopted the new strategy of attacking outdoor relief as a breach of the principles of political economy. Richard Whately, the Archbishop of Dublin and leading theorist of political economy among Irish academics, joined with the Irish landlords Monteagle, Radnor and Mountcashel as leaders of the campaign against outdoor relief. The economist and MP Nassau Senior supported them in the Commons by attacking outdoor relief as embodied in the Poor Law Extension bill.[137] A manifesto published by this group on April 2 declared that outdoor relief would "destroy the habits of industry and self-dependence" of the Irish.[138]

For all their rhetoric, in attacking Russell on the basis of economic principles Whately's group was really defending the interests of the Irish landlords. The records of their meetings show that they were "clearly motivated by fear that [outdoor relief] would lead to increased poor rates and therefore lower rentals."[139] The movement was one of landlords, not political economists; Senior, indeed, was isolated from his fellow economists in his opposition to outdoor relief.[140]

Most economists followed the example of George Poulett Scrope, who had also been critical of some aspects of the English New Poor Law.[141] Scrope was an anti-Malthusian who, along with J.S. Mill and W.T. Thornton, was a passionate enemy of Senior and others associated with the *Edinburgh Review*.[142] Though a "political economist," many of Scrope's ideas on Ireland diverged sharply from the standards of laissez-faire thought. The pamphlets with which he bombarded the government in support of useful works and Poor Law extension demonstrate his unorthodox tendencies. His *Irish Relief Measures, Past and Future* (1848) incorporated the arguments he had made in numerous pamphlets over the course of 1847. In it, he defended outdoor relief on humanitarian rather than theoretical grounds and encouraged the government to take a large role in relief, asserting that "the external power of the government *alone* can break the spell [of famine], by commencing the work of employment and improvement."[143]

As Scrope's contribution to the debate over outdoor relief shows, there was little consensus in this period on what constituted the "true" laws of political economy. Economists, politicians, and the public understood the term in widely differing fashions. Insofar as the economists had influence with the Whig minsters, their ideas survived only in a strongly diluted form.[144] Russell probably incorporated bits and pieces of the ideas of different economists into his policies, but on the whole he was unconstrained by their arguments or protests.

The attempts of Senior and the Irish landlords to prevent the introduction of outdoor relief proved futile. As the bill passed through the Lords in April and May, the Irish interests, mobilized by the Protectionists, were able to impose a variety of amendments on the bill to weaken its impact, including one that limited the duration of outdoor relief to one year. Whig and Peelite peers were able, however, to eliminate the last amendment by thirteen votes.[145] The Poor Law Extension Bill passed the Lords on May 18. Most Irish landlords felt like Palmerston, who called the legislation "a most drastic Black Dose." Lady Palmerston mourned that her husband would now be forced to send money to his Irish estate.[146]

THE END OF FAMINE RELIEF

In the summer of 1847 England washed its hands of responsibility for the famine. The end of government funding for soup kitchens took place on August 15, when the entire burden for relief was transferred to the Irish Poor Law. The government closed its depots in the west of Ireland. Many in England believed that the famine was over; politicians and the public took optimistic reports about the new harvest at face value.[147] The *Times* announced on July 2 that the famine had been "arrested" although the "moral plague" of the Irish people remained.[148] In a final gesture of goodwill, Wood announced on July 8 that the government would forgive half the debt incurred for soup kitchens, or about £4.5 million.[149] Famine conditions nevertheless continued in Ireland, and the poor law system was unable to significantly alleviate the starvation.

Several factors contributed to the government's refusal to resume aid to Ireland. One was a serious financial crisis, resulting from grain and railway speculation, that hit England in September. This crisis was greater than that of late 1846 and correspondingly produced near panic in England.[150] In the circumstances support for Irish relief did not exist, especially after the decision to forgive half of the soup kitchen debt. The *Times* remained preoccupied with the financial crisis through October and November, mentioning Ireland hardly at all. When it found time for Irish affairs it ignored the continued starvation, preferring to focus on the various "atrocities" of Irish peasants against landlords and Englishmen.[151] Russell, who had promised to help Ireland with £1 million saved from the soup kitchen fund in the spring, wrote to Clarendon on September 10 that "the falling off in the Revenue, still above one million sterling in two months, damages all my views of being able to help Ireland out of the savings of the loan."[152]

Any help that Russell might have been willing to propose for Ireland would almost certainly have been countered by the growing pessimism of his own cabinet. The changing public mood on the nature of the Irish people, spurred on relentlessly by the *Times*, was having its effect on the attitudes of the Whig cabinet. An increasing number of Russell's correspondents began urging him to come around to an understanding of the Celtic sources of Irish misbehavior as noted by the *Times*.[153] Wood's previous optimism had by the summer of 1847 entirely collapsed, and he was writing the prime minister letters despairing of "much good from what we do."[154] Clarendon, as yet new to his office, wrote hopefully of "a spirit of exertion & self reliance springing up that is entirely new in Ireland," though he deplored the "childish helplessness or reckless apathy" of the landlords.[155] Within a few months, however, his tone had entirely changed.

Clarendon's rapidly increasing panic over the state of unrest in Ireland soon led to a measure that the Whigs had hitherto been chary of instituting: coercion. The more level-headed Bessborough had successfully dampened Russell's fears on the subject.[156] Clarendon, by contrast, with his cries of "a savage spirit of disaffection, & tumultuous assemblages of persons,"[157] drove Russell to propose a coercion act on November 29. Even so, the prime minister could not help noting acidly to Clarendon that

it is quite true that landlords in England would not like to be shot like hares and partridges by miscreants banded for murderous purposes. But neither does any landlord in England turn out fifty persons at once, and burn their houses over their heads, giving them no provision for the future. The murders are atrocious so are the ejectments.[158]

Clarendon, unabashed, replied that he could not understand "how any Govt can think it expedient to leave 300,000 arms in possession of some of the most ferocious people on earth."[159] The passage of the bill on December 20 did little to placate Clarendon or others who shared his fears. By the spring of 1848 Clarendon's hitherto optimistic correspondence was overflowing with contempt for the Irish peasantry and "their absence of moral sense."[160]

The revolution of February 1848 in France and the subsequent turmoil in Europe led many Englishmen to share Clarendon's fears of revolution in Ireland. The *Times*, true to form, fanned the flames of public paranoia with accounts of a "rebel army" forming in Ireland.[161] Chartist demonstrations, which Clarendon and the *Times* linked to Irish agitation, increased the sense of danger.[162] Russell continued curiously obstinate in refusing to countenance further coercive measures, though Lansdowne and Palmerston joined with Clarendon in pressuring him. As tension continued to build throughout the summer, however, the rest of the cabinet moved to Clarendon's position.[163] Russell allowed for the suspension of *habeas corpus* on July 12, and the Young Ireland rising, a total fiasco, followed two weeks later.

It was perhaps symbolic of changing perceptions of the nature of the Irish problem that the government reacted to the rising by sending Lord Hardinge, fresh from putting down disturbances in India, to keep the peace in Ireland. By now what little sympathy the English government and people had for Ireland had been largely exhausted. Famine conditions continued in many areas, but England would now do nothing for relief. The *Times* bristled at the "monstrous ingratitude" of the Irish,[164] and if anyone in the government disagreed they no longer had the will to show it. A letter from Russell to Clarendon of February 1849 sums up the shifting public attitude and its effect on the government's position with respect to Ireland:

> The great difficulty this year respecting Ireland is one which does not spring from Trevelyan and Charles Wood but lies deep in the breasts of the British people. It is this—we have granted, lent, subscribed, worked, visited, clothed, the Irish millions of money, years of debate, etc. etc.—the only return is calumny and rebellion—let us not grant, clothe etc. etc. any more and see what they will do. . . . Now without borrowing and lending we could have no great plan for Ireland—and much as I wished it, I have got to see that it is impracticable.[165]

Russell visited Ireland in September 1848, followed by the Queen in a much-publicized visit in August 1849. Lord Fortescue wrote Russell on his return, "I fear your late visit to Ireland will not have opened to you better hopes or brighter prospects for its perverse & ill-fated People."[166] Victoria's visit, though on the surface occasioned by much goodwill, did little to eradicate a strong sense of despair among English politicians about Ireland. Clarendon hoped that the Queen's visit would convince the peasantry that "tranquillity is more profitable to them than rebellion wch [sic] will be a sort of guarantee for future good behaviour," beyond which he had few hopes to express.[167] Lord Dufferin wrote Russell plainly that the condition of the peasantry was "hopeless."[168] On this note Ireland practically disappeared as a subject in Russell's correspondence until his departure from office in 1852.

The famine, of course, did not finally end until around 1852. In 1849 conditions in Ireland were nearly as horrific as they had been in 1847, but there was little reaction from the English, aside from the Rate-in-Aid Act of May 1849, designed to share the burden of poor relief between poor and wealthy counties in Ireland, toward which the Treasury made a small £50,000 advance.[169] The Encumbered Estates Act, which the government passed in the same month, was little more than a gesture in recognition of the abysmal state of the Irish landlords. It allowed penurious landlords to sell off their estates more readily, but brought no commensurate reappraisal of assumptions made in 1847 that these same landlords would be able to pay the costs of famine relief through the Irish Poor Law.

CHANGING ATTITUDES

A perceived sense of self-interest was central to the reluctance of the British government to extend large-scale aid to Ireland during the famine. The government's measures in the first half of 1847 were, if inadequate, nevertheless hardly parsimonious. In that year alone the Exchequer devoted almost sixteen percent of its total expenditure to Irish relief.[170] Even though much of this was in the form of loans that would eventually have to be repaid, to an Englishman in 1847 it may have seemed that Britain would face economic ruin long before it had a chance to collect on these loans.[171] The *Times* reflected these fears when it complained that "want of money is the great complaint of the day," while English workers were sharing their meager incomes with the "shiftless" Irish peasantry.[172] Add to this the widespread hatred of the Irish landlords, who were supposed to have stashed away great reserves of money, and the anger felt at the Young Ireland rising of July 1848, and it may seem surprising that the government did anything for Ireland at all.

In this public atmosphere Irish relief would have been a difficult undertaking for the strongest of governments. For an administration as divided and politically insecure as Russell's, it was doubly difficult. Russell did not possess the personal authority or ability as an administrator that Peel undoubtedly did. Peel had the advantage of working with a cabinet composed largely of very able men; Russell's cabinet was mediocre by comparison. Peel's response to the Irish distress in 1845–1846 shows somewhat greater originality and flexibility of mind, but it is important to remember that he did not have to deal with distress on a scale that was even remotely comparable to the dimensions of the crisis that appeared just after he left office.

The idea that the Russell administration did not respond adequately to the crisis because of a doctrinaire adherence to the principles of economic dogmatism is too simplistic and should be discarded, even though some historians like Christine Kinealy continue to cling to it stubbornly. To be sure, the idea that limiting aid to the Irish was the best means of teaching them self-sufficiency and thus working moral reform, was integral to the ideas of many ministers including Peel and Russell. In some respects this attitude was symptomatic of a classical liberal outlook on human nature, but it was not synonymous with a laissez-faire conception of the workings of the economy. Russell and the Foxites, though very concerned with moral and economic reform, considered controlled government intervention and social legislation as an important means of achieving this. By no means was everyone agreed on the proper approach to developing self-sufficiency, as other historians such as Roy Foster, Peter Gray, Peter Mandler and Boyd Hilton have shown. These historians have been less successful in advancing alternate explanations for the behavior of the Whig government during the famine.

Religion has been advanced as an at least partial explanation for the reaction of both the Peel and Russell governments to the crisis in Ireland. Boyd Hilton, in a recent book, argues that economic and social policy-making in this period cannot be understood without reference to the religious attitudes of the ministers concerned. Through the 1840s, Hilton contends, moderate evangelicalism as generally associated with the Clapham school was the dominant mode of Protestant thought, with a commensurate influence on the minds of leading politicians, especially among Peelites and liberal Whigs. Misfortune, from the moderate evangelical perspective, was the result of human misconduct in not conforming to God's greater plan embodied in natural laws. Attention to natural laws, which were believed to coincide with those expounded by the ideology of laissez-faire, would be conducive to moral reform if not always to material progress.[173] The famine in this way of thinking might therefore naturally be seen as both the result of human improvidence and a God-given opportunity to work moral reform through avoidance of state intervention and attention to the natural workings of the economy.

Hilton's student Peter Gray further developed this thesis in a 1992 Cambridge Ph.D. dissertation, which he published as a book in 1999. While Hilton does little more than suggest that moderate evangelical thought influenced famine policy,[174] Gray attributes a profound influence to evangelical thought on the British response to the famine. His emphasis is primarily on the Peel government. Like Hilton, however, he argues that although moderate evangelicalism was less influential among the Whigs than the Peelites, it nevertheless exercised a disproportionate influence on policy through men such as Charles Wood and Sir Charles Trevelyan in the Treasury.

There are several problems with the "evangelical thesis" of understanding policy, not least being Hilton's failure to adequately answer the natural question of whether religion influenced economic thought or vice-versa. A more serious question is the extent to which British policy during the famine was noninterventionist. The Peel government, which both Gray and Hilton are at pains to suggest was significantly permeated with principles drawn from moderate evangelicalism, was in practice more interventionist as regarded the famine than the Russell administration. The Whigs, who are supposed to have in general been less subject than were the Peelites to moderate evangelical ideology, were in practice less interventionist than their predecessors in office. Although Russell and his supporters in the cabinet were inclined to do more in Ireland than they eventually conceived to be possible, there is little evidence to suggest that they were browbeaten into a laissez-faire stance by the evangelical economists in the Treasury. Hilton, indeed, has elsewhere repudiated the argument that the Treasury had a disproportionate influence within the cabinet.

The key to the inadequacy of the government's response to the famine lies in the changing course of public opinion. Peter Mandler has pointed in this direction by his conclusion that the "ethnic and national prejudice" of the English public stifled Foxite efforts at more interventionist legislation.[175] Mandler has put us on the right track, but—as we shall see in the next chapter—the complexity of the public reaction to the famine belies simplistic assumptions that the failure of famine relief can be attributed to "prejudice."

NOTES

1. Quoted in Norman Gash, *Sir Robert Peel: The Life of Sir Robert Peel after 1830* (London: Longman, 1972), 394.

2. Sir Robert Peel to Earl de Grey, August 22, 1843, Additional Manuscript 40478, ff. 160–166.

3. Ibid., August 24, 1843, f. 168.

4. Sir James Graham to Peel, November 24, 1841, Additional Manuscript 40446, ff. 142–144.

5. Graham to Peel, October 20, 1843, Additional Manuscript 40449, ff. 109–112.

6. Quoted in James L. Sturgis, *John Bright and the Empire* (London: Athlone Press, 1969), 128.

7. Ibid., 121–129.

8. See *Hansard* LX 630–677, 1064, 1088–1092; 4, 12 July 1843.

9. Peel to Graham, June 12, 1843, Additional Manuscript 40478, ff. 79–84.

10. Graham to Peel, May 6, 1843, Additional Manuscript 40478, ff. 39–44.

11. Peel to Edward Granville Eliot, January 6, 1845, Additional Manuscript 40480, ff. 503–504.

12. Graham had hoped that the trial would provide an occasion to separate O'Connell from the repeal movement, "and if by his venality we could blast his future influence, the Peace of a Nation might be secured" (Graham to Peel, October 20, 1843, Additional Manuscript 40449, ff. 109–112). O'Connell's conviction led Graham to congratulate Peel that "Not one life has been sacrificed: no additional Power has been asked or obtained by the Government: yet Agitation has been subdued and Law is now triumphant" (Graham to Peel, May 27, 1844, Additional Manuscript 40450, ff. 38–39).

13. Lord Broughton, *Recollections of a Long Life*, Lady Dorchester, ed. (London: John Murray, 1911), vol. 6, *1841–1852*, 88.

14. A packet of reports from the Provincial Bank of Ireland, sent to Peel from Goulburn on October 8, contains widely differing accounts of the same districts, some characterizing the blight as a "serious calamity," while others dismiss such accounts as "greatly exaggerated" (Henry Goulburn to Peel, October 8, 1845, Additional Manuscript 40445, ff. 219–226).

15. Peel to Graham, October 13, 1845, quoted in Cecil Woodham-Smith, *The Great Hunger* (New York: Harper & Row, 1962), 49.

16. It is worth emphasizing that unlike today, in 1846 there was no precedent whatever for official aid on such a scale.

17. Peel, speech to the House of Commons, April 17, 1846, *Parliamentary Debates* (Commons), 3rd ser., vol. 85 (1846), col. 721.

18. Mary E. Daly, *The Famine in Ireland* (Dundalk: Dundalgan Press, 1986), 74.

19. Ibid., 75.

20. Similar attitudes were evinced in handling distress among English workers. The government did, however, demonstrate less concern about "professional mendicancy" during the Lancashire cotton famine of the 1860s than it had in distributing Irish famine relief. In fact, many English writers used the supposed prevalence of beggardom among the Irish peasantry as opposed to that found among the English poor to demonstrate the extreme moral degradation of the former. The distinction between the English and Irish poor was less of kind than of degrees.

21. Peel complained to Lord Heytesbury that he was "being challenged by Protectionist opponents who keep repeating that we exaggerate the damage in Ireland." Peel to Lord Heytesbury, March 14, 1846, Additional Manuscript 40479, ff. 555–556.

22. Benjamin Disraeli, *Lord George Bentinck: A Political Biography* (London: Routledge, 1858), 254.

23. Cormac O'Gráda, *The Great Irish Famine* (London: MacMillan, 1989), 40.

24. *Times* (London), July 28, 1847.

25. Peel to Graham, March 26, 1845, Additional Manuscript 40451, ff. 49– 50.

26. Peel to Graham, December 3, 1845, Additional Manuscript 40452, ff. 46–51.

27. Peel, Cabinet memorandum, June 21, 1846, Additional Manuscript 40594, ff. 38–47.

28. Thomas Fremantle to Peel, November 20, 1845, Additional Manuscript 40476, ff. 556–559.

29. Heytesbury to Peel, October 27, 1845, Additional Manuscript 40479, ff. 517–518.

30. Dr. Lyon Playfair to Peel, November 5, 1845, Additional Manuscript 40577, ff. 376–380.

31. Richard Daly to Peel, October 4, 1845, Additional Manuscript 40575, ff. 136–137; Joseph Morris to Peel, October 30, 1845, Additional Manuscript 40577, ff. 192–193.

32. See for example the report of Charles O'Donnell, military secretary in Dublin, to Peel of June 15, 1846, Additional Manuscript 40593, ff. 347–350. Numerous alarmist reports from local landlords and magistrates are in HO 45/1080 and 1148.

33. D. Bain to Peel, October 21, 1845, Additional Manuscript 40576, ff. 144–149; Denis Moylan to Peel, October 27, 1845, Additional Manuscript 40577, ff. 46–47.

34. B.J. Lloyd to Peel, January 26, 1846, Additional Manuscript 40583, ff. 159–164.

35. J. Charlton to Peel, February 6, 1846, Additional Manuscript 40584, ff. 210–211.

36. Ramsey Goddard to Peel, December 5, 1845, Additional Manuscript 40580, ff. 266–267; Rev. R. Cobb to Peel, May 22, 1846, Additional Manuscript 40592, ff. 206–207; Dr. Berry King to Peel, November 18, 1845, Additional Manuscript 40579, ff. 81–82.

37. Thomas Ensor to Peel, April 25, May 20, 1846, Additional Manuscripts 40590, 40592, ff. 260–263, 114–119. Peel replied respectfully to the first of these letters.

38. Lyon Playfair to Peel, November 4, 1845, Additional Manuscript 40578, ff. 25–30.

39. Robert Traile to Peel, November 18, 1845, Additional Manuscript 40579, ff. 97–100.

40. William Buckland to Peel, November 28, 1845, Additional Manuscript 40580, ff. 3–4. In view of the racist theories being advanced at this time by a small coterie of scientists associated with Robert Knox, one might speculate that Playfair, Traile and Buckland, all learned in current theories of science and medicine, were influenced by Knox's ideas. I have found no evidence to substantiate this hypothesis, however.

41. Charles C.F. Greville, *A Journal of the Reign of Queen Victoria from 1837 to 1852*, Henry Reeve, ed. (New York: D. Appleton & Co., 1885), 103.

42. Stuart J. Reid, *Lord John Russell* (New York: Harper & Brothers, 1895), 147–148.

43. Lord Clanricarde to John Russell, March 11, 1846, PRO 30/22/5A, ff. 164–166.

44. Lord Clarendon to Russell, March 11, 1846, PRO 30/22/5A, ff. 159–160.

45. Charles Stuart Parker, ed., *The Life and Letters of Sir James Graham, 1792–1861* (London: John Murray, 1907), 2:52.

46. R.B. McDowell, *Public Opinion and Government Policy in Ireland, 1801–1846* (London: Faber & Faber, 1952), 177.

47. Mandler, *Aristocratic Government*, 170–175.

48. R.D. Collison Black, *Economic Thought and the Irish Question, 1817–1870* (Cambridge: Cambridge University press, 1960), 37–38.

49. Mandler, *Aristocratic Government*, 238.

50. Ibid., 6.

51. Ibid., 2–3, 19.

52. John Earl Russell, *Recollections and Suggestions, 1813–1873* (Boston: Roberts Brothers, 1875), 256.

53. John Prest, *Lord John Russell* (London: MacMillan, 1972), 74, 212, 262, 288.

54. See especially Woodham-Smith, *The Great Hunger*, 58, 105. Another historian has claimed that in Trevelyan "Ireland had its most ruthless and dedicated dictator since Cromwell." See Joseph M. Hernon, "A Victorian Cromwell: Sir Charles Trevelyan, the Famine and the Age of Improvement," *Eire-Ireland* 22 (1987): 20.

55. Peter Gray, "British Politics and the Irish Land Question," 246.

56. Jenifer Hart, "Sir Charles Trevelyan at the Treasury," *English Historical Review* 75 (January 1960), 102.

57. Bernal Osborne, speech to the House of Commons, January 19, 1847, *Parliamentary Debates* (Parl. Deb.) (Commons), 3rd ser., 89 (1847):127.

58. Woodham-Smith, *The Great Hunger*, 61.

59. Christine Kinealy, *This Great Calamity: The Irish Famine 1845–52* (Dublin: Gill & Macmillan, 1994), 88.

60. Prest, *Lord John Russell*, 237.

61. See, for example, a box of such reports for 1846 in HO 45/1080A.

62. George Poulett Scrope to Russell, May 2, 1846, PRO 30/22/5A, ff. 201–204; Daniel O'Connell to Russell, August 12, 1846, PRO 30/22/5B, ff. 345–346.

63. Russell to Lord Bessborough, June 29, 1846, PRO 30/22/5A, ff. 312–313.

64. Russell, speech to the House of Commons, August 17, 1846, *Parl. Deb.* (Commons), 3rd ser., 88 (1846):768.

65. Daly, *The Famine in Ireland,* 71.

66. Sir Charles Wood, speech to the House of Commons, August 17, 1846, *Parl. Deb.* (Commons), 3rd ser., 88 (1846):778–779.

67. Ibid., 30.

68. Quoted in Thomas P. O'Neill, "Food Problems during the Great Irish Famine," *Journal of the Royal Society of Antiquaries of Ireland* 82 (1952): 104–105.

69. Daly, *The Famine in Ireland,* 72.

70. *Parl. Deb.* (Commons), 3rd ser., 88 (1846): 775–778.

71. Russell to Duke of Leinster, October 17, 1846, in John Earl Russell, *Later Correspondence* 1:155–156; Russell, speech to the House of Commons, January 25, 1847, *Parl. Deb.* (Commons), 3rd ser., 89 (1847):430.

72. *Manchester Guardian,* February 3, 1847; Angus McIntyre, *The Liberator* (London: Hamish Hamilton, 1965), 292.

73. Woodham-Smith, *The Great Hunger,* 113.

74. Russell, speech to the House of Commons, August 17, 1846, *Parl. Deb.* (Commons) 3rd ser., 88 (1846):766.

75. Graham to Peel September 26, 1846, in Charles Stuart Parker, *Sir Robert Peel,* 3:463–464.

76. Ibid., 3:482–483.

77. *Times* (London), September 22, 1846.

78. Woodham-Smith, *The Great Hunger,* 113.

79. Daly, *The Famine in Ireland,* 78.

80. Ibid., 58.

81. Ibid., 81.

82. Russell to Bessborough, September 1, 1846, in John Earl Russell, *Later Correspondence,* 1:146.

83. Daly, *The Famine in Ireland,* 80–81.

84. John Earl Russell, *Later Correspondence,* 1:147.

85. Ibid., 1:150.

86. Ibid., 1:149.

87. Russell to Bessborough, December 1, 1846, PRO 30/22/5F, f.32.

88. Harriet Lister to Fanny Russell, August 23, 1846, PRO 30/22/5B, ff. 415–418.

89. Russell memorandum, September 24, 1846, PRO 30/22/5C, ff. 288–299.

90. Wood to Lord Bessborough, September 9, 1846, PRO 30/22/5C, ff. 87–92.

91. Wood to Henry Labouchere, October 2, 1846, PRO 30/22/5D, ff. 34–37.

92. Wood to Russell, December 2, 1846, PRO 30/22/5F, ff. 50–57.

93. Lord Lansdowne to Russell, October 13, 1846, PRO 30/22/5D, ff. 183–184.

94. Russell to Lord Auckland, September 23, 1846, PRO 30/22/5C, ff. 255–258.

95. Wood to Bessborough, December 21, 1846, PRO 30/22/5F, ff. 246–251.

96. Russell to Bessborough, December 28, 1846, PRO 30/22/5G, ff. 97–98.

97. Russell to Labouchere, December 28, 1846, PRO 30/22/5G, ff. 99–100.

98. Grattam, speech to the House of Commons, January 19, 1847, *Parl. Deb.* (Commons), 3rd ser., 89 (1847):123.

99. Ibid., 89 (1847):109.

100. This argument was, of course, by implication an attack on the Whig-Peelite decision to repeal the Corn Laws, also in Protectionist eyes the product of an obsessive attention to the principles of political economy.

101. Russell, speech to the House of Commons, January 19, 1847, *Parl. Deb.* (Commons), 3rd ser., 89 (1847):139.

102. Russell to Bessborough, February 14, 1847, PRO 30/22/6B, ff. 82–83.

103. *Times* (London), February 22, 1847. This subject will be treated more fully in the next chapter.

104. Greville, *Journal of the Reign of Queen Victoria*, 155.

105. Ibid., 217.

106. *Times* (London), February 25, 1847.

107. *Times* (London), January 9, 1847. Bessborough, himself an Irish landlord, complained for example that "I know that it is very difficult to induce the Times to do anything that they do not actually approve of but the daily paragraphs about Ireland & the Irish landlords are doing great mischief." Bessborough to Russell, January 14, 1847, PRO 30/22/6A, ff. 140–143.

108. *The History of the Times*, vol. II, *The Tradition Established 1841–1884* (London: *Times*, 1939), 57.

109. Tom Morley, "'The Arcana of that Great Machine': Politicians and The Times in the late 1840s" *History* 73 (February 1988), 40.

110. Ibid., 46.

111. Charles Greville to John Delane, November 13, 1846, Delane MSS, vol. 2, f. 47 in the archives of the *Times*, London.

112. Wood to Delane, September 19, 1848, Delane MSS, vol. 2, f. 49.

113. Russell, speech to the House of Commons, January 25, 1847, *Parl. Deb.* (Commons), 3rd ser., 89 (1847):437.

114. Ibid., 89 (1847):475.

115. George Poulett Scrope, *The Irish Relief Measures, Past and Future* (London: James Ridgway, 1848), 44–45.

116. Daly, *The Famine in Ireland*, 82.

117. Woodham-Smith, *The Great Hunger*, 171.

118. Prest, *Lord John Russell*, 248.

119. *Parl. Deb.* (Commons), 3rd ser., 89 (1847):426–440.

120. Lincoln to Peel, November 17, 1846, Additional Manuscript 40481, ff. 368–375.

121. Graham to Peel, January 3, 1847, Additional Manuscript 40452, ff. 199–204.

122. *Parl. Deb.* (Commons), 3rd ser., 89 (1847):773–804.

123. Wilbur Devereux Jones and Arvel B. Jackson, *The Peelites, 1846–1857* (Columbus: Ohio State University Press, 1972), 63; Kevin Nowlan, "The Political Background," in Edwards and Williams, *The Great Famine*, 159; O'Gráda, *The Great Irish Famine*, 52.

124. Disraeli, *Lord George Bentinck*, 274.

125. Bentinck to Cofton Croker, September 30, 1847, Additional Manuscript 41129, ff. 56–83.

126. Bentinck believed, as he told his father, that his "political fame" depended upon the success of the railway bill (Quoted in Jones and Jackson, *The Peelites*, 63).

127. David Large, "The House of Lords and Ireland in the Age of Peel, 1832–50," *Irish Historical Studies* 9 (September 1955):393.

128. Ibid., 393–394.

129. *Parl. Deb.* (Commons), 3rd ser., 89 (1847):109, 477.

130. Ibid., 89 (1847):848–858.

131. Large, "The House of Lords," 394.

132. John Earl Russell, *Later Correspondence*, 1:170.

133. O'Gráda, *The Great Irish Famine*, 46.

134. Ibid.; Black, *Economic Thought*, 196–197.

135. Nowlan in Edwards and Williams, *The Great Famine*, 160.

136. Jones and Jackson, *The Peelites*, 64.

137. Black, *Economic Thought*, 123.

138. *Times* (London), April 2, 1847.

139. Large, "The House of Lords," 392.

140. Black, *Economic Thought*, 122.

141. Ibid., 120–121.

142. Ibid., 30–31.

143. Scrope, *The Irish Relief Measures*, 67.

144. Black, *Economic Thought*, 243–244.

145. Large, "The House of Lords," 395–396.

146. Quoted in Prest, *Lord John Russell*, 252.

147. Woodham-Smith, *The Great Hunger*, 301–302.

148. *Times* (London), July 2, 1847.

149. *Parl. Deb.* (Commons), 3rd ser., 104 (1847):71.

150. Woodham-Smith, *The Great Hunger*, 304–305.

151. *Times* (London), November 16, 24–25, December 1–2, 1847.

152. Quoted in Woodham-Smith, *The Great Hunger*, 304–305.

153. For example, Lord Bedford to Russell, May 25, 26, 1847, PRO 30/22/6C, ff. 342–346, 352–354.

154. Wood to Russell, September 1, 1847, PRO 30/22/6F, ff. 5–14.

155. Clarendon to Russell, August 28, 1847, PRO 30/22/6E, ff. 226–234.

156. Russell wrote angrily to Bessborough on December 28 that "you have scarcely written me a word about the arming [of the peasantry]. I see that it goes on as vigorously as ever. I fear some bad outbreaks will occur before the Spring," and solicited his opinion on an arms bill. Bessborough replied flatly on December 30 that "I have not said much to you upon the subject of arms, because I have no great alarm upon the subject," and as for insurrection, "there appears to me not the most distant idea of it." In his somewhat embarrassed reply Russell continued to insist on "the rush for arms which has taken place in this untoward season. But I agree with you Arms Bills are very bad things." PRO 30/22/5G, ff. 97–98, 123–124; PRO 30/22/6A, ff. 25– 26.

157. Clarendon to Russell, October 23, 1847, PRO 30/22/6F, ff. 209–220.

158. Russell to Clarendon, November 15, 1847, PRO 30/22/6G, ff. 139–140.

159. Clarendon to Russell, November 17, 1847, PRO 30/22/6G, ff. 156–165.

160. Clarendon to Russell, February 5, 1848, PRO 30/22/7A, ff. 277–278. Clarendon's changing ideas were undoubtedly influenced by his close friendship with Delane. In stark contrast to Bessborough's suspicious attitude toward Delane, Clarendon wrote the editor that "You have done us a right good service here & I am much obliged to you." Clarendon to Delane, July 27, 1848, Delane MSS vol. 3, f. 46.

161. *Times* (London), April 19, 1848.

162. Prest, *Lord John Russell*, 285; *Times* (London), April 6, 1848.

163. Prest, *Lord John Russell*, 285–286.

164. *Times* (London), August 30, 1848.

165. Quoted in Mandler, *Aristocratic Government*, 252.

166. Lord Fortescue to Russell, September 26, 1848, PRO 30/22/7D, ff. 125–126.

167. Clarendon to Russell, August 16, 1849, PRO 30/22/8A, ff. 83–86.

168. Lord Dufferin to Russell, September 10, 1849, PRO 30/22/8A, ff. 181–184.

169. Woodham-Smith, *The Great Hunger*, 377–381.

170. Parliament, "Account of Public Monies Expended or Advanced by way of Loan in the Years 1845–8, for the Relief of Distress in Ireland," *Sessional Papers* (Commons), *1847–8, Sources for Famine Expenditure*, 1 September 1848, vol. 54, p. 16; "Expenditure of Ireland," *Sessional Papers* (Commons), *1849, Account of Net Public Income and Expenditure*, vol. 30, p. 181; "Public Income and Expenditure, from 1822 to 1849," *Sessional Papers* (Commons), *1850, Account of Net Public Income and Expenditure*, vol. 33, p. 158.

171. In 1853 the Aberdeen administration forgave all remaining debts on famine relief, which amounted to £3 million.

172. *Times* (London), May 12, 1847.

173. Hilton, *The Age of Atonement*, 14–16, 32. Hilton distinguishes moderate evangelicals from their more extreme millenarian coreligionists who generally denied the ability of humans to stave off national misfortunes but also were more likely to advocate state intervention to alleviate the effects of divine dispensations.

174. He characterizes most of the more influential ministers in both the Peel and Russell administrations as moderate evangelicals and suggests that this contributed to their reluctance to countenance state intervention.

175. Mandler, *Aristocratic Government*, 252.

4

The Famine and English Public
Opinion, 1845–1850

[I] am thinking of a tour in Ireland: unhappily [I] have no call I *desire* that
way or any way, but am driven out somewhither (just now) as by the point
of bayonets at my back. Ireland really *is* my problem; the breaking-point
of the huge suppuration which all British and European society now is.
Set down in Ireland, one might at least feel, "*Here* is thy problem. In God's
name, what wilt thou do with it?" [1]

The reluctance and disgust with which Thomas Carlyle regarded Ireland was as
characteristic of educated English opinion in 1849 as it would have been uncharacteristic in the first half of the decade. Before the famine, Ireland appeared to most observers as a perfect proving ground for the ideals of popular
liberalism. The English public did not deny the poverty of the country, but
convinced themselves that Ireland was rapidly improving, both morally and
economically, under the union. Her people, it was imagined, were thereby becoming reconciled to close relations with Britain.

   Educated opinion had initially faced the potato blight of 1845 and subsequent famine with an optimism characteristic of the prefamine years. Until
1847 the English public earnestly concerned itself with the Irish problem. It
did so, however, largely in the light of prefamine English social and political

preoccupations, such as the anti-Corn Law movement and the struggle between the "progressive" middle-class and the "feudal" aristocracy. The famine
seemed a God-given opportunity to implement prefamine schemes for moral
and social improvement, and to finally accomplish the work of amalgamating
England and Ireland as one. It also appeared to provide an instance in which
the benefits of free trade and enlightened middle-class management of government could be conclusively proven. The desperate and unique character of the
famine, in which perhaps one million Irish eventually died,[2] appears not to
have impressed itself upon the English psyche until the first months of 1847.

Unfortunately for Ireland, several circumstances conspired to halt and eventually roll back the English public's dawning realization of the dimensions of
the suffering caused by the famine. In 1847 and 1848 a combination of factors
worked a rapid change in the manner in which the English public perceived
Ireland. A growing sense that England was under siege by a variety of domestic
and foreign threats wrecked popular confidence in the possibility of working a
lasting solution to the Irish troubles, and transformed Ireland itself from an object of pity or desire to one of fear. The new intellectual current of scientific racialism, which had not itself contributed substantially to the initial change of
perceptions, capitalized on the loss of public confidence and gave enduring
ideological dimensions to what otherwise might have been a passing phase in
the popular outlook. By 1849 Ireland increasingly appeared as a moral quag-
mire destined to serve as a tool for the destruction of liberal ideals.

The famine has not as yet been seen as a watershed in English perceptions of
Ireland and the Irish. The period is instead usually seen as being simply one moment in the broader, unchanging pattern of nineteenth-century racism. This is
unfortunate, for study of this subject has a bearing on a number of wider issues
involving not only the nature of English perceptions of the Irish in the nineteenth century, but also the sources and dynamics of change in popular thought.

Several points should be evident from this chapter. The initial English response to the famine was not on the whole governed by any racist preconcep-
tions, but by the body of liberal prefamine assumptions about Ireland that were
discussed in chapter two. The racial interpretation of Ireland and Irish problems, which was so widespread in England in the latter half of the nineteenth
century, was in many respects the direct product of the politics of the potato
famine. The ideological foundations of racialist thought had been in place long
before the famine in the form of early "scientific" racism, and in this respect the
application of these ideas to the Irish problem after about 1850 may be seen as
simply one aspect of the popular diffusion of scientific thought. The profound
changes in popular perceptions that emerged from the famine were not themselves the product of new ideas, however. Instead, the new ideas of scientific ra-

cialism embodied and gave definition to changing social and political priorities that were themselves the result of domestic and foreign crises.

THE FAMINE AND LIBERALISM

In the autumn of 1845 Thomas Campbell Foster, commissioner of the *Times*, was busy prosecuting Delane's continued vendetta against Daniel O'Connell. Foster's anti-O'Connell polemic provoked angry replies from the Liberator, who characterized Foster as the "gutter commissioner"[3] of the *Times*. Delane replied in terms stronger than those to which he had hitherto been used, labeling O'Connell among other things a "wild beast."[4] Delane did not stop at rhetoric, however, and determined to ruin O'Connell's reputation by sending Foster to "expose" the poverty of the tenants on O'Connell's Kerry estates.[5] W.H. Russell, later to be celebrated as a correspondent of the Crimean War, arrived at Delane's behest to back up Foster's claims that O'Connell was among the worst of that ignoble race of Irish landlords. The resultant controversy would last through the summer of 1846.

This is not to say that Foster and the *Times* had no time for other matters, however. The commissioner's increasing insistence that racial difference was at the heart of Irish poverty had provoked a storm of protest not only among the Irish themselves, but also on the part of a multitude of English and Scottish writers. Apologia for his racial opinions occupied a large portion of his columns and also the editorial section of the newspaper itself.[6]

In the midst of these preoccupations the potato blight was not forgotten. In October an editorial expressed the "most serious apprehensions for the ensuing year"[7] and went on to describe the likely impact of a blight and possible famine on Ireland and its relations with England. Unlike newspapers such as the *Manchester Guardian*, whose more sober editorials expressed a comparatively optimistic viewpoint, the *Times* drew on Foster's criticism of the Irish peasantry to proclaim that they would have only themselves to blame for a famine, and that the English people would be quite justified in withholding any aid. After predicting that "the demagogue and the priest will deliberately stand between English charity and Celtic starvation," the leader-writer declared that

it cannot be concealed that there are also circumstances too likely to chill the hand of the giver. Besides that it is not in human nature, whatever it may be in grace, to give quite so freely to those who have all their days reviled and traduced the giver, who have leagued and conspired against him, and otherwise injured him to the utmost extent of their humble abilities, there is also the disheartening memory of former bounties lavished in vain.[8]

The arguments of Foster and the *Times* were not, however, initially well received in England. If the contents of the political and economic tracts, pamphlets and books printed from 1845 to 1847 about Ireland are any indication, hostility to Foster and optimism about Irish regeneration went hand in hand. The heartrending stories of mass starvation, which were chronicled in detail by the English press, did not suffice to destroy this fundamental optimism. English printers busily produced tract after tract advancing a multitude of solutions to the crisis. On the whole, the tone of these tracts was identical to those that had been published in the first half of the decade. Ireland's woes were blamed on a social and economic climate that was itself the product of past mismanagement and oppression. Ireland's hopes for the future were held to rest in amalgamation, "consummation" of the Union, and moral and economic reform through middle-class tutelage and the prudent management of relief.

The religious aspect of the liberal perception of the Irish problem is evident in many of these tracts, and became more overt in the famine years. The Queen's declaration of January 13, 1847 as a national day of fasting and humiliation is only one example of this. References to the blight and then the famine as "visitations of Providence" were common. These expressions did not, however, entail smug assumptions that the famine was just punishment for Irish iniquity, which the Irish must repent and atone for. Although the famine did for many appear to be a divine chastisement for human sinfulness, the burden of guilt was thought to be spread equally among peasants, landlords, and Englishmen. The Reverend C.H. Gaye, in a sermon delivered in response to the day of fasting and humiliation, expounded on the theme of guilt and retribution:

> Improvements may be made in the laws and administration of that unhappy country, in the culture of its soil, and in the social relations and moral habits of the people. The present catastrophe, I pray God, may be taken as a *signal* for improvement; it is, in truth, an *arousing* signal. . . . It would be hazardous, e.g. presumptuous, and uncharitable in the extreme, to interpret them . . . as token of the sufferers' peculiar sinfulness and hatefulness in the sight of God. Oftentimes, on the contrary, we know, they are tokens of Divine love. . . . [there is] guilt, absolute though not comparative guilt, in those on whom they fall . . . doubtless there is overmuch guilt in these islands, both one and the other of them.[9]

Distress in Ireland was not so much a means for atonement[10] as it was a God-given opportunity to work the moral and social reforms that had been dreamed about in the years before the famine. The purpose of responsible famine legislation would therefore not be to punish the unregenerate, but to work for long-term reform while relieving short-term suffering. As one woman asked,

> Can any great good be effected in this world without suffering, and that suffering proportioned to the good to be attained? It is a sad thought, and yet at this moment a very comforting one to me; for it is my fervent belief, that this famine opens a prospect of the future improvement of this country [Ireland].[11]

Improvement, many assumed, would take place only over the figurative, if not literal, corpses of the Irish landlords. Popular hatred of the Irish landlords carried over from the prefamine era, but in the famine years it became practically a monomania.[12] The greed of the landlords was largely blamed for the failure of public works projects in 1846 and the large-scale evictions that forced Irish paupers to emigrate to England. In the longer term, they were seen as having created the conditions leading to poverty and starvation in Ireland, although here the press admitted that the English government shared the blame for having given the landlords power in the first place.[13] Proposals that the landlords be compelled to support relief and accept the curtailment of their political and economic power were correspondingly popular. Any measure tending to strengthen the hand of the English, Scottish or Irish middle class in Ireland was, on the other hand, certain to find a good deal of support.

The sources of this popular hatred of the Irish landlords can only be summarized here. In the first place, it would be a mistake to overlook the reality of the cruelty and mismanagement that characterized ascendancy rule in Ireland.[14] This fact, well-chronicled in the prefamine years by English journalists, economists, novelists, historians and travelers, was even more evident in the first years of the famine. Starving peasants often found little sympathy from their landlords, who saw public works as pork-barrel projects useful only for the short and long-term economic gain they would bring to the proprietors themselves. The contemptuous and unfeeling language landlords used to describe the peasantry even at the height of the famine enraged English aid workers, who passed their anger on to educated opinion as a whole.

There were at the same time other aspects of antilandlord sentiment based on prejudice and ideology rather than observation. The Irish landed class was for many writers an extreme but nevertheless significant example of the inevitable failures of aristocratic government as a whole. The rhetoric surrounding the just-concluded debate over repeal of the Corn Laws fed naturally into criticism of Irish landlords during the famine years. The famine therefore appeared as an opportunity not only to improve the Irish but to demonstrate the superiority of middle-class ideals, including free trade, in the governance of the country.[15] The incompetence of the landlords to protect Ireland from famine was at the same time yet another argument against repeal of the union, which would, many assumed, have been followed by the installation of an Irish parliament dominated by landlords. Alexander Somerville saw the famine as yet another example of the principle that "it would be in the natural order of things for an Irish parliament of Irish landlords to legislate for themselves and against their tenantry and the great body of the people."[16]

It may be stated in addition that most English writers considered Irish landlords to be Irish even before they were landlords. They were usually referred to as a "race" that possessed all the degraded moral characteristics of their peasantry: violence, indolence, intemperance, thriftlessness, and domestic disorder and uncleanliness. English writers who aspired to religious tolerance also belabored Irish landlords with accusations of religious fanaticism. The fact that many of the landlords had originally descended from English or Scottish settlers was rarely pointed out except by themselves. Like the peasantry, however, the English considered the Irish landlords to be improvable, and success stories of improving landlords like Lord George Hill were often referred to by English writers anxious to set a good example.[17] In English perceptions of both Irish landlords and peasants, elements of race and class intertwined.

Forcing the landlords to support their peasantry through the Irish Poor Law, therefore, seemed well-calculated to work for the moral improvement of both peasants and landlords. Such a measure would, many believed, not only provide immediate relief without the "demoralization" assumed to be consequent on "gratuitous" aid, but also instruct the landed classes in their social duties.[18] Lord John Russell, among many others, believed that the antagonistic relationship between landlords and tenants and consequent social division of Ireland was of critical importance in the troubles of that island. A Poor Law on the English model (as opposed to its less comprehensive Irish counterpart) would help to heal these social divisions by teaching responsible behavior to all classes and forcing them to work together. As one author stated, "a stringent poor-law, viewed in relation to its effects upon the upper, and middle classes, is . . . calculated to promote the union and co-operation of those classes, and to perpetuate that union by the strong and enduring tie of private interest."[19] Furthermore, an extended Poor Law would not only ensure greater cooperation between landlords and tenants, but also forward the long-sought aim of instituting uniform laws and liberties throughout the British Isles.[20]

George Poulett Scrope was the most vocal of the many advocates of Poor Law extension, and elements of all these arguments may be found in his writings. The unwillingness of Irish landlords "to do their duty" to the peasantry necessitated in Scrope's opinion the use of "the strong hand of authority." They must be compelled to pay for relief of the starving through a strong poor law.[21] The regeneration of "the moral character of the Irish" in general that would follow would obviate the necessity of coercion in the future.[22]

The Poor Law Amendment Act of June 1847, with its uncompromising provisions for placing the burden for relief on Irish property,[23] effectively settled the issue for most writers. Nassau Senior had spoken out against it, rejecting in particular any provisions for outdoor relief, but his was an isolated voice, with the exception of Irish proprietors and some English Poor Law administrators.[24] For Scrope, however, the act did not go far enough. In the absence of a comprehensive system of land reform, he insisted, the moral regeneration of landlord and tenant might be strangled by the perpetuation of a feudal system of land tenure.

Many prominent political economists such as Senior, David Ricardo and Robert Lowe argued that Irish small-holdings were largely to blame for Irish agricultural inefficiency and overpopulation, and that the proper solution to the current state of affairs was to encourage emigration and land clearances, and thereby promote large-scale farming. For Scrope and John Stuart Mill, however, this program was both unjust and based on false premises. They rejected Malthusian population theory, arguing instead that the absence of tenant rights, exacerbated by landlord absenteeism and profligacy, was the true source of agricultural inefficiency. Measures for fixity of tenure, fair rents and compensation for agricultural improvements were in their view indispensable.[25]

As we have seen in the previous chapter, the efforts of Scrope and others to realize measures for land reform in Ireland proved abortive. Russell supported the extension of tenant rights, but for reasons of politics and personality was unable to win enough support in his cabinet to push any comprehensive measures through Parliament. Popular support for tenant rights in Ireland had before 1848 been based on images of landlord and peasant propagated in fiction and other literature. William Carleton was one of many who painted the picture of a long-suffering peasantry whose strong desire to improve was thwarted at the hands of cruel landlords manipulating an unjust land system to their own advantage. In the later years of the famine, popular support of tenant rights and other reforms would founder on changing perceptions of the Irish problem. Irish landlords by 1848–1849 no longer appeared as the sole villains in the Irish drama, and were widely admitted by the English public to be at least in part the victims of circumstance.[26] Peasants, conversely, no longer appeared simply as victims but also as perpetrators of Irish poverty.

In the first years of the famine, however, Scrope and Mill maintained with confident determination the idea that the Irish peasantry were not only wholly redeemable but substantially innocent of the *Times* charge that they were responsible for their own predicament. Both men took Foster severely to task for his racial opinions, which they rejected *in toto*. Scrope wrote contemptuously of the "nonsense bruited about as to some supposed Celtic incapacity for industry," insisting that the Irish were "as industrious as any people under the sun" but only degraded by circumstances.[27] Mill sneered at "Mr. Foster's indolent Celt."[28] In one editorial written for the *Morning Chronicle* in October 1846, Mill stated:

> A people have been for half a thousand years under such a *régime* as this [in Ireland], and men wonder at them for their indolence, and their want of enterprise, and their improvident marriages. They must be something more than human if they were not, in these particulars, all that they are charged with being. But to tell us in all gravity, that because they are all this, therefore they are so by nature and because of a difference of race, is a thing which might rouse the indignation even of persons not very quickly moved to such a sentiment, if that were a proper object of indignation which is perhaps only an aberration of the intellect.[29]

Landlords were the primary but not the only villains in the sad story of Irish moral degradation leading to poverty and famine. The humble potato stood menacingly next to the rapacious landlord as a protagonist needing to be either reformed or eliminated. The letters Peel received urging him to work for the replacement of the potato by anything from bread to macaroni were in fact very much reflective of public opinion. Here too, as in the case of land or poor law reform, the moral factor was central to arguments in favor of the replacement of the potato crop with something more wholesome. The ease with which the potato could be cultivated convinced many writers that its use was morally degrading. The blight appeared as a divine hint and opportunity to transform Irish morals through the cultivation of wheat. For one writer, grain, in "the skill and labour required for its production, and the complicated processes necessary to convert it into human food, would have employed, and trained to habits of industry and thoughtfulness, each rising generation," thus spreading "the influence of civilization."[30]

SYMPATHY AND CHARITY

Any scheme for state-sponsored emigration would have appeared as an admission of defeat in the fight for Irish reform. Through 1847, most writers remained opposed to the idea, and the statement of one author that "any practicable scheme of extensive emigration would seem to be invaluable, as tending at once to set free the limbs of industry, and to give room for the application of that capital and skill which must lay the foundation of future prosperity,"[31] was an exception to the rule. Arguments against emigration centered partly on the assumption that the Irish could be reformed at home and need not be sent abroad, and partly on the injustice of allowing Irish landlords to rid themselves of paupers for whom they were responsible, but there were other, more practical reasons as well. Most obviously, the poorer class of emigrants might be expected to travel no farther than Liverpool, where they would increase the burden on English poor-rate payers. The wealthier and therefore more desirable elements of the population, meanwhile, could be expected to travel to America or Australia.[32]

The Malthusian principles that one might expect to have been used in support of emigration were often ignored and sometimes specifically debunked. Overpopulation, at least until 1847, was usually a landlords' argument used to justify their inability to support their tenants and to lay the blame for Irish poverty at the door of improvident marriages that were supposedly encouraged by the priesthood. English writers generally denied that Ireland was overpopulated at all, or, if they admitted the principle of overpopulation, blamed it on the landlords because of their supposed complicity in the moral degradation of the peasantry.[33] With any substantial degree of land and social reform, then, the population problem, if it existed at all, could be expected to disappear; emigration, therefore was unnecessary.

Proselytism, like emigration, attracted few adherents among those seeking a long-term solution to Irish poverty. Given the common belief that religious intolerance was at the root of many of Ireland's problems, proselytism seemed not only unnecessary but evil. Irish Protestant attempts to capitalize on famine distress to effect mass conversions, particularly in those cases in which ministers exchanged food in return for attendance at Protestant schools or lectures, came in for violent criticism in England. For every pamphlet that joyfully recounted the deathbed conversions to Protestantism of starving Irish peasants,[34] there were many more that viewed such efforts with revulsion, echoed in the exclamation of one woman that "the idea of mixing up proselytism with relief" had been suggested by an "evil spirit."[35]

Vilification of the Irish priesthood was not widespread, with one major exception. The exception, unsurprisingly, was the *Times*, which remained true to its anti-Catholic tradition.[36] Numerous editorials noted the supposed preference of priests for tithes and agitation over poor relief, and expressed the fear that they would seek to enhance their own position by manipulating and pro-

voking the peasantry into an uprising. It is difficult to find the same sort of attitude elsewhere. Indeed, journalists, aid workers and others were through 1847
almost unanimous in their praise for the behavior of the Irish clergy. Accounts
of their devotion to the suffering in common with their Protestant brethren
bred hopes that the famine would inaugurate an enduring pattern of Catho-
lic-Protestant cooperation in caring for the peasantry.[37]

Aid workers were in the forefront of those playing down any fears of popular
unrest being instigated by priests, repealers, or anyone else.[38] The collapse of
tourism in Ireland during the famine forced English readers looking for "first
hand" portraits of the Irish people to turn to the many chronicles of suffering
that were published by aid workers.[39] Not surprisingly given their purpose as
fund-raising devices, these tracts present the Irish in the most optimistic light
possible. Peasants appear not as brute beasts living in filth and indifferent to
their fates, but as suffering, often childlike innocents. Their patience in misery
is often remarked upon, as is their kindness and generosity, but most emphasized is their desire for education and instruction in the wiser ways of English
prudence, thrift and forethought. Comments on race were uncommon, and
where they appeared were accompanied by specific remarks on the tractability
of racial boundaries. Mrs. Frederic West, for example, added to her comments
on Irish racial characteristics the statement that "religion and education will, it
is to be hoped, correct the deep dark passions which so often accompany a very
ardent temperament; and which have come to the Irish by descent from the
fervent blood of the Milesians and Spaniards."[40]

The success of these tracts may be measured in part by the contribution of
private charitable organizations to relief. Politicians did not expect much from
private charity, and were themselves often cynical about the value of contributing to organizations such as the British Association.[41] Lord Lincoln, for example, wrote Peel that "the calamity is so far beyond the powers of a private
subscription that if I had not held office in Ireland I should not have been
much inclined to take part in it but under the circumstances I shall send £50 or
£100 if you have any intention of subscribing."[42] While the public charitable
effort was hardly overwhelming, it did not justify Peel's gloomy prediction that
"there will be no hope of Contributions from England for the mitigation of this
Calamity—Monster meetings—the ungrateful Return for past kindness—the
subscriptions in Ireland to Repeal Rent and O'Connell Tribute—will have dis-
inclined the Charitable here to make any great exertions for Irish Relief."[43]
Cecil Woodham-Smith has estimated that private contributions for relief in
Ireland amounted to £505,000 overall in the course of the famine (more than
twice that coming from American sources),[44] but the multitude of private

charities outside the British Association and the Quakers makes it likely that the figure was actually somewhat larger.

Many writers nevertheless viewed charitable subscriptions for the needy with a measure of suspicion. They considered charitable societies themselves, and in particular the British Association, which worked through government offices, to be susceptible to bureaucratization and subsequent "jobbing" and corruption. More important, however, was the concern that the improper distribution of private relief would hinder the process of moral regeneration for which the famine was supposed to be such a golden opportunity:

> Dreadful as the Irish destitution is well known to be, a mere subscription bears some faint analogy to indiscriminate relief. The donor does not feel that he has produced a permanent effect; it is true, that he has fed the hungry, but he has not employed them, or improved their condition, and money so spent is partly thrown away.[45]

The purpose of charity was not simply to provide short-term relief, but to work a lasting moral and economic reform in Ireland. Private charity was therefore almost uniformly offered only in cases of extreme want (insofar as that could be determined) and was often accompanied by moral and economic education. In this respect famine relief took on characteristics similar to the sort of middle-class philanthropy being practiced on English workers. The inculcation of proper domestic habits of thrift and cleanliness, for example, appeared to be of prime importance in Irish relief missions.[46] Aid workers needed therefore not only to distribute food to peasants, but also

> to enter their cottages, and to talk to them about the management of their children and their domestic concerns: to shew them economic modes of preparing their meals; to point out the mischief of uncleanliness and idleness; to set them an example, to rebuke and commend them according to circumstances, and to exercise that beneficial influence which higher position, and the power to do little acts of kindness, and the voice free from the harsh tones of party and religious difference, naturally give.[47]

Most private charitable organizations offered aid only under severe restrictions. Even the Quakers, whose supposedly selfless and impartial efforts during the famine are legendary, resisted indiscriminate almsgiving and avoided providing food in areas where it was readily available from local merchants.[48] They based their attitude on a belief that the "Irish were not innately debased, but were so from long poverty and lack of opportunity."[49] The attitudes of William Bennett, a Quaker who spent much of 1847 dispensing charity in Ireland and writing pamphlets calling for more private subscriptions, were in keeping with those of his coreligionists. Although Bennett laid much emphasis on the moral degradation of the Irish peasantry, he was concerned to demonstrate to the English public that carefully managed charity[50] could work a profound change in the character of the people. In making this statement he was fully conscious of his opposition to a growing trend in England of racial and religious "prejudice" against the Irish. He rejected these attitudes in vehement terms, describing them as the result of "fear, of interest, or the want of faith in principle," and denied that there was "anything in the national character fatal to improvement."[51] The Irish were, he insisted,

> our fellow creatures,—children of the same Parent,—born with our common feelings and affections,—with an equal right to live as any one of us,—with the same purposes of existence,—the same spiritual and immortal natures,—the same work to be done,—the same judgment seat to be summoned to,—and the same eternal goal.[52]

He flatly stated in addition that the Irish were

> not in the centre of Africa, the steppes of Asia, the backwoods of America,—not some newly-discovered tribes of South Australia, or among the Polynesian Islands,—not Hottentots, Bushmen, or Esquimeaux,—neither Mahomedans nor Pagans,—but some millions of our own Christian nation at home, living in a condition low and degraded to a degree unheard of before in any civilized community.[53]

Ireland's current misery was, he insisted, a product of "the remnants of the hereditary and selfishness of the old feudal times," as a result of which Ireland had been treated as neither "a Sister" or "a Bride" but "as a captive slave won by the force of arms, kept by coertion, and therefore unattached and restless, miserable, and easily to be won by others."[54]

The defensiveness evident in Bennett's writings was a product of the continuing efforts of the *Times* and others to impugn the Irish race. It would appear, however, that in 1847 Bennett still spoke for the mainstream of English opinion. James Tuke, another Quaker, was equally concerned to demonstrate that under similar conditions "Saxon and Celt would be alike indolent and fainthearted."[55] Alexander Somerville, traveling in the island as a correspondent for the *Manchester Examiner*, also specifically rejected "that general but doubtful assertion, that a Celtic population is not constitutionally fitted for commerce and industrial enterprise."[56] Like Bennett and many others, he denounced "the injustice and evil of the feudal privileges of land and landlords," arguing that they were largely responsible for the famine. Political economy as a moral and economic system appeared to Somerville by contrast as "the very essence of humanity, benevolence, and justice," which would rescue the country.[57]

For all of Somerville's opposition to the pessimistic pronouncements of the *Times* on race, his ideas as a whole evince aspects of a new trend of racial theory. Not only did he use the terminology of race more freely than had been characteristic of most prefamine writings, but when he did so it was often with the implication that while some characteristics of race were mutable, others were not:

> The Saxon race, as represented by the English and lowland Scotch, would seem to have more aptitude for self-emancipation than the Celtic race as represented in Ireland; or rather more impatience under servitude, out of which arises the aptitude for commercial enterprise, which practised through many generations, becomes the Saxon inheritance, and would become the inheritance of any race if that race were fairly set in motion.[58]

The hints of bitterness against the Irish peasantry that appear in Somerville's writings were beginning to creep into many English accounts of the famine. Echoing the *Times*, he complained that the "munificent contributions from England" were ultimately being paid for "by Englishmen who work, who take off their coats to work, and sweat with their coats off."[59] He noted by contrast that many of the Irish peasantry appeared to be starving themselves in order to save money to buy arms while all the time refusing to pay their rents.[60]

THE TIMES AND THE RISE OF RACIALISM

The growing note of popular pessimism was reflected in the increasing stridency after 1847 of advocates of a reinterpretation of the Irish problem on racial grounds, oblivious to the angry criticism of their stance by men such as Scrope, Mill and Bennett. By the early months of 1847 the *Times* had placed itself in the forefront of the new conceptual trend of racialism. As we have seen, Delane and his staff hardly responded to the onset of the famine with generosity. However, growing Irish misery aggravated an already cynical frame of mind to the point where leader writers began to vent their disgust in a series of extraordinarily hateful articles. A leader of February 22 set the standard for many to follow:

Remove Irishmen to the banks of the Ganges or the Indus—to Dehli, or Benares, or Trincomalee, and they would be far more in their element there than they are in the country to which an inexorable fate has consigned them. Under a tropical sun they would hug themselves in the consciousness of perpetual warmth and periodical famines. They would fold their arms and wait the coming calamity, if not with philosophy, at least with composure. They would bend beneath it and perish by hundreds in unrepining patience. When it had passed away, they would moralize and make pilgrimages. But the idea that human exertions could mitigate the inflictions of Heaven, or that evils that had been repeated for centuries could ever be prevented in future, would be denounced as impious or insane. The failure of crops and the terror of tempests would be the only interruptions to a life of indigent contentment and indolent endurance. Besides these they would know no cares and no griefs. But their destiny has not permitted them this concurrence of temper and climate. They are Asiatics in an European latitude and on an European soil. Their nature is in endless conflict with itself. Urged, by the exigencies of a position which they could not prevent, to desultory exertions which they cannot continue, they relapse after a brief excitement of tumultuous industry into their natural slough of acquiescent poverty. And when, as now, poverty has been blighted into destitution, their temper and instincts suggest no cure and no prevention but the alms of alien beneficence and the provision of alien wisdom.[61]

In direct contradiction to those who continued to advocate the extension of English laws and liberties to Ireland as the best hope for the regeneration of the island, the *Times* advanced the hypothesis that the Irish were racially unsuited for English institutions:

Ireland has a people whose character bears a stronger affinity to that of the Bengalese or the Cingalese than of any Teutonic family, or even their kindred Celt. To this people we have communicated popular institutions and Saxon laws. Peculiarly adapted to the fostering warmth of a tropical sun and a tropical despotism, they have been forced to shiver in the temperate regions of constitutional liberty, and to exchange the appropriate inertness of parental tyranny for the bustling excitement of a popular Government. The consequence is obvious.[62]

The continued outspoken hostility of many writers to the racialist pronouncements of the *Times* would appear to indicate that in 1847 the educated

English public as yet by no means despaired of their prefamine confidence in the potential regeneration of the Irish people. The Whig government, however, was impressed by the *Times* as "that base exponent of the basest of existing things—*English public opinion*."[63] At the very least, its statements were believed to have "produced a considerable impression on the Publick Mind."[64] Assumptions on the part of some ministers of the supposedly "anti-Irish mood" of the English and Scottish people appear to have been based largely on the statements of the *Times*, even in periods when charitable activity and donations for the starving were flourishing.[65]

Government relief measures had been subject to little popular criticism before 1847. The miserable failure of the Whig public works program in 1846 did not goad even the *Times* into attacking the government;[66] the *Manchester Guardian* in reporting Russell's relief program for 1847 simply stated, "We are by no means prepared to offer any suggestions on this subject."[67] For the largest portion of the British press, the Irish landlords and peasantry remained the preferred scapegoats for the failures of antifamine measures. Although there were many suggestions for additional legislation in favor of social reform, the assumption was usually that Russell shared these desires and would get around to implementing them once he could muster enough support to overturn the opposition of the Irish landlords. By the summer of 1847, however, ministers appear to have been convinced that the public mood had become so profoundly anti-Irish as to preclude any further substantial relief measures.

They could find evidence for this not only in the pages of the *Times*, but also in other sections of the popular press. *Punch*, for example, true to its general tendency to follow trends in the *Times*,[68] began to adopt a more pessimistic tone on Irish issues in this period. As Roy Foster has argued, this was partly the product of a change in editors and partly representative of a changed public perception of the Irish problem in the face of famine.[69] Peter Gray, elaborating on Foster's points, demonstrates that *Punch* followed contemporary opinion in, at first, welcoming the famine as an opportunity to improve the Irish out of some of their more improvident habits. Though continuing to mock Orangeism, the magazine expressed the popular belief that the famine was a work of providence intended to wean the Irish from the corrupting moral influence of the potato. By December 1846, however, *Punch* gave vent to growing frustration over supposed Irish intransigence and ingratitude, and began to print jokes and cartoons that blamed Irish poverty on the Irish. Only at this point may one begin to find cartoons which "simianize" Irish features in the manner that was to become standard for the rest of the century.[70]

To what may we attribute the transformation of public perceptions of the Irish problem in 1847 and 1848? In essence, it took place in reaction to a series of perceived domestic and international threats to the stability of Great Britain, none of them having much to do with Ireland itself. At home, a financial crisis threatened the economic equilibrium of the country and seemed to preclude the massive outlays of money that would be needed to feed the Irish. The Chartist agitation of 1848 raised the specter of popular revolt in England, while at the same time a growing influx of Irish immigrants threatened to "infect" English and Scottish working men with Irish habits. The Young Ireland rising of 1848 caused not only fury at Irish "ingratitude," but stimulated further fears that Irish immigrants and Chartists would combine to cause an insurrection in England. Abroad, a potential European food crisis in 1846 and 1847 spelled possible danger for England and argued against any large food shipments to Ireland. More crucially, the continental revolutions of 1848 first distracted the English public from the continuing Irish distress, and then threatened to spill over into Great Britain in the wake of Chartist and Irish nationalist disturbances.

Too many people, warned one author, were laboring under the "delusion" that a "famine in England" was impossible.[71] In reality the English public was anything but overconfident on this point. As early as 1845, the government took care to publicize the fact that food shortages in Continental Europe and Scotland made it exceedingly difficult to procure food.[72] By 1846, indeed, the highlands of Scotland were experiencing a food crisis very similar to that ravaging Ireland.[73] England, to which the blight had also spread in the summer of 1845, was of course not dependent on the potato, but even so it was widely believed that the potato blight in combination with the spread of bad grain harvests from the continent might result in severe food shortages in England. Thomas Carlyle wrote to Charles Gavan Duffy in March 1847 that "starving Ireland will become starving Scotland and starving England in a little while."[74] Those writers who chose to emphasize the potato blight as an instrument of providence also pointed to the possibility and even likelihood that the English as well as the Irish might be subjects of divine chastisement.[75]

A series of financial crises in 1847 contributed to the apocalyptic mood and appeared to some as the precursor of a social catastrophe in England. These crises, driven by food and railway speculation, came in the critical months of February and September when the Irish famine was at its height. As we have seen, they placed the Treasury under great pressure and convinced the government that large expenditures for relief were unwise, helping first to defeat Bentinck's railway bill and then leading the government to renege on its promise for further aid to Ireland after the summer of 1847.[76] The financial uncertainty also frightened and preoccupied the English public, however, and the crisis of September 1847 was especially traumatic. The *Times* almost completely ceased coverage of Irish distress, and for several weeks concentrated exclusively on the economy. Other periodicals and the public in general were likewise distracted and further pushed the Irish famine into the background.[77]

The possibility of unrest among the English poor was a threat implicit in the danger of spreading food and economic crises. The Chartist agitation of 1848 gave form to the specter of social unrest and added credence to the idea that an Irish peasant could not be fed without taking food out of the mouth of an English worker, thereby spurring the latter to anger and even revolt. Conversely, the tenuous character of the English worker as sober, industrious and law-abiding might be weakened by the increasing presence of Irish immigrants in English industrial districts.

It was but a short step from viewing Ireland as a sick patient in need of a moral cure (an image frequently used in depictions of Ireland), to seeing Irish paupers as carriers of a moral plague that might contaminate even the most stolid English workers, engendering "a spirit of discontent" and making either a rising or a general collapse of English industry inevitable. As a result, England might "sink from her high estate to the level of those whose sorrows she has so long deplored."[78] This fear led the normally level-headed economist George Poulett Scrope to exclaim that the continuation of this process would "spread through Britain the gangrene of Irish poverty, Irish disaffection, and the deadly paralysis of industry that necessarily attends upon these elements of evil."[79] The Irish peasants were no longer even for Scrope objects of sympathy, but carriers of a moral disease:

> [W]astefully consuming whatever they obtain, whether by alms, by plunder, or from public charity, spreading misery, disease, and disaffection over the land, and endangering the public tranquillity, the security of property, the permanency of our social institutions, and the safety and integrity of our empire.[80]

Ireland itself seemed to provide ample evidence for the supposed propensity of the Irish for violence and unrest. In the wake of O'Connell's death in 1847 and the subsequent collapse of the Repeal Association, rural unrest spread to many parts of Ireland. Starvation and evictions contributed to it, but for the most part it was the same old story of poverty, faction and land hunger. The absence of any political channel for grievances led to an increase in sporadic violence, including assassinations.[81] The Crime and Outrage (Ireland) Act of November 29, 1847, did little to dampen British fears; indeed politicians and writers through the spring of 1848 almost unanimously predicted a rising in Ireland. Under the circumstances the Young Ireland rising in July was no surprise, but it gave substantially more strength to the cries of "monstrous ingratitude" with which many had been abusing the Irish since the summer of 1847.

Although the 1848 insurrection was in reality a pathetic affair, in the context of the prevailing European unrest and the Chartist disturbances it seemed a harbinger of things to come. Newspapers, fresh from focusing almost obsessively on the financial dislocation of the last months of 1847, found themselves in the first half of 1848 immersed in continental affairs, where uprisings appeared to be spreading like wildfire across Europe. Ireland's continuing woes got short shrift by comparison, until the island threatened to become a springboard for revolution. When England turned its attention back to Irish affairs in the spring and summer, therefore, it did so in an entirely defensive manner. The *Times*, like the *Manchester Guardian* and other newspapers, ignored the ongoing famine almost completely, while the very small (in comparison with the Repeal Association) Young Ireland movement loomed large as a revolutionary fraternity of "Irish traitors" forming a "Rebel army" and preparing to throw the British Isles into civil war and social chaos.[82]

The collapse after 1847 of English charity for Ireland was one product of these apparent threats to Great Britain. The relief drive of January 1847 that had been launched in response to the "Queen's letter" had raised £171,533; a similar drive in October of the same year was a complete failure, raising little more than the £10,000 garnered by a final call for charity in 1849.[83] Englishmen who felt in danger themselves were unlikely to continue giving freely to those whom they considered part of the forces threatening them. The *Times*, whose grudging support of donations for Ireland in the winter of 1846–1847 had changed to outright hostility by the summer of 1847, was in the forefront of the drive to cut off all aid, both public and private, to the Irish. After declaring in August that the famine was over, harvests were good, and employment readily available in Ireland, the *Times* completely ignored the resurgence of starvation over the following two years. The newspaper bitterly attacked a charity drive launched in October of that year, and in February 1849 denounced a proposal made in parliament for a government grant of £50,000 to the distressed.[84] The Quakers ended their famine relief program in the summer of 1847 and the British Association ran out of funds in the autumn of 1848, though starvation deaths were at their highest level since early 1847.[85]

The collapse of the charitable impulse toward Ireland coincided with a changing Irish perception of the nature of English intervention. The intellectual process of separation between the Irish and the English was in this sense not wholly one-sided. The Irish, like the English, responded to the famine with a prodigious quantity of printed material.[86] The tone of these tracts was from the beginning critical of English relief measures as being not sufficiently generous. Their rhetoric was nevertheless almost identical to that being used by English authors. Irish writers admitted the moral degradation of the peasantry, and advocated relief measures predicated on the need to work moral reform and legal uniformity between England and Ireland. With the exception of a few extreme Protestant writers, most Irish writers hotly contested racialist ideology and advanced traditional liberal theories of human equality. As one Irishman exhorted his English readers,

> Seize, then, the opportunity to amalgamate as one, Ireland with England's people. Fear not the idle stories of the past; look but upon the present, and think of the glorious future which the guidance and help of England may accomplish. England has laboured for, and won her glories by her labour. Teach Ireland, and she will win glories too—not for herself alone, but for the general weal. Lead her kindly now, and she will rush to your foremost ranks in the hour of danger.[87]

The famine, however, worked a change in Irish opinion just as it had in England. Here the source of change was the evident failure of liberal ideals to prevent starvation or even to work any sort of lasting change in the habits of the peasantry or the relationship of the two countries. Political economy and its associated theories of human nature and human relations, which before the famine had found many advocates in the better-off portion of the Irish population, came increasingly to appear as a foreign philosophy. English moral and political standards began to seem demonstrably inapplicable not only to Irish conditions but to the Irish people themselves. By 1847 and 1848 calls appeared in Ireland for the creation of an "Irish political economy" tailored to the peculiarities of the Celtic race. With the failure of the relief measures of the English government, which most Irish perceived as acting under the dictates of English political economy, the idea grew in Ireland that "political economy's mission of assimilating Ireland to England [had] failed; concomitant with its decline was an increased emphasis on Ireland's difference from England."[88]

Anglo-Irish fiction by writers such as W.H. Maxwell and William Carleton further expressed this process of separation. W.H. Maxwell had in his earlier work partially suppressed his already dim view of the Irish peasantry. His 1845 history of the 1798 Irish rising, though hateful enough, was masked in a veneer of respectable phraseology expressing the hopeful prospects for Irish regeneration. Writing in the wake of the 1848 rising he no longer felt any such compunctions, and confidently informed his English readers of the depravity of the Irish people. Sternly declaring to the "Celts" that "you have alienated the sympathies of those who so often dragged you through starvation," Maxwell contemptuously dismissed an idea that had worried many English before the famine: that a neglected Ireland could turn to America or France for support. Ireland, Maxwell declared, was so utterly worthless that no one else could be bothered to take care of her:

> Is there a European state to whom you would not be an encumbrance; nay, a regular nuisance? Were you auctioned tomorrow, Lamartine would not bid a five-franc piece; and as bad as a Pennsylvanian bond may be, Polk would prefer it to an investment in Pike securities.[89]

The key to maintenance of the union in Maxwell's mind was not moral and social reform; instead, "a ton or two of gunpowder and a coil of rope will do the job."[90]

In 1847 William Carleton had been the first major author to directly address the tragedy in a novel, *The Black Prophet*. Carleton treated his subject with uncharacteristic delicacy, being careful to avoid insinuations of rabble-rousing on the part of the Catholic clergy, and stating magnanimously that outrages brought about by hunger "ought to be looked upon with the most lenient consideration and forbearance by the executive authorities."[91] The villain of the story, Darby Skinadre, is a Dickensian character, a greedy Irish merchant who scolds the peasantry for their lack of industry and refuses them aid without proper payment.[92] None of the characters in the story, however, are presented as being irrevocably bad, their many faults being presented as products of their environment.

The Black Prophet was widely read and praised, but its liberal tone was not to be repeated in Carleton's subsequent novels. In the last years of the famine Carleton not only unleashed the anti-Catholic feeling that he had kept buried for years, but wrote novels increasingly hostile to the Irish people themselves. *The Emigrants of Ahadarra* (1848), meant to expose the plight of Irish emigrants, also served as an anti-Catholic polemic. The peasant characters of this novel are far less sympathetic than any of Carleton's earlier creations, though the author was careful to state that their faults were not due to "any constitutional deficiency in either energy or industry that is inherent in their character."[93] *The Tithe Procter* (1849) and several other novels in the 1850s, however, explicitly denounced the Irish people for their supposed ingratitude and inhumanity.[94] The change in tone was due in part to Carleton's anger at the Young Ireland rising of 1848, but also likely had something to do with the changing mood of his readership.

The silence of English novelists in the face of the famine is indicative of the collapse of the market for novels on Irish subjects after 1847, despite the apparently limitless potential for drama provided by the event.[95] Aside from some sentimental poetry and penny-dreadfuls, no English fiction substantially addressed the subject during the famine years, nor did anything of note appear for the rest of the century. The once-flourishing literary genre that had taken Ireland and the Irish people as a rich source for fiction was, in the wake of the famine, becoming unpopular in England and by the early 1850s had almost completely disappeared.[96] Whereas in the early 1840s English readers had eagerly read numerous novels addressing Irish social issues, by the early 1850s their taste for "social reform novels" was sated by English rather than Irish settings.[97]

Lowbrow fiction eventually filled the gap left by the disappearance of middle- or highbrow fiction in the Irish genre. In the late 1840s the emergence of cheap, often violently anti-Catholic literature in this genre was no more than a tendency. By the first years of the ensuing decade, it was as we shall see a definite trend. "Paddy" reemerges in these works as a dirty, violent, ignorant and priest-ridden fool. The writers make little effort to excuse his behavior or to express hope for his future; and one fictional Englishman, when returning to Ireland after a seven year absence, notes "the immutability of men and things in this interesting country."[98] "Improvement" in these works has less to do with economic and social reform than with religious conversion. In one novel dating from the end of the 1840s, the machinations of a predatory priest to make a peasant girl into a nun are foiled by a Protestant Sunday-school. The anonymous author concludes the narrative with this lecture:

> Gifted with natural good sense and abilities, with acuteness and penetration into character beyond his supposed amount of cultivation, deep gratitude for favours, and equal resentment for injuries, the Irishman, in his craniological developments, presents strong features and remarkable contrasts. His perception of wrong and right are curiously at variance with his general conduct; and a constitutional sluggishness of disposition is almost the only natural ground on which we can account for his general debasement (as a peasant class) in the social system, or his tame and abject submission to the domination of the Irish priesthood.[99]

The emergence of this sort of literature coincided with a growing confidence on the part of Protestant evangelists. Their calls for the evangelization and conversion of Ireland did not congeal into a broadly supported movement until the beginning of the 1850s. In the last years of the 1840s, however, it is possible to detect a note of complacency and assurance in the manner by which they harangued the British public. At the same time, the zeal with which their opponents had condemned proselytism in 1846–1847 had by 1848–1849 begun to disappear. The furious fire and brimstone diatribe of one "Minister of the Gospel" was extreme but not uncharacteristic, when he described the famine not as a lesson for all humanity, but as God's wrath against the "impenitent" Catholic Irish. Here are no prescriptions for long-term reform, but a simple quick-fix solution, which the author assumes his English readership would gladly support: throw the priests out of the country.[100]

The shift in public attitudes evinced in charity, literature and elsewhere, did not initially entail an abrupt change in philosophy. At first, old arguments were merely justified in new terms. Teaching the Irish to fend for themselves was once a moral imperative; *letting* the Irish fend for themselves became not only a physical necessity but also a means of retribution for Irish ingratitude. Making the landlords support their own poor became less a means to the end of social reform than a necessity due to domestic and international threats to English prosperity. Within a decade, however, these ideas, originally an almost unconscious response to perceived domestic and international threats, had found definition in the arguments of a hitherto small but strident group of racialist philosophers. And just as racialism gave definition to the anti-Irish public mood of 1848–1850, the latter gave life to racialism as an idea and helped to transform it from a minority theory to a popular and enduring ideology.

Racialist propaganda from 1845–1847 was undoubtedly a small factor in the shaping of public attitudes toward Ireland. The power and influence[101] of the *Times* in this regard should not be underestimated, and the artfully stated racialism of the editors likely convinced some readers of the newspaper to see the Irish in similar terms. As we have seen, in 1846 and 1847 critics of racialism remained both confident and vocal. After 1848, however, antiracialist arguments appeared in print much less frequently, and those that did so increasingly took the tone of challenging established opinion. It is highly unlikely that this evidently rapid change in public attitudes was due to the force of intellectual persuasion. Racialism was instead seized upon as a vehicle for the expression of popular opinions that were hardening in the face of perceived threats to the stability of the British state and society.

The latter half of the 1840s marked a transitional phase in racial theory as it was understood by scientists. James Cowles Prichard's Lamarckian vision of the impermanence of racial characteristics was still widely accepted. Critics sought to modify rather than condemn the received wisdom. Robert Chambers in *Vestiges of the Natural History of Creation* (1844) advanced a vague neo-evolutionary notion that he called "recapitulation." All men were of the same species, Chambers argued, but at different stages of development. He did not address in detail the question of what exactly drove the process of development except to say that it mirrored that undergone by children in the womb. Charles Hamilton Smith in *The Natural History of the Human Species* (1848) attempted to import to Britain a system of "racial typology" that had been popular in France since the beginning of the century. This theory made cultural differences subject to racial characteristics and divided humanity into white (the most superior), African, and Asian "types." It did not differentiate within each type, and also assumed the common ancestry of humanity.[102]

Anyone determined to make a case for immutable Irish racial inferiority might have done so with reference to the notion of racial typology, by hinting that the Irish were not fully white. Mrs. Frederic West, for example, was convinced of the "Eastern and Pagan origin" of the Irish round towers, which she compared to the Taj Mahal and other Indian architecture.[103] She referred to the Irish language as "Celto-Phoenician Irish" and speculated that the ancestors of the Celts had originated in the Middle East, reaching Ireland via North Africa and Spain.[104] As we have seen, however, she also explicitly stated that with education the Irish were capable of the same standards of civilization as the English and Scottish. Most writers before 1848 did not speculate at all on the racial origins of the Irish beyond vague ideas as to their affinity with the French.[105]

L.P. Curtis and his supporters have pointed to the *Anglo-Saxon*, a journal that had its birth in the first years of the famine, as a typical example of the profound racism of English thought in this period. Despite its title, however, this journal was very much a product of its time. The opening address to the first issue described members of the Saxon race as "not Angles, but Angels."[106] In a subsequent issue, however, it sought to answer the question of "who are the Anglo-Saxons?"

> All who speak, and think, and read in the English Language in its present form and fashion. . . . As a family name, it does not exclude the Celt, whether Irish, Scotch, or Welsh; the two families are rapidly blending into one, and it is only natural to retain the name of the predominating element.[107]

Even phrenology added up to little more at this time than a vague series of ideas rather than a coherent system of thought. The boundaries that one phrenologist drew between English ("Industrious, Inventive, Noble, generous and brave") and Irish ("Generous, Careless, Flabby, Laborious & brave") were much less distinct than those between Irish and Africans ("Stupid, Indolent, Mischievous and profane") or Asians ("Inventive, Mischievous, Cunning, Indolent & Cowardly").[108]

Robert Knox's campaign in favor of a more tightly defined concept of race is particularly significant in the context of the nebulous definitions that prevailed at the end of the 1840s. Knox was a peculiar figure. Born in Edinburgh in 1791, he studied anatomy in Paris under Georges Cuvier, originator of the theory of "racial typology" later popularized in Britain by Charles Hamilton Smith. Upon returning to Edinburgh and becoming a lecturer in anatomy, he became a practitioner of dissection. In 1828 he became involved in scandal by unknowingly dissecting the victims of the murderers Burke and Hare, and in the resulting popular uproar was burnt in effigy. He alienated yet more people through his outspoken radicalism and antiimperialism. He began to promote his racial theories in a series of articles in the *Medical Times* in the early to mid-1840s, and in 1845 delivered a series of lectures on the same subject in Manchester and other cities, gaining considerable notoriety.[109] His magnum opus, *The Races of Men*, was published in 1850.[110]

Knox thoroughly rejected the contentions of Prichard and others who had "ascribed the moral difference in the races of men to fanciful causes, such as education, religion, climate &c." Racial characteristics, he declared, were utterly immutable whatever the environment.[111] Where others had at least loosely placed Celts in the same racial class as Saxons, Knox stated that the Irish were as different from, and inferior to, the Saxons as were the "Esquimaux."[112] The cry of amalgamation, he argued, was a pipe-dream. Intermarriage could have no long-term effects, nor could extending English laws and liberties to Ireland. "The experiment has been going on already for 700 years," he wrote. "I will concede you seven times 700 more, but this will not alter the Celt."[113] Government in Ireland should be based upon the fact that "Ireland is not a colony, but merely a country held by force of arms, like India; a country inhabited by another race."[114] His prescription for the future was cynically pragmatic:

> The [Celtic] race must be forced from the soil; by fair means, if possible; still they must leave. England's safety requires it. I speak not of the justice of the cause; nations must ever act as Machiavelli advised: look to yourself. The Orange club of Ireland is a Saxon confederation for the clearing the land of all papists and jacobites; this means Celts. If left to themselves, they would clear them out, as Cromwell proposed, by the sword; it would not require six weeks to accomplish the work.[115]

As these statements indicate, the comparatively cheery pre-1845 visions of the English-Irish "marriage" as a peaceful and complementary union were coming under attack. At the end of the 1840s most writers continued to take for granted Scrope's assumption that "Britain is wedded for good or ill to Ireland."[116] The increasingly apparent need for coercion in Ireland, however, made it seem that the union must be maintained not only by moral persuasion, but also by physical force. Knox's theories pointed to a growing trend of thought that would discard the marriage ideal entirely by claiming that Saxons and Celts were racially incompatible.

In the early 1850s, Knox's ideas would be widely disseminated, controversial and very influential.[117] He emerged as a central figure in the polygenist movement, which denied the common origins of the races of humanity and had been gaining strength since Prichard, the arch-apologist of monogenism, had died in 1848.[118] In the context of the late 1840s, Knox's ideas are particularly important because they represent a substantial break from the past in perceptions of the Irish and racial theory more generally. To be sure, Knox was not the first to advance opinions of this sort. He was, however, the first to state them concisely in clear, scientific terminology. Thomas Campbell Foster and the *Times*, by contrast, popularized the use of the word "race" with reference to the Irish and did their best to convince the public that the peasants were protagonists rather than victims in the tragedy of Ireland, but they did not construct a coherent theory of race in Ireland.

THE FAMINE AS WATERSHED

The continuing debate over the impact of the famine in Ireland has often focused on the question of whether the years 1845–1852 may justly be described as marking a "watershed" in Irish social history. Whatever the merits of each side of this debate, there is no question that in another sense the famine was indeed a watershed, that is, in its impact on English perceptions of Ireland and the Irish. The last two chapters have traced the process by which the famine and the events associated with it broke down the liberal consensus of the first half of the 1840s about the need and attainability of Irish reform. The next chapter will demonstrate how the uncertainty and pessimism that marked the last two years of the 1840s coalesced into a new and reasonably well-defined popular perspective by the end of the 1850s. It would be going too far to say that one perspective, or discourse, "replaced" the other. More accurately, a minority opinion became a majority opinion, changing and evolving in the process.

NOTES

1. Thomas Carlyle, journal entry for May 17, 1849, in *Reminiscences of My Irish Journey in 1849* (New York: Harper & Brothers, 1882), iii.

2. Daly, *The Famine in Ireland*, 99.

3. *Times* (London), October 7, 1845.

4. *Times* (London), October 2, 1845.

5. Maurice R. O'Connell, ed., *The Correspondence of Daniel O'Connell* (Dublin: Blackwater Press, 1972), 7:343–344.

6. See chapter two.

7. *Times* (London), October 18, 1845.

8. *Times* (London), October 18, 1845.

9. C.H. Gaye, *Irish Famine, A Special Occasion for Keeping Lent in England* (London: Francis and John Rivington, 1847), 11– 13.

10. Boyd Hilton has made much of the idea that the burden of atonement for past mistakes was on man. In fact evangelical religious doctrine held that Christ Himself atoned for man's misdeeds, and that man's proper response to divine chastisement was not atonement but moral reform.

11. W.S. Gilly, ed., *Christmas 1846, and the New Year 1847, in Ireland. Letters from a Lady* (Durham: G. Andrews, 1847), 4.

12. Maria Edgeworth's *Castle Rackrent* (1800) and *The Absentee* (1812) had capitalized on antilandlord sentiment decades earlier.

13. James S. Donnelly, Jr., "'Irish Property Must Pay for Irish Poverty': British Public Opinion and the Great Irish Famine," in Chris Monash and Richard Hayes, eds., *"Fearful Realities": New Perspectives on the Famine* (Dublin: Irish Academic Press, 1996), 60–62.

14. Joel Mokyr, *Why Ireland Starved: A Quantitative and Analytical History of the Irish Economy, 1800–1850* (London: George Allen & Unwin, 1983), 210.

15. It should be emphasized that support for the "businesslike" management of Ireland did not necessarily entail a rejection of aristocratic government. The Whigs, after all, were manifestly aristocratic, but as many authors pointed out some members of the landed class ran their estates very effectively on sound middle-class principles. One might draw a parallel with the Crimean War, which appeared to a portion of the English public as an opportunity to demonstrate the superiority of the businesslike manner of making war.

16. Alexander Somerville, *Letters from Ireland during the Famine of 1847*, K.D.M. Snell, ed. (Dublin: Irish Academic Press, 1994), 98.

17. Lord George Hill bought 33,000 acres of land in Gweedore, County Donegal, in 1838. He found the minds of the peasantry "far degenerated below the human standard" but by residing on his property, learning the Irish language, redistributing land, encouraging education and fighting temperance, he claimed to have changed them entirely within a few years. In his mind, his experiments proved that emigration was a false panacea for Irish poverty; he insisted that the country was not overpopulated (Lord George Hill, *Facts from Gweedore: with Useful Hints to Donegal Tourists* [London: Hatchard and Son, 1846], 16, 25–40). Hill's work was very widely quoted by other authors.

18. Black, *Economic Thought*, 120–121.

19. *Thoughts on National Education, as an Instrument of National Prosperity; and as a Mode of Diffusing amongst the Labouring Classes in Ireland Habits of Industry, Frugality, and Forethought; with an Introductory Chapter* (London: Thomas Cautley Newby, 1847), iv.

20. Although most economists hoped to harmonize the Irish and English economies through the natural operation of market forces and standardization of laws tending to allow the free operation of these forces, most accepted that some government intervention was necessary for this purpose (Black, *Economic Thought*, 242).

21. George Poulett Scrope, *The Irish Relief Measures, Past and Future* (London: James Ridgway, 1848), 19.

22. Ibid., 48.

23. Donnelly, "'Irish Property Must Pay for Irish Poverty,'" 60–61.

24. Black, *Economic Thought*, 122–123.

25. Richard Ned Lebow, "J.S. Mill and the Irish Land Question" in John Stuart Mill, *John Stuart Mill on Ireland, with an Essay by Richard Ned Lebow* (Philadelphia: Institute for the Study of Human Issues, 1979), 3–6.

26. Donnelly, "'Irish Property Must Pay for Irish Poverty,'" 70–73.

27. Scrope, *The Irish Relief Measures*, 83.

28. *Morning Chronicle*, October 15, 1846, quoted in Mill, *John Stuart Mill on Ireland*, 17.

29. *Morning Chronicle*, October 10, 1846, quoted in Mill, *John Stuart Mill on Ireland*, 6. By the 1860s Mill had changed his tune and was more willing to consider the possibility of an innate corruption in the Irish moral character (Lebow, "J.S. Mill and the Land Question," 7–8).

30. *Thoughts on Ireland* (London: James Ridgway, 1847), 37.

31. "An Englishman," *An Earnest Plea for Ireland* (London: John Ollivier, 1848), 8.

32. George Poulett Scrope, *Letters to Lord John Russell, M.P. on the Further Measures Required for the Social Amelioration of Ireland* (London: James Ridgway, 1847), 7–13.

33. Daly, *The Famine in Ireland*, 66–67.

34. *A Brief Account of the Famine in Ireland* (London: J.H. Jackson, 1847), 18–22.

35. W.S. Gilly, ed., *Christmas 1846, and the New Year 1847, in Ireland*, 46.

36. John Walter II, who owned the paper until his death in 1847, was a country gentleman who "hated O'Connell, his programme, and his religion." His son John Walter III took over the proprietorship of the *Times* in 1847. Though an early disciple of the Oxford movement, he nurtured a lifelong hostility to Catholicism (*History of the Times*, 2:8, 47).

37. "James Hack Tuke's Narrative of the Second, Third, and Fourth Weeks of William Forster's Visit to some of the Distressed Districts in Ireland," in *Distress in Ireland* (London: Edward Newman, no date), 1.

38. Lord Dufferin and the Hon. G.F. Boyle, *Narrative of a Journey from Oxford to Skibbereen during the Year of the Famine* (Oxford: John Henry Parker, 1847), 8.

39. Until the stimulus provided by the Queen's visit to Ireland in 1849, leisure travel to the island was almost wholly nonexistent.

40. Mrs. Frederic West, *A Summer Visit to Ireland in 1846* (London: Richard Bentley, 1847), 142. An advocate of national schools, Mrs. West claimed that Irish children, once educated, could reach or even excel the same standards of civilization common among the English and Scottish. She suggested that adults were by contrast unredeemable once corrupted by early influences (ibid., 193–214).

41. This organization was founded on January 1, 1847 by Stephen Spring Rice and run by substantial merchants. It was funded by private subscription (including £2,000 given by Queen Victoria), and distributed aid through government apparatus. It raised £470,000 in the course of the famine, giving a sixth of this amount for relief in Scotland (Woodham-Smith, *The Great Hunger*, 169–170).

42. Lincoln to Peel, January 5, 1847, Additional Manuscript 40481, ff. 398–399.

43. Peel, Memorandum to Cabinet, November 1, 1845, Additional Manuscript 40577, f. 267. Peel and Russell, as we have seen, tended to be less optimistic about the chances of a peasant uprising. Their fears were not reflected in print before about 1848, with the notable exception of the *Times*.

44. Woodham-Smith, *The Great Hunger*, 245–246. According to Mary Daly, the charitable response to the great famine was proportionately smaller than it had been during similar but smaller crises in 1822, 1826 and 1831. She attributes this to the increasingly powerful belief that the landlords needed to be taught to support their own poor (Daly, *The Famine in Ireland*, 42–43).

45. *Distress in Ireland: Outlines of a Plan for Employing Funds to Be Raised by Subscription in England, in Such a Manner, That in Relieving the Destitute, Their Condition May Be so Far Improved as to Prevent the Necessity for Aid in Future Years* (London: James Ridgway, 1847), 5.

46. Poor domestic habits seemed the surest evidence of Irish moral degradation. In most novels in the "Irish peasant" genre, a peasant's moral state was best discernable by reference to his personal and domestic hygiene.

47. W.S. Gilly, ed., *Christmas 1846, and the New Year 1847, in Ireland*, 6. The author of this quotation practiced what she preached. On one occasion, she rebuked the starving mother of seven children for not having weaned her two-year-old child: "Believe me, it required no small effort to stand firmly on that wretched floor, and to talk firmly to that wretched mother; but if I had given way, and turned hysterical too, who was to do *my* duty?" (ibid., 18).

48. Daly, *The Famine in Ireland*, 89–91.

49. Helen E. Hatton, *The Largest Amount of Good: Quaker Relief in Ireland, 1654–1921* (Kingston and Montreal: McGill-Queen's University Press, 1993), 7–8.

50. He contrasted this to the disasters to be expected from any reliance on government-sponsored or "gratuitous relief."

51. William Bennett, *Narrative of a Recent Journey of Six Weeks in Ireland, in Connexion with the Subject of Supplying Small Seed to Some of the Remoter Districts: With Current Observations on the Depressed Circumstances of the People, and the Means Presented for the Permanent Improvement of Their Social Condition* (London: Charles Gilpin, 1847), 139, 142–143.

52. Ibid., 29.

53. Ibid., 138.

54. Ibid., 145–147.

55. James H. Tuke, *A Visit to Connaught in the Autumn of 1847* (London: Charles Gilpin, 1848), 29.

56. Somerville, *Letters from Ireland*, 177.

57. Ibid., 127, 134.

58. Ibid., 177–178.

59. Ibid., 56.

60. Ibid., 54–55.

61. *Times* (London), February 22, 1847.

62. *Times* (London), February 25, 1847.

63. Fitzwilliam to Russell, November 16, 1847, PRO 30/22/6G, f. 171.

64. Edward Twistleton to Sir George Grey, Dec. 26, 1846, HO 45/1080B.

65. Wood to Bessborough, December 21, 1846, PRO 30/22/5F, ff.249–250.

66. The close connections Delane and his leader-writers had with many Whig leaders no doubt precluded outright criticism.

67. *Manchester Guardian*, January 27, 1847.

68. Gray, "*Punch* and the Great Famine," 27.

69. Foster, *Paddy and Mr. Punch*, 174–178.

70. Gray, "*Punch* and the Great Famine," 27–29.

71. *The Famine as Yet in Its Infancy; or, 1847 Compared with the Prospects of 1848, 1849, &c. Addressed to Every-Body* (London: Hamilton, Adams and Co., 1847), 5.

72. Daly, *The Famine in Ireland*, 72.

73. Relief in Scotland was based on the same moral and economic principles that were applied in Ireland. Although private aid to Scotland was proportionately greater than that given to Ireland, the government cut off state aid to both countries in August 1847 (T.M. Devine, *The Great Highland Famine* [Edinburgh: John Donald, 1988], 111–116).

74. Thomas Carlyle to Charles Gavan Duffy, March 1, 1847, in Charles Gavan Duffy, *Conversations with Carlyle* (New York: Charles Scribner's Sons, 1892), 25.

75. The *Times* described the Irish famine as only one aspect of a "world visitation" (January 16, 1847).

76. Mandler, *Aristocratic Government*, 252–253.

77. Woodham-Smith, *The Great Hunger*, 306.

78. Mrs. K.C. Maberly, *The Present State of Ireland, and Its Remedy* (London: James Ridgway, 1847), 12.

79. George Poulett Scrope, *How to Make Ireland Self-Supporting; or, Irish Clearances, and Improvement of Waste Lands* (London: James Ridgway, 1848), 28.

80. Ibid., 30.

81. Woodham-Smith, *The Great Hunger*, 324–329.

82. *Times* (London), April 11, 19, 1848.

83. Kinealy, *This Great Calamity*, 161–162.

84. Ibid., 165, 240.

85. Ibid., 237.

86. Although many Irish writers had their tracts printed in Dublin, London publishers also printed a large number of books and pamphlets by self-professed Irishmen during the famine.

87. Jasper W. Rogers, *Facts for the Kind-Hearted of England! As to the Wretchedness of the Irish Peasantry, and the Means for Their Regeneration* (London: James Ridgway, 1847), 34–35.

88. Boylan and Foley, xii, 10. The further development of Irish thought on this subject after the famine will be traced in the next chapter.

89. W.H. Maxwell, *The Irish Movements: Their Rise, Progress, and Certain Termination; with a Few Broad Hints to Patriots and Pikemen* (London: Baily Brothers, 1848), 20–21.

90. Ibid., 57.

91. Carleton, *The Black Prophet*, 247.

92. Alexander Somerville suggested that Skinadre was not a villain at all, but a hero: "what would have become of those people if Darby Skinadre had not had meal to sell to them? Would they not have perished utterly? Instead of being a cruel hard-hearted man, he was a benefactor whom they should have blessed and prayed for" (Somerville, *Letters from Ireland*, 174).

93. William Carleton, *The Emigrants of Ahadarra: A Tale of Irish Life* (London: Simms & M'Intyre, 1848), 267.

94. Wolff, *William Carleton*, 113–118.

95. Some scholars have recently advanced arguments that the famine had a profound impact on contemporary English literary efforts. Elsie Michie, for example, argues that "the Irish cataclysm is not so much absent from the Brontës novels as it is virtually invisible," speculating that Heathcliff in *Wuthering Heights* (1847) and Mr. Rochester in *Jane Eyre* (1847) are simianized Irishmen in disguise (Elsie Michie, *Outside the Pale: Cultural Exclusion, Gender Difference, and the Victorian Woman Writer* [Ithaca, N.Y.: Cornell University Press, 1993], 55). These arguments are imaginative but difficult to take seriously.

96. Wolff, *William Carleton*, 122.

97. Barbara Hayley, "'The Eerishers are marchin' in leeterature': British Critical Reception of Nineteenth-Century Anglo-Irish Fiction," in Wolfgang Zach and Heinz Kosok, eds., *Literary Interrelations: Ireland, England and the World*, vol. 1, *Reception and Translation* (Gunter Narr Verlag Tübingen, 1987), 48.

98. R.F. Walond, "Mr. Smith's Irish Love," in *Paddiana; or, Scraps and Sketches of Irish Life, Present and Past* (London: Richard Bentley, 1847), 37.

99. *Paddy's Leisure Hours in the Poor House; or, Priests, Parsons, Potatoes, and Poor-Rates* (London: John W. Parker, 1849), 67.

100. "Minister of the Gospel," *The True Source and End of Ireland's Destitution; Together with an Appeal, to British Christians, on Behalf of Ireland* (London: John Snow, 1849), 26–30.

101. And, one might add, irresponsibility.

102. Banton, *Racial Theories*, 28–53.

103. West, *A Summer Visit to Ireland in 1846*, 19–22.

104. Ibid., 279–281.

105. Even the writer R.F. Walond, who postulated the "immutability" of the Irish in his short stories, was careful to disassociate them from any affinity with the Africans. In one story he compares Irish peasants who are substantially reformed through their conversion to Protestantism with a "converted" African who declares to some English philanthropists: "'Once I bery bad man ('Poor thing!')—go quite naked. (Sensation.) Kill fader, moder, shild . . . ven meet Mr. Smith, blessed Mr. Smith! him say, No roast shild—bery bad roast shild.' " After learning to wear shoes and trousers, and read the "good book," the African "never more roast shild" but otherwise remains much the same (Walond, "The Mendicity Association" in *Paddiana*, 258).

106. *The Anglo-Saxon* (London: Longman, Brown, Green, and Longmans, 1849), January 1849: 3.

107. Ibid., July 1849: 5–6.

108. J.C. Lyons, *The Science of Phrenology, as Applicable to Education, Friendship, Love, Courtship, and Matrimony, etc.* (London: Aylott and Jones, 1846), endpiece.

109. Knox wrote that at the time of his lectures "I had the great question of race, the all-absorbing question of the day, wholly to myself" (Knox, *The Races of Men*, 20–21).

110. *Dictionary of National Biography*, 11:331–333; Banton, *Racial Theories*, 58.

111. He argued also that races could survive only in the regions which they had been created to inhabit—so that European settlements in Africa, Asia and even North America were doomed to eventual extinction.

112. Knox, *The Races of Men*, 14.

113. Ibid., 13, 53.

114. Ibid., 375.

115. Ibid., 379.

116. Scrope, *Letters to Lord John Russell*, 59–60.

117. His impact was according to Nancy Stepan "immediate" (Stepan, *The Idea of Race in Science*, 41).

118. Ibid, 41.

5

Aftermath of Disaster: Public Perceptions of the Irish Question, 1850–1860

In 1860 Charles Kingsley wrote a letter to his wife recording some of his observations during a trip to Ireland:

> I am haunted by the human chimpanzees I saw along that hundred miles of horrible country [in Sligo]. I don't believe they are our fault. I believe there are not only many more of them than of old, but that they are happier, better, more comfortably fed and lodged under our rule than they ever were. But to see white chimpanzees is dreadful; if they were black, one would not feel it so much, but their skins, except where tanned by exposure, are as white as ours.[1]

Had Kingsley made such remarks in 1840, his contemporaries would have singled him out as an eccentric. Twenty years later such a depiction of the Irish was, if not typical, unexceptional. In the years between 1840 and 1860 a profound shift had taken place in the way the English public saw the nature of the Irish problem and not least of all the Irish people themselves.

This chapter will trace the process in the 1850s by which these changes in public perceptions took place. The loss of public confidence in liberal ideals that had been wrought by the famine provided the impetus for change in the latter half of the 1840s. These ideals died hard, however, and the attempts of racialist scientists and philosophers to construct a new understanding of Ireland and the Irish in the early 1850s met at first with sometimes bitter resistance from English and Irish alike. Overcoming this resistance could have been a slow process, but a number of factors helped the transition to occur with almost startling rapidity. Perhaps the most important of these was the postfamine perception of Ireland as a land of opportunity, a land for settlement and evangelization, and ultimately a frontier region. Governed by these ideas, pro-settlement writers and others borrowed racialist terminology to build a new image of the Irish as willing, natural and perpetual workers and servants.

Irish immigration, which in this decade appeared to many English to have reached epidemic proportions, sparked a commensurately fearful response that drew on the language of racialism as a means of resisting contamination of English working class respectability by Irish moral degradation. At the same time, many Irish writers began in these years to conceive their relationship with England in terms that borrowed much English racialist language. Absolute and unchanging distinctions between Saxon and Celt were advocated as a means of preserving Irish national identity against the encroachments of both racialist colonialism and liberal assimilationism, which appeared anything but benign after the disastrous events of 1845–1852.

Racialism did not supplant liberalism in the sense of any wholesale conversion of English public opinion to the new theories. Instead, the language of racialism crept gradually into popular discourse, to the extent that even those who angrily repudiated Robert Knox used much of the new terminology of race in doing so. At the same time, elements of the older ideas persisted in the arguments of the racialists themselves, who did not abandon hope of the economic development of Ireland, though for them the role of English and Scottish businessmen in this mission was less that of benevolent tutors than settlers and colonial masters.

In the 1840s, the gendered conception of the English-Irish relationship as a marriage had assumed a symbiotic and complementary, if in practice unequal, relationship between the countries. In the 1850s Irish difference was more sharply and harshly defined. England and Ireland appeared less frequently as husband and wife, and more often as master and servant or colonizer and colonized. Their unity, while often still justified in gendered terminology and by natural law, was now said to be based on economic power and physical force. Affection and attraction between the two was no longer conjugal, but the love of master for servant and vice versa. The Irish role in either case was, of course, ultimately subservient. The effect of the change on the English view of reformist legislation for Ireland was however, profound, as any comparison of the legislative records of 1840–1845 and 1850–1870 will show.

THE TRIUMPH OF RACIALISM

Robert Knox proclaimed in 1850 that "race is everything: literature, science, art—in a word, civilization, depends on it."[2] In saying this he was doing no more than repeating what he had been saying for years, but in the last stages of the famine his words had a resonance among the English public that they had not had before. Many writers either lauded Knox's ideas *in toto* or, more frequently, integrated aspects of them (primarily the idea of race as an immutable category) into their own outlook on the Irish question. Others denounced them as foolish or even criminal, but few indeed were those who felt confident enough to throw them out altogether. Confusion characterized the greatest number of responses to racial theory as applied to Ireland, leaving open the question of whether Irish characteristics were "indigenous to the soil, or the effects of early education and example."[3] Whatever their position, none ignored the issue of race, which by the end of the decade occupied a prominent part of almost everything written about the country.

Race did not of course mean the same thing to everybody in the 1850s any more than it had in the 1840s. Polygenism, or the argument for the separate origin of the races of men, had nevertheless by this time supplanted monogenism among the scientific community as the most widely accepted racial theory.[4] Racial theorists therefore generally held several fundamental beliefs in common, even as they disagreed about many other issues. While Knox found by the middle of the decade that his insistence on race as a fixed category dividing peoples and nations from each other had become accepted by the majority of his colleagues, by no means did everyone draw the same conclusions from this "fact" as he did.

George Ellis, a physician and one of the most prominent ethnologists of his day, agreed with Knox on most of his assertions concerning the origin and immutability of racial difference. Although Knox and Ellis were agreed that the differences between the Saxon and Celtic races required perpetually distinctive legislation for each, they held widely differing conceptions of what this separate treatment entailed. For Knox, as we have seen, it meant that the Irish were to be ruled strictly by force and possibly even eventually wiped out. Ellis by contrast used these arguments to justify a policy that was largely paternalistic.[5] The Celtic affinity for despotic government, Ellis believed, permanently disqualified them from the liberties enjoyed by the English. Left to themselves they would become like "France on a minor scale," with domestic "turbulence" and poverty, rule by despotic demagogues and, in addition, a warlike and anti-English foreign policy.[6] This same proclivity for despotic rule, however, appeared to him well suited to the imposition of strong English overlordship, as the Irish were "easily contented, easily managed, easily governed" so long as they were ruled fairly and firmly.[7] He advocated the establishment in Ireland of what amounted to permanent coercion acts, including district fines for outrages, in combination with state endowment of the Irish Catholic clergy, extensive settlement of the country by English small proprietors, and firm and fair Saxon control of the Irish economy.[8]

The Celtic race in Ellis's estimation was characterized by pugnacity, "licentiousness," sociability, dishonesty, hospitality, lack of "moral courage," and vulnerability to priesthood and despotism.[9] The Saxon, "the direct antithesis of the Celt," had according to Ellis an innate "love of adventure and aggrandizement," a "love of liberty" and the "democratic spirit," and a propensity for orderliness, though he also tended to be arrogant and selfish.[10] For Knox, these differences between Celt and Saxon clearly argued for the inferiority of the former, but Ellis stated firmly that the Celts "were not to be treated as an inferior race." In general he rejected the idea that "the admission of natural differences between two races implies, on the whole, the necessary inferiority of one of them."[11] As Ellis realized, however, a large portion of the public would be incapable of going any further than "the presumption that mental *difference* implies mental *inferiority*." He hoped that by getting the "political economists" to see that one did not follow from the other, he could reassure them that what he considered to be a proactive policy for Ireland was compatible with acceptance of modern racial theory.[12]

Many racialists and liberals alike either did not see Ellis's distinction or denied its validity. Opponents of racialism, whose resiliency in the face of the advance of the new ideas should not be underestimated, often lumped all racialists together as prophets of Irish inferiority who saw no purpose in treating them as anything other than slaves. In 1851, the winner of the £200 prize offered by the London publisher John Cassell for the "Best Essay on the Moral, Social, and Political Condition of Ireland" stated that "The idea that there is something inherent in the Roman Catholic religion, or in the Celtic race, which presents an insuperable bar to industrial progress, is refuted by a mass of evidence which social science can rarely obtain."[13] R.G. Latham, an ardent apologist for James Cowles Prichard's theories, wrote a supplementary chapter to a reprint of Prichard's *The Eastern Origin of the Celtic Nations* in 1857, arguing that "the miserable spirit of partizanship . . . which delights in contrast between the Kelt and Anglo-Saxon (each glorified at the expence of the other, according to the nationality of the writer), scarcely deserves notice in scientific works."[14] Richard Tuthill Massy, a doctor and phrenologist whose somewhat hysterical prose can have done his cause little credit, did not deny the importance of race but savaged those who used it as an argument for Irish inferiority as opposed to Irish difference. The "blunderings" of the *Times* in particular, he argued, had detracted from the fact that religion, not race, was at the heart of the Irish troubles.[15]

Opposition to racial theory, which made a point of denying Irish-English compatibility, sometimes entailed upholding marriage as a conceptual tool for understanding the union. John Garwood, writing in 1853, used language typical of 1840s liberals in portraying the union as a symbiotic, marriage-like relationship in which English and Irish characteristics would unite to create a more balanced whole.[16] S.R. Hole, an Oxford undergraduate, admitted in 1859 that the marriage had been a troubled one, but did not rule out hope for the future:

> The wedding . . . has not been, as yet, productive of much happiness; but you must remember, that if the husband has been harsh at times, and disagreeable, the conduct of the lady has been very aggravating and suspicious. Hath she not flirted with *Monsieur* and *Jonathan?* Hath she not decked herself with ribbons of obnoxious hue, and gone after strange priests, whom John Bull honoureth not?[17]

Whereas the idea of marriage had permeated much of the written material on Ireland in the first half of the 1840s, however, in the early 1850s the concept appeared much less frequently as a rhetorical device. The conclusions drawn from "observation" of the feminine Irish nature were also increasingly different from what they had been before. Qualities that in the early 1840s would have appeared to most writers as potential solvents of the hard English nature and therefore arguments for assimilation, now appeared as evidence for the necessity of separate treatment of the two nations. In the 1840s the debates between Tories and Whigs over the question of whether Ireland should be treated differently from England generally boiled down to whether coercion should be applied there. In the 1850s little had changed in this respect. Separate treatment meant coercion and the denial of basic English liberties for which the Irish were not only unready, but never would be ready.[18]

Most English writers continued to take for granted the femininity of the Irish character. Richard Tuthill Massy, in his discourse on Irish physical characteristics, noted in the Celtic skull a "love of approbation" and of "display," and in his hands "eloquence of movement," "gracefulness and versatility," and "fineness and susceptibility"; as for the Celtic shoulder, "by some it would be called effeminate."[19] The Reverend Samuel Garratt spoke at length on the "gracefulness of the Irish," contrasting it with the "manliness" of the English.[20] For Lord John Manners, "the essentially poetical" Irish character was a "physiological fact."[21] In the 1850s, however, belief in Irish femininity no longer led inexorably to use of the language of marriage as a means of accomplishing English-Irish integration and symbiosis. Insofar as the relationship continued to be seen as a marriage, it was a marriage based on force rather than natural, conjugal affection.

Just as the growing use of the language of race changed the meaning of gendered terminology in the Irish context, it crept into and diluted the arguments of those who tried to attack racial theory directly. Confusion and timidity were often the result, and certainly attacks on racialism in the 1850s lacked the confidence and coherence of those made even in the late 1840s. Richard Tuthill Massy accepted many racialist presuppositions about immutable Celtic and Saxon characteristics even as he passionately derided the racialists for concluding that Ireland was forever doomed to servitude and degradation.[22] John MacElheran, a member of the Royal College of Surgeons in Edinburgh, argued in an address to the British Association for the Advancement of Science not that race was mutable or unimportant, but that the Saxon race was less pure and ultimately inferior to the Celtic.[23] Harriet Martineau's 1852 *Letters from Ireland*, in many respects a repetition of the sort of arguments for Irish improvability that had been the vogue in the early 1840s, are interspersed with intimations of something dark and unchangeable in the Irish character, disgust for the "Hottentot Kraals" in which the peasantry lived, and brooding over whether real change in the country would ever take place.[24]

Thomas Carlyle's confused, pessimistic and cynical meditations on Ireland and Irish problems at the end of the 1840s were in many respects typical of the opinions held by his English contemporaries. The journal that he kept of a journey to Ireland is curiously transitional, combining elements of a wistful liberal hope for improvement, and an angry contempt for Irish incapacity to improve. A close attention to Irish racial characteristics pervaded his journal, and Carlyle eventually discerned "five or six type-physiognomies, which I could recognize as specimens of Irish *classes* of faces," including the "angry-bewildered" and "a bland big tiger face . . . this is of a mixed breed, I think a North-country face."[25] He added, however, his impression of "the air of faculty *misbred* and gone to waste, or more or less 'excellent possibility much marred,' in almost all these faces."[26] On the whole, he leaned toward the conclusion that whatever may have been possible for Ireland in the past, it was not "patchable" in the future, and that the "one *true* station in the universe" for the poor Irish "is *servants*, 'slaves' if you will; and never can they know a right day till they attain that."[27]

The sentiments depicted in Nassau Senior's journals of his visits to Ireland in the 1850s and 1860s are similar to Carlyle's. While noting the improvement of the Irish abroad and mildly lauding the effects of the Irish Poor Law and the Encumbered Estates Act, Senior also expressed in 1861 his despondence at the minimal changes achieved in the habits of the Irish people since 1844 and repeatedly harped on the evils of Catholicism in Ireland.[28] He recounted without comment the contemptuous evaluation by an Irish landlord of "the opinion—still, I believe, cherished by many of the English Liberals—that Ireland can prosper under English institutions" and expressed his own disgust at the "un-intelligent faces" of the Irish beggars.[29] His revulsion at the "villages of wigwams" inhabited by Sligo peasants led him to declare his dislike for "a people so ignorant, so prejudiced, and so illogical, as the lower Irish."[30]

The continuing phenomenon of Irish poverty disgusted many English travelers who had hoped that English tutorship would uplift the people. Hope in the 1840s had appeared in the form of evidence of increasing Irish self-sufficiency. In the 1850s, English writers who visited Ireland had little to say about improvements in Irish moral or economic habits, finding cause for optimism instead in the spreading of English colonists across the countryside. John Forbes noted with approval in 1852 the English settlements dotting Connemara. The danger appeared to be only that poverty and agricultural backwardness would scare them away.[31]

In the 1840s most writers had seen settlement as a temporary phenomenon aimed at the education and regeneration of the Irish. In the following decade, self-enrichment rather than self-sacrifice was usually urged as an instigation to settlement. Numerous tracts urged the colonization of Ireland in the 1850s. Famine, many argued during the late 1840s and also after it had ended, had acted as a purgative. Its effects, however distressing in many respects, also heralded an era of opportunity. The "famine of 1847," one London land agent noted, had "caused a great revolution in the internal economy of Ireland, and apparently laid the foundation for a new order of things."[32] The economic potential of Ireland that had been observed in the 1840s remained in the 1850s, but the obstacles that had prevented economic exploitation of the island had disappeared in the intervening years. Overpopulation (one writer stated with unintentional irony) no longer stood in the way of investment as it had before, and while the Encumbered Estates Act had freed the land, the national infrastructure was improving with English help, and the Irish themselves were becoming more docile.[33]

One prospective settler wrote that he saw two sources of possible doubt in the minds of those who were considering moving to or investing in Ireland. These doubts, which "like nursery rhymes, have fixed themselves on their minds," were "doubt as to the security of life and property; [and] Pat's applicability to either mental or physical labour."[34] The first concern was allayed by assurances of the peaceability of the countryside. Firm measures for coercion and a powerful police force were now in place to prevent the sort of outrages that had been so common before the famine.[35] The possibility that the Irish might want to seek revenge for English treatment of them during the famine was never considered. After all, as many authors stated again and again, the Irish could not be other than profoundly grateful for the aid the English had so generously provided them in those years.

The second doubt was more troubling. Robert Knox's racial theory could offer little reassurance, given how the Scottish physiologist liked to portray the Irish as unregenerate brutes who must either be cleared out of their country altogether or kept down by perpetual and extreme measures of coercion. How could such creatures be made to work for an English master? Moreover, the old liberal argument for the regeneration of Ireland and the Irish as a moral duty was in the 1850s increasingly outmoded. In any case, liberalism implied that English movement to Ireland was only a temporary phenomenon until the Irish could learn to care for themselves, and therefore offered limited support for those who saw settlement and colonization as permanent propositions.

A conception of the Irish race was therefore developed that avoided both extreme racialism (or Orangeism) and liberalism. The Irish as presented by pro-settlement writers were a clearly and permanently distinct race, but their racial attributes were held to particularly suit them for both work and servitude. Their undoubted indolence was rarely held to be constitutional, but their lack of self-reliance was.[36] Under firm but benevolent management, they were easily kept in line by those who acquired the "knack" of dealing with them: "Once get this knack, and you may do what you please with them; they are easier to manage than any other people."[37] Physically, meanwhile, they made excellent laborers:

> The mind and spirit of the man, it is proved, may be properly toned; while, considered merely as a source of animal power, there is no race whose physical conformation is more perfectly developed. The Irish are the tallest, the strongest, and the heaviest of British subjects.[38]

The Cornish owner of a Irish copper mine praised his workers by saying that they were "much more manageable than his own countrymen, and worked contentedly for much smaller wages," and that "nothing could exceed the attention, industry, and soberness of the men."[39]

In the estimation of these writers the Irish could not only be made to work, but were in fact yearning to do so for English masters. The English were, they told themselves, not disliked but greatly loved and admired in Ireland.[40] As one Englishman represented it, the Irish admiration of the English stopped little short of worship:

> Irish peasants . . . are beginning to . . . duly appreciate and value, the brain-power, judgment, and, above all, indomitable perseverance and energy, of Saxons. So that no longer is England branded as an island full of wrath, hatred, and oppression towards Ireland, but rather as the "Grave mother of majestic works, / From her isle-altar looking down; / Who, God-like, grasps the triple forks, / And King-like, wears the crown."[41]

Making Ireland attractive as an area for settlement also involved its redefinition as an exciting frontier region full of both opportunity and adventure. The "wild west of Ireland"[42] in particular invited descriptions of this sort, being a largely unexplored area with supposedly limitless economic potential and "wild," primitive inhabitants. The "bold and romantic" geography of the west was central to its charm, and attracted many eloquent descriptions.[43] According to one settler, "There is a freshness, a cheerfulness, a constant variety, a union of softness and grandeur about the scenery of the West of Ireland that . . . make it one of the most desireable places of settlement in the world."[44] The dark complexion (often attributed to Spanish or Middle Eastern ancestry) of the inhabitants was noted along with accounts of their primitiveness.[45] One popular guidebook described this region as the "Wild West," attributed "Arab" and "gipsy" ancestry to the people who lived there, and argued for settlement of the area even as it described the mark that the "Saxon in Ireland" was already beginning to make there.[46]

This tendency to portray Ireland as a frontier region carried by implication a comparison of the Irish people with "wild" natives such as the American Indians. The American Indians had been a favorite subject of European writers since the eighteenth century. In the first half of the nineteenth century, romanticism and antiindustrial sentiment helped to popularize the notion of the Indians as "noble savages," whose simplicity, closeness to nature, chastity and poetic attributes were held to be the result of their distance from the corrupting forces of industrialism. Though easily manipulated by their "priests," their piety and gentleness were supposed to be shed only under the more extreme instances of oppression to which white settlers subjected them. Indian attributes could, many Europeans believed, hold the key to the reform of rampant industrialism. Assimilation was held to be the proper goal of European settlement, a goal that was fostered by the assumption of Indians' racial affinity with the Europeans but hindered by the widely condemned brutality of white frontiersmen.[47]

In the middle of the nineteenth century, Ray Allen Billington has argued, a drastic shift began to take place in the way in which Europeans viewed the Indians. Nature no longer seemed to purify, but rather to corrupt those who remained close to it. The Indians thus increasingly appeared as "ignoble savages," "a decayed race, steeped in vice and indolence, unable and unwilling to adjust to the modern world, and hence doomed to rapid and justifiable extinction."[48] Their degeneracy, combined with the gospel of inevitable progress and the common assumption that the land they possessed was full of economic potential, led many Europeans to believe that white conquest and colonization, not assimilation, should be the European ambition in America.[49]

Sir Francis Head, the former governor of Canada, made a direct connection in this respect between the Irish and other "aboriginal" races such as the American Indians. All such peoples, Head wrote, "innocently revelling in what is usually called a state of Nature," were doomed by "the stern decree of Providence" to be "melted away, as they themselves figuratively express it, 'like snow before the sun.'" The Irish, indeed, might be expected to succumb and be "swept away" by the march of progress and civilization even more quickly than most, given that "they are NOT, like the Red Indians and other aborigines, the lawful owners of the soil on which they sleep," which in fact belonged to "another race" in the form of the Anglo-Irish ascendancy. Head was predicting not extermination for the Irish, but their wholesale emigration, though he allowed that some by completely renouncing their heritage and culture might remain and be absorbed into the new order.[50]

Similarities between English portrayals of the Irish and the American Indians appear in other respects as well. Prefamine English literature often described the Irish as simple, mystical creatures who were close to nature and whose ancient nobility had been degraded by centuries of Anglo-Irish oppression. Assimilating with and civilizing the Irish did not necessarily mean modernizing them, for the attributes of their character that kept them close to nature were held to be complementary to the qualities that made the English a successful urban and industrial people.[51] In the 1850s, Irish peasant culture seemed no longer romantic but thoroughly wretched and degraded. Assimilation with such a people was an impossibility, but their suppression and the colonization end enrichment of their land was an idea that seemed both good and inevitable.

A change in the way the English public viewed proselytism in Ireland accompanied the redefinition of the country as an American-style frontier region. Respect for Irish religion and culture had been a byword among liberals of the 1840s, when social control in Ireland seemed achievable by means of moral and economic reform. In the years following the famine, disillusion with the old ideals may have made religious conversion seem a practical alternative, especially for a people who were increasingly being associated with the "heathen" of America. Evangelization, therefore, seemed to many to be as integral to the march of civilization in Ireland as it was assumed to be in America.

Protestant attempts to convert the Irish became more common and more aggressive in the late 1840s and early 1850s.[52] Irish Protestants formed the vanguard of this movement. Their missions often sprang out of soup kitchens or local relief societies that had been formed during the famine when, to the disgust of many English observers, food had been offered in return for Sunday-school instruction by Protestant preachers. In some areas, in particular a number of small islands off the western coast, they were successful in converting whole districts and formed model Protestant communities, of course advertising them for all they were worth. As always, they carried on an active propaganda war among the Irish in the form of itinerant preaching, and provoked angry and sometimes violent responses from the Catholic peasantry. The resulting incidents and inevitable "martyrdoms" gained due notice in the tracts and leaflets with which the Irish Protestants waged their parallel propaganda campaign in England, calling confidently for help from their English and Scottish evangelical brethren.[53]

The call did not go unheard. A number of organizations such as the Scottish Reformation Society and the British Evangelical Alliance sprouted in England and Scotland, and sent preachers to join the battle for souls in Ireland. Not a few of these preachers were roughly handled in the course of their duties. Rather than suffer their humiliations in silence, representatives of these organizations sent infuriated letters to English officials, protesting the "molestation" of preachers in their "labour of love" and demanding tough measures against those to blame.[54] The true culprits in their view were not the poor, deluded peasantry but their priests, who according to one account, "have been the actual, although invisible, ringleaders of the mobs in Ireland, by denouncing the Ministers referred to from their altars, and stirring up the deluded votaries to riot and bloodshed."[55] The "leniency on the part of our Rulers," another complained, "only encourages the Popish priests of Ireland to bolder and more daring acts of encroachment."[56] Lord Palmerston as Home Secretary appears to have generally passed such reports on to officials in Dublin without comment, though in one instance he minimized the provocations offered by these preachers in noting that "the Catholics incessantly put forward the Principle of religious equality, and they cannot reasonably refuse equal personal security to Persons engaged in explaining or recommending the Doctrines of both Religions."[57]

British evangelicals also brought their case before the English people, publishing tracts that described their efforts to roll back the tide of "Papal darkness," the results of which one author described as "remarkable and encouraging" despite "the priests having everywhere stirred up the people against it."[58]

In the 1840s, as described in chapter two, the English public had generally viewed this sort of spectacle with a jaundiced eye, expressing disgust at the disorder resulting from fanaticism on both the Catholic and Protestant sides. Popular opinion on this subject was much more divided in the 1850s. Some English writers continued to repeat the argument that the English should "first elevate the Irish people in the social scale, and then appeal to their judgement on religious questions."[59] For many others, however, the end of the famine had inaugurated a period of religious as well as economic opportunity in Ireland. Ireland appeared to them to be finally and definitively turning to Protestantism, a development that had "in the wonderful order of God's providence, resulted from the famine. The *immense* sums of money so freely and generously raised in England at that time," argued John Garwood, "did much apparently to open the Irish heart."[60] Others who doubted the ultimate possibility of creating a Protestant Ireland still could not but "highly approve" of any efforts in this direction.[61]

If the growth of tourism in Ireland is any indication, religious disturbances appear not to have dampened the attraction of the country as a travel destination. Optimism at the prospects for settlement and religious conversion in Ireland no doubt contributed to making the country attractive for tourists, but so did Ireland's own "natural," even feminine appeal. One tourist advocate used this terminology to represent Ireland's allure:

> With a warm heart she will welcome you; with lip-liveliness and sparkling language she will entertain you; with impulsive zeal she will conduct you over her diversified demesne, and bring under your eye scenes where "Grace and Terror smiling stand / Like sisters hand in hand."[62]

Tourism in Ireland had ground practically to a halt in the latter half of the 1840s after a period of popularity in the first half of that decade. In the 1850s, several travelers noticed that it was much harder to get away from the crowds of tourists than it had been in earlier years. This was especially true in resort areas such as the lakes of Killarney, where S.R. Hole noticed with disgust how tourists mutilated trees and spread graffiti over ruins.[63] In keeping with the change of attitudes towards Ireland in the intervening years, however, the type of tourist visiting there had changed, being no longer limited only to pleasure-seekers. As one observer noted in 1852,

> Whereas, in former years summer tourists in Ireland consisted of persons of rank and fashion—of invalids in search of health, and pleasure-seekers in search of increased animal and mental enjoyment—the majority of the crowds of English pilgrims this year to the "Isle of Saints" consist of manufacturers from Manchester, cloth-workers from Leeds and Bradford, warehousemen from Liverpool, merchants from London, and rich tradesmen and thriving shopkeepers from every part of England—all with one eye for the picturesque, and another for discovering new outlets for the profitable investment of capital.[64]

Travel guides reflected this in their attention to the opportunities for the development of trade and industry in Ireland.[65]

The growth of tourism in the early 1850s was accompanied by the appearance of a fairly well-organized tourist industry. Publishers took advantage of the phenomenon by publishing pocket guides for use during travel, in addition to travel accounts such as Thackeray's or the Halls,' which had been more common before the famine.[66] The Dublin publisher James McGlashan listed twenty-eight such works for tourists in an 1852 advertisement, including handbooks for investment as well as others on scenery, history, culture and "superstitions."[67] The 1853 "Great Industrial Exhibition" in Dublin was a popular attraction, providing an opportunity for English and Irish railway companies to offer package tours for those interested in taking in the sights of Ireland after touring the exhibition. The Chester and Holyhead Railway Company, for example, offered one-month package tours from May to September 1853 for £6. 5s. first class from London (or £4 from Liverpool), which included transportation to Dublin for the exhibition, and then to Cork, Cove, Mallow, and Killarney, with optional excursions to Belfast.[68] Sir Francis Head attested to the popularity of a similar tour that had been offered in the previous year, observing that in Westport the inn "was overflowing with English tourists, each carrying in his or her right hand a pea-green 'Handbook,' that had been given gratis at Euston Station."[69]

While the primary concern of many travel books and tour guides published in the 1850s was to attest to the economic potential of Ireland, the racial heritage of the Irish people also came in for a great deal of attention. Irish architecture, particularly in the form of "ancient" constructions such as the round towers, was often described as being, as one guide put it, of "an oriental parentage . . . connected with sun or fire worship."[70] The hospitality of the "Celts" was frequently noted, but so were their physiological characteristics. Whereas travel accounts dating from before the famine often devoted a great deal of attention to the supposedly ongoing process of the moral and economic improvement of the people, travel guides of the 1850s, while dwelling at length on Ireland's physical capabilities and the growth of English settlement there, had little to say about any changes in the habits of the Irish people themselves.[71]

Tourism, settlement, proselytism and racialism were integral to the ongoing process by which Ireland was recreated in the English public image as a frontier country. In the process Ireland was gradually moved out of the position she had earlier enjoyed as a member of the British family of nations. More and more, the Irish problem was being considered as an imperial rather than a domestic issue. Ireland increasingly appeared as a colony rather than a "sister isle"; a servant rather than a mate. The Irish people were no longer unfortunate relatives impoverished by force of circumstance, but natives degraded as a result of their own natures. This new image of Ireland and the Irish helped not only to justify economic exploitation of the island, but also served as a counter to what was for the English one of the most unsettling phenomena of the decade: Irish immigration to England and Scotland.

IRISH IMMIGRATION

In the last years of the 1840s, as the famine receded into the background in English minds, immigration became an ever more pressing issue. It was the central Irish issue of the 1850s, and to a great extent it determined the development of English perceptions of the Irish after the famine. Irish immigration was of course nothing new; large numbers of Irish had been entering England since the beginning of the century. In the 1840s and 1850s, however, the rapid influx into Britain of thousands of impoverished Irish coincided with a shifting popular perception of the Irish that was based less and less on goodwill and more on fear. The still-fresh memory of working-class unrest in English cities in the 1840s, combined with continuing financial instability and continental disturbances, made England appear potentially vulnerable to destabilization caused by immigration.

Solely in terms of numbers, the Irish influx was unprecedentedly large. From 1841 to 1851 the number of Irish-born residents of Britain rose from 419,256 to 727,326 and continued to grow to a total of 806,000 in 1861 before gradually declining thereafter.[72] Local figures varied widely, though it was felt most strongly in Lancashire, western Scotland and London. Liverpool was the most likely port of debarkation for Irish who traveled to England either as a place of permanent residence or as a way-station on the road to America. City authorities estimated that in 1847 alone 296,231 Irish landed in Liverpool, and by 1853 a total of 586,332 had arrived. Of course many of these moved on elsewhere, but even so the percentage of the Irish-born population of Liverpool had risen from 17% in 1841 to over 22% in 1851.[73]

English commentators tended to blame this phenomenon on the evictions carried out by Irish landlords, or on overpopulation. In reality a number of factors acted to drive Irish emigration to England. The foundation had been laid by the collapse of Irish cottage industries earlier in the century, and by the flooding of Irish markets with cheap English agricultural products, against which the outmoded and heavily encumbered Irish agricultural system could not compete. Of course the catastrophic social conditions in Ireland during the 1840s and 1850s had much to do with the burst of emigration in these years, but even then high demand for labor in England pulled immigrants there more than conditions in Ireland pushed them.[74] One major difference between the immigrants of the 1850s and those that had preceded them was that in earlier years they had been primarily from Belfast and the northeast, while in the 1850s they were largely poor peasants from the south and east of the country.[75] Assimilation of the immigrants was accordingly a more difficult proposition for the English than it had been before.

Urban historians disagree about the extent to which the Irish population of English cities was segregated into ghettoes. Lynn Lees has shown that while the urban Irish were not for the most part locked in ghettoes, they were also not integrated into English areas, but were "relegated to the side streets and back alleys of their neighborhoods. They lived close to the English, but they remained apart."[76] Although the "ghetto Irishman" was not the norm, for most contemporary English the distinction between Irish and English districts of cities was clear enough; a sort of "mental ghettoization" was taking place.[77] Ghettoes did exist, because of an "Irish tendency towards self-segregation" and a number of socioeconomic factors.[78] Irish labor, both male and female, tended to be limited to unskilled positions that, with some exceptions, English workers spurned. Urban Irish families were structured little differently from those of their English working-class counterparts,[79] but poor living conditions and their general poverty led to disproportionate Irish involvement in petty crime.[80]

Religion was a divisive issue between English and Irish workers, but should not be overestimated and was not simply a matter of Catholic versus

Protestant. Although Catholicism was one factor contributing to Irish self-segregation in English cities, public incidents of anti-Catholicism were not dependent on the prevalence of Irish residents in any particular region. Working-class periodicals and literature, though hardly speaking of the Irish in glowing terms, rarely held their religion against them.[81] In practical terms, the most significant difference was that the Irish went to church while the English workers, though retaining residual Protestant identities, for the most part did not.[82] Indeed, English Catholics found little in common with their Irish coreligionists, whose faith in the 1850s still remained largely uninfluenced by the codification of liturgy and church authority wrought during the counter-Reformation. Rome at this time was only beginning to encourage proselytism aimed at enforcing religious uniformity among the Irish communities in England.[83]

Tensions between Irish and English workers were primarily the product of fears over job competition. Most contemporary observers were convinced that the Irish drove down wages, and made no secret of their opinions,[84] often expressed in apocalyptic terms. Henry Grant, for example, wrote in 1850 that "hordes upon hordes of famishing Irish are flocking over to England, to lower a labour-market already too deeply depressed."[85] It is surprising that these fears did not produce more hostility on the part of English workers than they did. For the most part, the reaction of English workers went no farther than indifference or silent contempt, though at times it flared into outright hostility and even violence.

Incidents of violence between English and Irish workers were much less common than contemporary commentators, and some modern historians, have made them out to be. Disturbances that occurred before the beginning of the famine, such as attacks by English railway navvies on Irish workers in England, Wales and Scotland in the spring of 1846, were hardly noticed by contemporaries.[86] In the early 1850s, however, violent confrontations of workers and immigrants appeared to some middle-class observers to presage the beginning of a moral regression of English workers. Local magistrates and police involved in dealing with these disturbances were, however, surprisingly impartial in their apportionment of blame, which they generally distributed equally between English and Irish and attributed to religious and economic causes.[87]

English working-class periodicals reflected these tensions, but on the whole did not adopt the language of scientific racialism. Working-class perceptions of the Irish as expressed in these periodicals from 1840 to 1860 appear in fact to have been only slightly influenced by the priorities of educated English opinion. Assimilation and improvement made as little impression upon them in the 1840s as did race and biology in the 1850s. In the decade under consideration here, descriptions of the Irish as brutish louts were common but appear to have been rarely elaborated into arguments for Irish racial inferiority. The general tone was not uniformly hostile; at times the editors of English working-class newspapers even tried to make common cause with the Irish.[88]

This possibility of cooperation between English and Irish workers often appeared as more of a threat to middle-class Englishmen than did the sporadic outbreaks of clashes between them. Despite the Irish reputation as strikebreakers, they were just as often prominent on the other side of the picket line.[89] The threat of substantial Irish involvement in English working-class politics never fully materialized, however, despite the high profile of a few radicals of Irish descent such as Bronterre O'Brien and Feargus O'Connor.[90] Daniel O'Connell's repudiation of Chartism encouraged large numbers of Irish to abandon that movement, but the few that remained were enough to frighten many English observers. Irish Chartists segregated themselves, or were segregated from, their more numerous English cohorts, going so far as to march separately from the rest during the presentation of the 1848 Chartist petition to parliament. Even marching apart, however, they retained a prominence that caused many English to overestimate their influence.[91]

Placating the English workers, and incidentally keeping them separate from and even antagonistic to the Irish, became a priority of local legislators. Legislation enacted at the expense of Irish immigrants could be justified as a measure in favor of both English ratepayers and workers. Pressure on poor rates fueled a campaign led by the *Times* and the poor law guardians in Liverpool and Manchester to extend and enforce laws for the removal of Irish paupers from England. In Liverpool, poor rates had doubled from 2s 1d to 4s 1d in 1847 alone.[92] The adverse impact this had on the pocketbooks of property holders was matched by the offense it offered to popular principles, which held that Irish landlords were responsible for Irish poverty and therefore as well for provision for the Irish poor. The London government therefore responded with the Poor Removal Act of June 1847, which allowed local authorities to remove to Ireland any Irish-born pauper who did not have official approval for settlement in England. Under this act, 67,513 Irish were removed between 1847 and 1853, though many more simply decided to forego poor law relief in order to avoid detection.[93] In the long run, however, as the authors of this legislation well knew, their efforts to remove the Irish paupers would have only a slight effect.[94]

The Radical politician and Quaker John Bright was gravely alarmed by the implications of Irish immigration, becoming from the beginning of the famine an important spokesman against it even as he rejected the undercurrent of racialism that marked the attitudes of many of his contemporaries. He was not above taking advantage of the tensions between English and Irish workers, however, to deflect blame upon the latter for hardships that English workers might otherwise have attributed to English mill owners. In the course of a protest to parliament against unrestricted Irish immigration in December 1847, Bright commented that "many of the evils which in times past have been attributed to the extension of manufactures in [Lancashire] have arisen from the enormous immigration of a suffering and pauperized people driven for a sustenance from their own country."[95]

Like most of his contemporaries, Bright blamed Irish landlords for the condition of their peasantry and demanded that they take responsibility for their own poor rather than evicting them and therefore unloading them on the English. A trip to Ireland in 1849 only confirmed him in this opinion, which he was to reiterate again and again, while condemning racial and religious prejudice as "subterfuges of the oppressor."[96] The unequal and unjust treatment of the country by the Anglo-Irish ascendancy, he wrote Richard Cobden in 1851, worked "a wide & silent cruelty, beggaring, demoralizing, & destroying multitudes of our people."[97]

Though Bright appears not to have ever spoken explicitly on the subject, most English middle-class observers were, as we saw in the last chapter, deeply alarmed by the possibility that Irish immigration would spread a moral plague among the English working-class population.[98] Significantly, the comparatively small number of middle-class, respectable Irish who settled in England were accepted readily enough.[99] Irish paupers and working poor, however, appeared to threaten the tenuous respectability and moral integrity of the English worker, and thereby ultimately the framework of English society. A petition from the Select Vestry of Liverpool to Sir George Grey in 1849 expressed the vestrymen's desire "to save their own poor from the contagious demoralization" consequent upon the influx of Irish paupers.[100]

More ominous was the danger that the Irish would transmit to the English not only their moral degradation, but also their propensity for social revolution, a danger that for Thomas Carlyle conjured up visions of "the Irish Giant—named of Despair, . . . advancing upon London itself, laying waste to all English cities, towns and villages."[101] Preventing the realization of this awful prophesy necessitated separation of English and Irish working-class populations, both physically and conceptually. The measures that the national and local governments undertook to effect this found justification in the emergence of a new rhetoric with strong racialist elements, which emphasized and reinforced differences between English and Irish. Assimilation came under increasing attack as a dangerous policy that might degrade the English without improving the Irish, rather than working to the benefit of both. Integration as fostered by immigration was held not only to hurt the character of English workers, but also, paradoxically enough, to deprive Ireland of some of her best citizens, who once in England had metamorphosed to the dregs of humanity.[102]

Attention to the living conditions of the urban Irish in English cities seemed to support fears of the degenerative influences of Irish immigration on English working-class society. Ironically, the appearance of widespread popular concern about slum conditions in English cities coincided with the beginnings of large-scale Irish immigration, and the former were therefore often blamed on the latter.[103] As Lord Ashley said in a speech in January 1848 at Bath, "Was it not found that where the Irish appeared wages were lowered, respectability disappeared, and slovenliness and filth prevailed?"[104] The Irish were believed to have a strongly adverse effect on both wages and crime rates, though in reality their impact in both areas was minor.[105] Local middle- and high-brow periodicals made much of Irish crime statistics, and selectively published court reports emphasizing the stupidity and degradation of the criminals.[106]

One major work of fiction dating from this period addressed the danger of social disorder as a product of Irish immigration. This was Elizabeth Gaskell's *North and South* (1855), in which an industrialist uses unskilled Irish laborers to counter a strike called by his English workers. Misunderstanding between workers and masters is the proximate cause of the strike, but the introduction of the Irish element elevates the conflict to the level of class warfare. Gaskell's Irish do not appear on the scene as aggressive criminals or revolutionaries, but as timid, incompetent workers easily manipulated by their social superiors or their priests. They do not willingly provoke violence, which is instead the result of bigotry on the part of the English workers, who call the strikebreakers "Irish blackguards" and spread "exaggerated stories" of their "ignorance and stupidity."[107] Gaskell advances the idea of moral contamination, however, in a subtle manner. The violence of the English workers is not portrayed as typical for them; their usual reaction to hardship is, as the heroine Margaret Hale muses, to stand like "granite." The ringleader of their strike, a worker named Boucher, is however not English at all, but of "Irish blood," as his passionate, violent behavior and eventual suicide demonstrate.[108] When Boucher's death brings closure and a peaceful resolution to the crisis (as well as a departure of the Irish), Margaret is left to meditate that "if the world stood still, it would retrograde and become corrupt, if that is not Irish."[109]

The overt and subtle dangers of Irish corruption of English cities made controlling them more important than ever before. Unfortunately, given the decline of liberal ideals and the spread of racialism, this was also an exceedingly tricky business. If the immigrants could not be entirely removed, and their race prevented their moral reform along the lines that had been envisaged by the liberals, what was to be done? Evangelization, many Englishmen argued, was the answer for the Irish in England, just as it appeared to be for those who remained in their own country.

The Anglican Reverend Samuel Garratt, speaking before the Church of England Young Men's Society in late 1852, directly confronted the racial problem and decided that while preventing assimilation it could be a great advantage in the work of evangelization. The Galatians to whom St. Paul had preached an epistle were, Garratt argued, essentially the same people as the modern-day Irish, and had even spoken in Gaelic. Their racial characteristics were also similar:

> There is the same disposition to receive with affectionate warmth those who preach the Gospel to them, the same willingness to be in bondage and want of the full appreciation of the freedom of Christ, the same openness to the witchcraft of seducing teachers, and we find the same difficulty which is intimated as existing among the Galatians in raising the tone of practice, and maintaining the purity of doctrine.[110]

He exhorted his audience to take these and other racial characteristics into account when preaching to the Irish, which should be done after the model of St. Paul: "You must speak to them as if they were children. And they are more easily reached by the heart than the head."[111]

IRISH CONTRIBUTIONS

Immigration added momentum to the creation of sharper boundaries in English minds between themselves and the Irish who threatened to engulf them. Irish writers too found their own reasons to emphasize the differences between themselves and the English, and in doing so borrowed many ideas on race that were becoming current in England. Seamus Deane has argued that the emergence among the Irish of a cohesive sense of their own national character was "in response to the earlier English (or British) definition,"[112] and Edward Said's assertion that the self-images of colonized peoples form and change partly in response to those expressed by the colonizer certainly appears to hold true in the Irish instance.[113]

In the early nineteenth century, the Irish poet and historian Thomas Moore had worked to inculcate among the Irish a positive notion of difference, partly in opposition to negative portrayals of his country by England in the past, and partly as a means of countering the efforts of liberal calls for integration and assimilation. Ireland as defined by Moore and the Irish themselves, "had a unique character, a unique destiny and a glorious past."[114] Some Irish historians in the same period used the not yet generally accepted ideas of race in the same cause.[115] English and Irish political economists, meanwhile, advanced the work of amalgamation by spreading their moral and economic ideas through Irish schools and universities. Professors in Dublin, Belfast and Galway cooperated with them, as did members of the Church of Ireland hierarchy and representatives of the government in Dublin.[116]

In the aftermath of the famine, Irish writers discarded many of the ideas they believed they had been force-fed in the 1840s, even as they used others—in particular the English depiction of Irish nature as essentially feminine—as a springboard for the advancement of a racial sense of Irish difference. Like some of the English racialists, the Irish used the new theories as a vehicle for attacking political economy. The values associated with domesticity and the family, as one Irishman informed the Irish Statistical Society in 1859, demonstrated that "the family and not the individual [was] the true unit to be considered in social questions."[117] English legislation in Ireland needed to be adapted to the peculiarities of the Irish racial character, right down to music education, which in Ireland required "a homeliness in tunes as well as in words, if they are to touch the heart."[118]

Thomas Boylan and Timothy Foley have concluded from this that "from the end of the 1850s women, Catholics, and Celts contributed to what one might call a 'feminisation' of values in Ireland which constituted a radical questioning of the English, Protestant, and 'male' discourse of political economy."[119] This feminization of values was in fact nothing new. In the 1840s Irish writers like William Carleton and Thomas Moore had described Irish qualities in feminine terms. What was original about Irish thought in the 1850s was the specific association of these qualities with racial characteristics and the use of them as a weapon against political economy, rather than as evidence for the advantages to be accrued from English-Irish assimilation.

Irish writers used the language of race in attacking English racialists and liberals alike. The *Dublin Evening Post* in the course of a long diatribe against Knox and the *Times* dubbed "John Bull" as "half man and half beast," adding that "we know that anything good they have in England, is French, that is to say, Celtic—and anything vile is German, that is to say, Anglo-Saxon."[120] Other Irish writers expressed contempt for the ideal of assimilation by taunting Irishmen who tried to be like Englishmen. Among English writers, jibes at these would-be Englishmen became common from the 1850s;[121] for the Irish, this attitude apparently developed earlier. The Irishman Jasper Rogers recounted in 1847 his meeting with one such person:

I had the *honour* to meet at dinner recently, a person of this class, [who] said, 'I aam pe-fectly ce-tain no one caaen know that I aam an I-ishman,' and at the next instant, turning to a servant, he added, 'Po-ta, if you *plaze*.' When this thoroughly low-bred Irishism came out I could not help smiling, and caught at the same moment the eye of a lady opposite, who seemed greatly amused. In a few minutes after, she said . . . 'Pray, may I help you to a potato'—the killing reply was, 'Pon my hona' I neva' *ate* pittatis at all at all.' [122]

In a letter to the *Limerick Reporter*, John MacElheran lamented, "Oh! it is melancholy, it is sickening, to hear Irishmen aping English impudence and English pronunciation. These wretches, who prefer English bastard names to their honourable patronymics, should be kicked out of Irish society."[123]

Irish history, as always, was a weapon in the hands of both Irish and English writers. Irish historians throughout the nineteenth century emphasized the mythical and heroic in their history.[124] English historians who interpreted it in the 1850s no longer argued for the past victimization and future improvement of Ireland, but demonstrated the existence of a sort of Irish *sonderweg* arising out of the racial and moral inferiority of her people. A historical textbook published in 1855 traced Celtic Irish racial origins to Spain and North Africa. In prehistoric times, this author argued, Ireland had been inhabited by "a wealthy, learned, and polished nation" of "people who came from the east," fire-worshipers who had constructed the famed Round Towers before dying out long before the Celts settled the island.[125]

Thomas Wright's history of the British Isles up to the Christian era achieved a synthesis of British and Irish history with the new racial teaching. In the introduction to his work he stated that "we have to do with the races of mankind," and proceeded to reconstruct British history "according to the system now generally adopted by ethnologists."[126] According to this scheme, the earliest inhabitants of Britain were the Celts, who had entered western Europe first by way of the Mediterranean before being driven to the British isles by the more powerful Germanic tribes. The mass of the Celtic population of Britain before the Saxon invasion was according to Wright made up of "serfs, without civil influence or even civil rights; the mere slaves of the superior orders," and were in addition "priest-ridden" by the Druids.[127] After being conquered but not assimilated by the Romans, they were driven out (again not absorbed) by the "Teutonic" Saxon invasion in the fifth century. The Saxons proceeded to create in England "between the aristocratic feeling of the Saxon landholders, and the republican principles that existed in the towns . . . under the balancing influence of the crown, the modern political constitution."[128] The Celts in

Cornwall, Wales, Scotland and Ireland meanwhile remained "a barbarous people, who were much less than the Saxons capable of benefitting by the Roman civilisation with which they came in contact."[129]

The history of Ireland before the English conquest in the twelfth century was presented by historians in much the same terms. It was a "savage nation" of barbarians racked by fratricidal warfare,[130] whose divisions blinded them to their own poverty and made them susceptible to conquest.[131] Although the oppressive treatment of Ireland by the "feudal" English government in the first centuries after the conquest came in for frequent condemnation, the results of attempts at assimilation were not always assumed to have been positive. One historian, writing in reference to the mingling of English settlers and native Irish in the fourteenth century, did not condemn settlement but warned of the possible consequences when the settlers failed to maintain their distance from the native Irish:

> The intermixture of the two nations was now carried on to a greater extent than it had ever been before and, what was very singular, the more civilized race adopted the language, dress, habits, and laws, of the barbarians, instead of teaching them the arts of civilization, which would seem to have been the more natural course.[132]

Natural laws, it would seem, did not remain infallible.

Historians no longer approached the long history of Irish poverty and suffering after the conquest with the sort of humility and self-reproach that had characterized the works of Smiles and others in the 1840s. They usually attributed Irish backwardness instead to some mixture of race and religion, which according to Sir George Nicholls "united to prevent the growth of that orderly gradation of classes, and that sympathy between one class and another, which exist in every well-conditioned community."[133] The English government, Sir Francis Head asserted, was manifestly "*Not Guilty*" for Irish suffering, which he attributed solely to the machinations of the Irish priesthood.[134] The history of Ireland since the eighteenth century was also presented in less optimistic a light than it had been in the 1840s, when the picture had been one of gradual but steady progress and inevitable amalgamation. Nicholls persisted in hoping for the "blending and eventual amalgamation of the two peoples" but had to admit that little progress had been made in this area so far, despite the best efforts of the English government.[135]

The famine, which might otherwise have appeared as a powerful argument against smug assurances that Ireland was better off in the union, was deftly dodged by most historians. In her textbook on Irish history, Julia Corner reiterated the claim that English government "is better for [the Irish] than any they could substitute for it," but in several pages on the history of Ireland between 1845 and 1855, she devoted all of one paragraph to the famine. She did not, in fact, even call it a famine, writing instead that "the deepest distress and suffering were spread over the country," which led to "large subscriptions" and "several millions of money."[136] Sir George Nicholls expended more effort than had Corner in describing the famine, but did little more than recount in a self-satisfied manner the extent of aid given by the English,

> until the repeated failures caused apprehensions as to the perpetuity of the burden, and seemed to point to the necessity of compelling the Irish people to abandon the treacherous potato, which it was thought they would hardly do, so long as they could turn to England for help whenever it failed them.[137]

IMPLICATIONS OF RACIALISM

English perceptions of the Irish underwent a profound change for the worse after the potato famine. While the attitude prevalent in the first half of the 1840s can hardly be called enlightened, it did at least entail a significant amount of attention to the sufferings of the Irish and a desire to ameliorate them. R.N. Lebow's observation that "it rarely occurred to Englishmen that many of these alleged traits [of the Irish] might be the *result*, not the *cause*, of poverty";[138] is patently false in the context of the period 1840–1845. For the decade after the famine, however, the statement has some relevance. In the 1850s, reforming the Irish and easing their sufferings was no longer a priority. Instead, separating them from the English (particularly English workers), controlling them effectively, and making use of their land moved into the forefront of the English agenda.

This agenda was supported by a view of the Irish people that emphasized the permanence of their character and condition. Their misfortunes were no longer seen so much as the product of past mistakes as they were in the nature and destiny of the Irish themselves. Keeping them happy, not reforming them, was of the essence, for the failure of what was assumed to have been the great experiment of liberalism during the famine had demonstrated the futility of attempting to raise them to an English standard of civilization. Ireland was no longer British, but colonial.

NOTES

1. Frances Eliza Kingsley, ed., *Charles Kingsley: His Letters and Memories of His Life*, 2 vols. (London: Henry S. King, 1877), 2:107. This letter is often quoted as a typical example of English attitudes towards Ireland in the nineteenth century, though as we shall see it was more representative of the 1850s and 1860s than of the 1840s.

2. Knox, *The Races of Men*, v.

3. Catherine M. O'Connell, *Excursions in Ireland during 1844 and 1850* (London: Robert Bentley, 1852), 16. The author was unrelated to Daniel O'Connell.

4. Stepan, *The Idea of Race in Science*, 40–45.

5. It is interesting to note that, while both Knox and Ellis assigned the Scottish, Welsh and northern Irish to the Celtic race, neither addressed the question of whether a distinct legislative system should be applied to them.

6. Ellis saw French behavior during the revolutions of 1848 as fresh evidence for the instability of the Celtic character (George Ellis, *Irish Ethnology Socially and Politically Considered; Embracing a General Outline of the Celtic and Saxon Races; with Practical Inferences* [London: Hamilton, Adams and Co., 1852], 3, 61–63).

7. Ibid., 147.

8. Ibid., 49–96, 146–150. Ellis's ideas dovetailed with the redefinition (to be described later in this chapter) in these years of Ireland as a frontier area ripe for settlement and development. William Bullock Webster, himself often referred to by others as the primary spokesman for settlement in this period, pointed to Ellis's book as providing a theoretical basis for his version of Ireland's ideal future (William Bullock Webster, *Ireland Considered as a Field for Investment or Residence* [Dublin: Hodges and Smith, 1852], 117–118).

9. Ellis, *Irish Ethnology*, 27–40.

10. Ibid., 16–26. Ethnologists differed immensely concerning the purity of the Saxon race. Some treated it as a monolithic entity; for others it was "more or less hybrid" (R.G. Latham, MD, *The Ethnology of the British Islands* [London: John VanVoorst, 1852], 260).

11. Ellis, *Irish Ethnology*, 153.

12. Ibid., iv–v.

13. William Edward Hearn, *The Cassell Prize Essay on the Condition of Ireland* (London: John Cassell, 1851), 4.

14. R.G. Latham, supplementary chapter to James Cowles Prichard, *The Eastern Origin of the Celtic Nations*, 383.

15. Richard Tuthill Massy, MD, *Analytical Ethnology: The Mixed Tribes in Great Britain and Ireland Examined, and the Political, Physical, and Metaphysical Blunderings on the Celt and the Saxon Exposed* (London: H. Bailliere, 1855), 143, 157.

16. John Garwood, *The Million-Peopled City; or, One-Half of the People of London Made Known to the Other Half* (1853; reprint, New York: Garland Publishing, 1985), 255–256.

17. S.R. Hole, *A Little Tour in Ireland* (London: Bradbury & Evans, 1859), 91.

18. Lord John Manners, *Notes of an Irish Tour* (London: J. Ollivier, 1849), 51.

19. Massy, *Analytical Ethnology*, 12–19.

20. Garratt, "The Irish in London" in Rev. Thomas Nolan, ed., *Motives for Missions. A Series of Six Lectures Delivered before the Church of England Young Men's Society* (London: Sampson Low and Son, 1852), 217–218.

21. Manners, *Notes of an Irish Tour*, 51.

22. According to Massy, Celtic facial characteristics betrayed an "austere and cunning" appearance indicative of the "man of the revolution." The Saxon face was by contrast typical of the "plain blunt man." Yet Massy was one of the most ardent opponents of Knox (Massy, *Analytical Ethnology*, 14–15).

23. MacElheran claimed Shakespeare as a representative of the Celtic race and dwelt at length on "Saxon deformity" and "degeneracy." Most English were according to MacElheran just as Celtic as were the Scottish and Irish (John MacElheran, *Celt and Saxon: Address to the British Association, on the Ethnology of England; Letters to "The Times" and other Journals, on the Races of Celt and Saxon* [Belfast: R.D. Read, 1852], 4–6).

24. Harriet Martineau, *Letters from Ireland* (London: John Chapman, 1852), 190–191, 218.

25. Carlyle, *Reminiscences of My Irish Journey in 1849*, 19. Carlyle also compares Ireland with Dahomey and Madagascar, a reference to African affinities that had been exceedingly rare before the famine.

26. Ibid., 20.

27. Ibid., iii–iv, 210.

28. Nassau William Senior, *Journals, Conversations and Essays Relating to Ireland*, 2 vols. (London: Longmans, Green, and Co., 1868), 1: viii.

29. Ibid., 2:8, 29.

30. Ibid., 2:167, 178.

31. John Forbes, MD *Memorandums Made in Ireland in the Autumn of 1852*, 2 vols. (London: Smith, Elder and Co., 1853), 1:210, 259.

32. Thomas Scott, *Ireland Estimated as a Field for Investment* (London: Thomas Harrison, 1854), 19.

33. Ibid., 19–29.

34. Mr. Eastwood to William Bullock Webster, July 27, 1852, quoted in Webster, *Ireland Considered as a Field for Investment or Residence*, 7.

35. Ibid., 5.

36. Ellis, *Irish Ethnology*, 81–82.

37. Pistis (pseudonym), *A Trip to Ireland, with Observations on Killarney and Its Neighbourhood* (London: C. Mitchell, 1850), 18–19.

38. Webster, *Ireland Considered as a Field for Investment or Residence*, 46–47.

39. Forbes, *Memorandums Made in Ireland in the Autumn of 1852*, 1:30.

40. John Henry Ashworth, *The Saxon in Ireland: Or, the Rambles of an Englishman in Search of a Settlement in the West of Ireland* (London: John Murray, 1851), 53.

41. Charles Richard Weld, *Vacations in Ireland* (London: Longman, Brown, Green, Longmans, & Roberts, 1857), 357.

42. Ibid., 13, et seq.

43. George Preston White, *A Tour in Connemara, with Remarks on Its Great Physical Capabilities* (London: W.H. Smith & Son, 1849), x.

44. Ashworth, *The Saxon in Ireland*, 97.

45. White, *A Tour in Connemara*, 20–21; Ashworth, *The Saxon in Ireland*, 17; *Black's Picturesque Tourist of Ireland* (Edinburgh: Adam and Charles Black, 1854), 202–205.

46. *The Tourist's Illustrated Hand-Book for Ireland* (London: John Cassell, 1853), 187–189.

47. Ray Allen Billington, *Land of Savagery, Land of Promise: The European Image of the American Frontier in the Nineteenth Century* (New York: W.W. Norton & Co., 1981), 13–20, 46, 114, 135.

48. Ibid., 105–106, 124.

49. Ibid., 219. Billington's argument that changing perceptions of the Indians were the product of the triumph of utilitarian ideas in mid-nineteenth century Europe does not ring true, but for our purposes the question of how perceptions changed is significant even if the question of why they changed is left open.

50. Sir Francis Head, *A Fortnight in Ireland* (London: John Murray, 1852), 148–150.

51. Luke Gibbons, "Race Against Time: Racial Discourse and Irish History," *Oxford Literary Review* 13, 1–2 (1991), 100–101.

52. Donal A. Kerr, *"A Nation of Beggars"? Priests, People and Politics in Famine Ireland, 1846–1852* (Oxford: Clarendon Press, 1994), 207.

53. *Popery in Ireland as Exemplified in the Experiences of a Ragged School Teacher* (London: T. Hatchard, 1857), 5. This is only one of a large number of such tracts dating from the 1850s that are extant in the British Library.

54. John Finch, Chairman of the British Organization of the Evangelical Alliance, memorial to Lord Palmerston, September 8, 1853, HO 45/5129A.

55. Berkeley Addison, Chairman of the Scottish Reformation Society, memorial to Lord Palmerston, August 9, 1853, HO 45/5129A.

56. George Lyon, Chairman of the Scottish Reformation Society, memorial to Lord Palmerston, November 4, 1853, HO 45/5129A.

57. Lord Palmerston, note dated August 12, 1853, appended to memorial of Berkeley Addison to Palmerston, August 9, 1853, HO 45/5129A.

58. *Evangelization in Ireland in 1853; Being a Brief Narrative of the Mission of One Hundred Ministers of the Gospel in the South of Ireland, During the Autumn of 1853* (London: Partridge, Oakey, and Co., 1854), 3.

59. "The Editor and Sole Proprietor of the Hull Advertiser," *Brief Notes of a Short Excursion in Ireland, in the Autumn of 1852* (London: Whittaker & Co., 1853), 34.

60. Garwood, *The Million-Peopled City*, 284.

61. Head, *A Fortnight in Ireland*, 155.

62. George W. Asplen, *A Lively Sketch of a Trip to Killarney and the South of Ireland* (London: A.W. Bennett, 1858), 45.

63. Hole, *A Little Tour in Ireland*, 158. One 1853 tour guide spoke of the "unparalleled number of strangers who . . . flocked to the Irish shores for the first time last summer" (*The Tourist's Illustrated Hand-Book for Ireland*, 21).

64. "Editor and Sole Proprietor of the Hull Advertiser," *Brief Notes of a Short Excursion in Ireland*, 6.

65. *Black's Picturesque Tourist of Ireland*, 205, 256.

66. Travel writing in the sense of Thackeray or the Halls was on the decline after 1850, C.J. Woods has argued, largely because of the growing preponderance of rail travel, as a result of which "the traveller savoured less of the countryside he passed through at high speed; and travel, in Europe at least, became more common, and so other people's accounts less interesting" (C.J. Woods, "Irish Travel Writings as Source Material," *Irish Historical Studies* 28 [November 1992], 173). The prolific publication of generic travel guides, however, more than filled the gap left by the decline of traditional travel writing.

67. Advertisement in *The Irish Tourist's Illustrated Handbook for Visitors to Ireland in 1852* (London: Office of the National Illustrated Library, 1852).

68. Front-page advertisement in *The Tourist's Illustrated Hand-Book for Ireland*.

69. The handbook was given to all who signed up for a Chester and Holyhead Railway tour. Head, *A Fortnight in Ireland*, 151.

70. *The Tourist's Illustrated Hand-Book for Ireland*, 17.

71. The works of the Halls and Thackeray dwelt at length on Irish social and moral conditions, whereas *Black's Picturesque Tourist of Ireland*, like most other travel guides published in the 1850s, had nothing whatsoever to say on the subject.

72. It should be noted that these figures do not include either seasonal migrant workers, whose numbers ranged from sixty to one hundred thousand per year from 1841 to 1851, or second-generation Irish (M.A.G. O'Tuathaigh, "The Irish in Nineteenth-Century Britain: Problems of Integration," *Transactions of the Royal Historical Society*, 5th ser., 31 [1981], 151, 153).

73. Frank Neal, "Liverpool, the Irish Steamship Companies and the Famine Irish," *Immigrants and Minorities* 5:1 (March 1986), 31, 34–35.

74. Lynn Hollen Lees, *Exiles of Erin: Irish Migrants in Victorian London* (Manchester: Manchester University Press, 1979), 24.

75. Ibid., 39.

76. Ibid., 63.

77. Graham Davis, "Little Irelands," in Roger Swift and Sheridan Gilley, eds. *The Irish in Britain 1815–1939* (London: Pinter, 1989), 113.

78. O'Tuathaigh, "The Irish in Nineteenth-Century Britain," 159.

79. The Irish in England married earlier and had fewer children than did those remaining in Ireland. Urban English families were slightly more likely to be extended than were urban Irish families, which were more often nuclear (Lees, *Exiles of Erin*, 124–127, 135–136).

80. W.J. Lowe, *The Irish in Mid-Victorian Lancashire: The Shaping of a Working-Class Community* (New York: Peter Lang, 1989), 103.

81. D.G. Paz, *Popular Anti-Catholicism in Mid-Victorian England* (Stanford: Stanford University Press, 1992), 57–58.

82. John Werly, "The Irish in Manchester, 1832–1849," *Irish Historical Studies* 18 (March 1973), 345–350.

83. Lees, *Exiles of Erin*, 170–175.

84. Fergus D'Arcy, "The Irish in 19th Century Britain: Reflections on their Rôle and Experience," *Irish History Workshop* (1981), 8.

85. Henry Grant, *Ireland's Hour* (London: Thomas Hatchard, 1850), 3.

86. David Brooke, *The Railway Navvy: "That Despicable Race of Men"* (London: David & Charles, 1983), 112–17.

87. The HO 45 files in the Public Record Office in Kew contain copious police accounts, personal testimonies, and official reports on English-Irish disturbances throughout the British Isles in the 1850s. There is no space to survey them here; suffice it to say that they are generally not concerned with predicting the consequences of unrest, but in determining its causes, a task in which the officials concerned seem to have been remarkably dispassionate. Their typical moral judgment on these affairs may be summed up by Palmerston's laconic comment on one such account that "Blows & Stones are not fit arguments to be used in theological Discussion" (Lord Palmerston, note appended to memorial of Berkeley Addison, Chairman of the Scottish Reformation Society, to Palmerston, August 9, 1853, HO 45/5129A).

88. Lowe, *The Irish in Mid-Victorian Lancashire*, 147; Paz, *Popular Anti-Catholicism*, 58.

89. D'Arcy, "The Irish in 19th Century Britain," 9.

90. Ibid., 7.

91. Lees, *Exiles of Erin*, 226–250. Irish involvement in nationalist politics was by comparison much more significant, though it did not manifest itself in truly threatening form until the Fenian crisis of the late 1860s (D'Arcy, "The Irish in 19th Century Britain," 10).

92. Neal, "Liverpool . . . ," 32.

93. Ibid., 51–53.

94. D'Arcy, "The Irish in 19th Century Britain," 4.

95. Quoted in R.A.J. Walling, ed., *The Diaries of John Bright* (London: Cassell, 1930), 95.

96. John Bright, "Speech Notes on Ireland," October 25, 1849, Additional Manuscript 43392, f.36.

97. John Bright to Richard Cobden, September 25, 1851, Additional Manuscript 43383, f. 209.

98. The cholera epidemics (known as "Irish fever") that followed large-scale Irish immigration into cities like Liverpool encouraged this perception (Neal, "Liverpool . . . ," 39).

99. Foster, *Paddy and Mr. Punch*, 289.

100. Augustus Campbell to Sir George Grey, April 13, 1849, HO 45/2674.

101. Thomas Carlyle, "Downing Street" (1850), quoted in Seamus Deane, "Irish National Character 1790–1900," in Tom Dunne, ed., *The Writer as Witness* (Cork: Cork University Press, 1987), 99.

102. For example, C. Locock Webb, *Suggestions on the Present Condition of Ireland, and on Government Aid for Carrying Out an Efficient Railway System* (London: Smith, Elder & Co., 1852), 11.

103. Davis, "Little Irelands," 104.

104. Ibid., 115.

105. Jeffrey G. Williamson, "The Impact of the Irish on British Labor Markets During the Industrial Revolution," in Roger Swift and Sheridan Gilley, eds., *The Irish in Britain 1815–1939*, 136, 156; Roger Swift, "Crime and the Irish in Nineteenth-Century Britain," in ibid., 163–167.

106. Frances Finnegan, *Poverty and Prejudice: A Study of Irish Immigrants in York 1840–1875* (Cork: Cork University Press, 1982), 173–174.

107. Elizabeth Gaskell, *North and South* (London: Oxford University Press, 1973), 178, 228.

108. Ibid., 308.

109. Ibid., 400.

110. Rev. Samuel Garratt, "The Irish in London: a Lecture Delivered on Monday, Dec. 6th, 1852, at the Music Hall, Store Street," in Nolan, ed., *Motives for Missions*, 186.

111. Ibid., 191.

112. Deane, "Irish National Character," 91.

113. Said, *Culture and Imperialism*, 35–70.

114. Deane, "Irish National Character," 95.

115. Gibbons, "Race Against Time," 103.

116. Boylan and Foley, *Political Economy and Colonial Ireland*, 17–117.

117. Quoted in ibid., 148.

118. Quoted in ibid., 127.

119. Ibid., 150.

120. Quoted in MacElheran, *Celt and Saxon*, 21, 26.

121. Brian V. Street, *The Savage in Literature: Representations of "Primitive" Society in English Fiction 1858–1920* (London: Routledge & Kegan Paul, 1975), 104–105.

122. Rogers, *Facts for the Kind-Hearted of England!*, 13.

123. Quoted in MacElheran, *Celt and Saxon*, 60.

124. David Cairns and Shaun Richards, *Writing Ireland: Colonialism, Nationalism and Culture* (Manchester: Manchester University Press, 1988), 52–53.

125. Julia Corner, *The History of Ireland: From the Earliest Period to the Present Time.* Adapted for Youth, Schools, and Families (London: Dean and Son, 1855), 5–10.

126. Thomas Wright, *The Celt, the Roman and the Saxon: A History of the Early Inhabitants of Britain, Down to the Conversion of the Anglo-Saxons to Christianity* (London: Arthur Hall, 1852), vii, 1.

127. Ibid., 4.

128. Ibid., 436.

129. Ibid., 453.

130. Corner, *The History of Ireland*, 9–18.

131. Robert A.M. Stewart, *New and Popular History of Ireland from the Beginning of the Christian Era to the Present Time* (London: John Cassell, 1851–1852), 1:15.

132. Corner, *The History of Ireland*, 81.

133. Sir George Nicholls, *A History of the Irish Poor Law, in Connexion with the Condition of the People* (London: John Murray, 1856), 13.

134. Head, *A Fortnight in Ireland*, 245.

135. Nicholls, *A History of the Irish Poor Law*, 72.

136. Corner, *The History of Ireland*, 185–188.

137. Nicholls, *A History of the Irish Poor Law*, 357.

138. Lebow, *White Britain and Black Ireland*, 40.

Conclusion

The period 1840–1860 was a defining moment in the history of English-Irish relations in the nineteenth century. In practical terms, its consequences were disastrous, although not irreversible. In the short term, the abandonment of liberal ideas in the 1850s meant the end of reformist legislation for Ireland until the era of Gladstone.[1] It is true that the Peel and Russell administrations from 1841 to 1852 had failed to carry out any very significant or lasting reforms for Ireland, and that what they had been able to achieve in the island was often doomed to failure because of its basis in misguided principles of economy and morality. Given two more decades, however, government predicated on the economic and moral reform of Ireland and the Irish might indeed have been able to improve conditions in the country significantly. Russell in particular was full not only of good intentions for Ireland but also of numerous plans for its regeneration, including schemes for extensive land reform and pacification of Irish political and religious grievances. Were it not for the potato blight, which crippled his administration, Russell's legacy in Ireland might well have been that of hero rather than villain.

The interest and optimism with which the English regarded Ireland in the first half of the 1840s was wholly absent in the two decades following the famine, during which the legislative record was abysmal. Admittedly, the legislative inertia that marked the Palmerston administrations from 1855 to 1865 was not peculiar to Ireland but extended to English domestic policy as well. At the same time, it is clear that there was little public pressure for reform in Ireland until after the Fenian agitation of the late 1860s, which had brought the issue of Irish poverty once again to the fore. Unlike the English reaction to the repeal agitation of the 1840s, which had remained fundamentally optimistic despite fears of an Irish rising, the response to Fenianism was remarkably savage—reflecting the differences in climate between the 1840s and the 1860s.[2]

The efforts of William Gladstone to carry through a program of social and political reform in Ireland (including home rule) from the 1870s to the 1890s might at first appear to mark a general return to the liberal idealism of the 1840s. In fact, however, he was fighting a losing battle against what had by the last quarter of the century become a virtual popular consensus of racialism. The great Liberal prime minister's social and political outlook had been formed in the 1840s, when he was a rising young star of the Peelite faction in Parliament. Like Russell, Gladstone remained to the end of his life true to the liberal view of Irish regeneration.

By the end of the century, as L.P. Curtis has ably shown, racialist ideas dominated popular thought on Ireland. The greater coherence lent to scientific thought on race by the emergence of Darwinism and its associated theories added a force and malevolence to English perceptions of the Irish that had not existed even in the 1850s. English writers and caricaturists insisted again and again on the bestiality and subhumanity of the Irish, used these "facts" as weapons against Gladstonian reform. The roots of this attitude are traceable to the events surrounding the Irish famine in the middle of the century. The painful and very gradual dissolution of racialism would commence only in the beginning of the next century.

HISTORICAL TRENDS

The change in attitudes that marked the period 1840–1860 was not, it should be emphasized, unprecedented. English perceptions of the Irish have for centuries followed a pattern alternating between the pessimistic and the optimistic. Periods of several decades in which most English observers looked ahead to increasing cooperation and integration between the two countries were usually punctuated by shorter periods in which social or military crises in Ireland, such as those of 1641 and 1798, stirred feelings of bitterness and contempt. English hostility, while it lasted, involved the adoption of punitive, and the abandonment of reformist, legislation, but generally softened in one or two decades unless another crisis occurred to renew it.

The fact that a change in public perceptions of Ireland took place between 1840 and 1860 does, however, run counter to the still commonly accepted view that English perceptions of the Irish were uniformly hostile and even racist throughout the course of recorded history. More interesting and relevant is the degree to which the English view of the Irish was predicated upon, and shifted in connection with, English preoccupations in the areas of economic and moral philosophy, science, and politics. Popular views of religion, the economy, science, gender relations, class relations, imperial stability and defense, and imperial growth all had their impact on English attitudes toward the Irish. It is important to remember, however, that the process went both ways, for events in Ireland such as the repeal movement, the famine, the 1848 rising and emigration all affected the way in which educated Englishmen viewed many of these issues. Opinions went both ways in another respect as well, for English and Irish attitudes were defined to a great degree in relation to each other.

The emerging doctrines of moral and economic liberalism fueled the optimism that marked the five years before the famine. Attitudes toward Ireland in these years were partly defined in terms of recent theories about human nature and origins, and natural law both moral and economic. At the same time, Irish pressure for repeal of the Act of Union forced the English to define their own attitudes in reaction, by stressing the union as natural and justifying it by both history and the future. Irish history showed what the country would descend to without enlightened, liberal English rule; hope for Ireland's future rested wholly upon the unfettered exercise of English rule. The idea of the British family of nations, and more particularly of the English-Irish union as a marriage, was advanced to demonstrate the impossibility of a separation.

The period 1846–1852 presented the English with a rapidly changing set of social, political and economic circumstances in both England and Ireland. In Ireland, the central event was of course the famine, which exposed the fallacy of liberal government and, in appearing to reverse the march of Irish moral and material progress, belied the Whig notion of Irish history as a steady progression toward prosperity and civilization under English tutelage. The social and economic dislocation arising from the famine, in combination with the 1848 Young Ireland rising, added urgency to fears developing in England over financial crises and threats of revolution spreading from the continent. The Irish threat to England was given concrete form in the masses of Irish immigrants who fled their own country in search of relief and employment. The 1848 Chartist petition appeared to presage possible class conflict in England, and although fears of an outright social explosion had died down by the beginning of the 1850s, the threat of moral contamination of English workers by the Irish remained.

This apparent danger fueled both physical and conceptual separation of English and Irish. Conflict, and especially cooperation, of English and Irish workers had to be prevented. Assimilation was in this respect a patently inappropriate ideal to pursue. Assimilation in the form of the extension of English laws and liberties to Ireland was also inadvisable given the apparent necessity of harsh coercion measures there to prevent social unrest or revolution. The huge expenditures which the English believed they had made in 1846–1847 demonstrated the dangers of integration on another level. The supposed unwillingness of the Irish to improve themselves, combined with their apparent ingratitude, made it seem that a continuation of liberal policies would entail endless expenditure for no clear return, at a time when England's economy seemed anything but stable. For most Englishmen, spending too much on Ireland threatened not only to empty their own pockets, but also to enrage the English workers who might be forced to share their last loaf with an ungrateful and indolent Paddy.

Changes in scientific attitudes toward human nature did not at first drive, but were themselves driven by, events in Ireland and shifting political and economic priorities in that country. The Irish degeneracy supposedly demonstrated by the events surrounding the famine lent racialists both physical "proof" and, more important, an emotional edge to their theories. Anger at the Irish for their ingratitude for English relief funds and unwillingness to make use of them was very widespread in the last years of the famine. Racialism provided an outlet for this anger at the same time as it conveniently shifted the blame for the Irish catastrophe from the English to the Irish themselves. It also proved its usefulness in providing a conceptual framework for the separation of English and Irish without weakening the dominant position of the former.

In the 1850s, though racialism no doubt proved convincing for some who studied the arguments of its theorists, its main function was to justify English policy toward the Irish in both Ireland and England. Maintaining separation between Irish immigrants and English workers continued to be a priority throughout the famine, but so did the reversal of this process through Saxon colonization and settlement of Ireland. The settlement movement of the 1850s was a reaction to the famine in another respect, for it purported to take advantage of the "clearance" of Irish incumbrances on land and overpopulation that had followed that disaster. Racialism justified colonization in several respects, most notably by reinforcing the idea of the English as a dominant people, and also by aiding in the construction of a view of the Irish that emphasized their docility and suitability for work. Evangelization in Ireland took the place of moral and economic tutelage as the proper means for social control in that country, being necessitated by the racialist denial of the efficacy of liberal methods and the settlers' need to maintain stability in Ireland.

Gender runs as a constant thread in English perceptions of Ireland throughout this period. This element of English thought is traceable back to the beginnings of relations between the two countries. A number of qualities of character generally associated with the Irish, particularly their simplicity, hospitality, vanity, emotionalism, and their love of music, poetry and folklore, were "feminine" or child-like traits that had been ascribed to them by the English since the twelfth century. In the seventeenth century one English writer went so far as to compare Irish geography with the female anatomy.[3]

Here again what had changed in the first half of the nineteenth century was not the fundamentals of English thought, but their form, which in taking on the trappings of liberal theory found it necessary to embody its gendered conception of the Irish in a rhetoric of marriage. The weakening of liberalism in the aftermath of the famine did not, of course, remove the gendered conception of Irish nature, but changed its form. The femininity of Irish nature was used not to justify complementarity and assimilation, but to emphasize and reinforce differences in power and social freedom between the two peoples.

Irish subservience to England was an element of fundamental continuity in English thought between 1840 and 1860, as indeed it had been for several centuries before. In the early 1840s, subservience was defined in terms usually of wife to husband, but also of student to teacher or patient to doctor. Ruling Ireland carried with it a moral duty to improve, instruct, or "cure" the country so as to cement the bond of its union with Britain. In the 1850s, Ireland's role was increasingly seen as little more than willing servitude. It would be untrue to say that the ruler had no moral duties. These duties had changed, however, from being limited to ruling Ireland in fairness and justice, to having no element of moral or economic uplift aside from the mission to evangelize. Even the moral mission of evangelization, however, was never advanced as a means of raising the level of the Irish to near-equality, but as a way to make them happy where they were.

A strong element of continuity therefore underlay all of the changes that appeared on the surface of English perceptions of the Irish from 1840 to 1860. Whether the dominant note in the English mood was optimism or pessimism, Ireland always remained at best a junior partner in the union inhabited by people fundamentally different from the English. At no time in this period did the English public come to terms with the possibility that the Irish might be capable not only of cooperating with or imitating the English, but also of emulating, becoming independent from, and even outstripping the English in civilization, wealth and power. The rise of racialism was in this respect only what Edward Said has called a "codification of difference" that more strictly defined differences that were already assumed to exist.[4]

The continuities that undoubtedly persisted in English perceptions of the Irish throughout the course of relations between the two countries should not blind us to the fact that changes in popular attitudes could be profound and have a significant practical impact on policy. It should be clear from these chapters that the one-dimensional view of English perceptions of the Irish that still prevails among many scholars is wholly unsuited to serious historical research. Attention to the complexities of English language and popular thought is essential if we are to properly understand the ideas (or lack thereof) behind official policy in Ireland and the reasons for the ultimate failure of English government in that country.

NOTES

1. Patrick O'Farrell, *England and Ireland since 1800* (London: Oxford University Press, 1975), 28.

2. Much of L.P. Curtis's evidence for the belief in innate Irish inferiority that he claims to have characterized English attitudes throughout the nineteenth century is in fact drawn from cartoons and books produced during the Fenian crisis in the late 1860s.

3. John P. Harrington, *The English Traveller in Ireland: Accounts of the Irish through Five Centuries* (Dublin: Wolfhound Press, 1991), 15.

4. Said argues that this trend was associated with the rise of scientific racism in the mid-nineteenth century and extended across the whole spectrum of imperial thought (Said, *Culture and Imperialism*, 130).

Bibliography

PRIMARY SOURCES

"Agricola." *Suggestions on the Best Modes of Employing the Irish Peasantry, as an Anti-Famine Precaution. A Letter to the Right Hon. Sir Robert Peel, Bart.* London: Hatchard and Son, 1845.

Anonymous. *A Brief Account of the Famine in Ireland.* London: J.H. Jackson, 1847.

Anonymous. *The Comical Sayings of Paddy from Cork, with His Coat Buttoned Behind.* Glasgow: 1840?

Anonymous. *Distress in Ireland. Outlines of a Plan for Employing Funds to Be Raised by Subscription in England, in such a Manner, That in Relieving the Destitute, Their Condition May Be so far Improved as to Prevent the Necessity for Aid in Future Years.* London: James Ridgway, 1847.

Anonymous. *Evangelization in Ireland in 1853; Being a Brief Narrative of the Mission of One Hundred Ministers of the Gospel in the South of Ireland, during the Autumn of 1853.* London: Partridge, Oakey, and Co., 1854.

Anonymous. *The Famine as Yet in Its Infancy; or, 1847 Compared with the Prospects of 1848, 1849, & c. Addressed to Every-Body.* London: Hamilton, Adams and Co., 1847.

Anonymous. *The Measures Which Can Alone Ameliorate Effectually the Condition of the Irish People.* London: J. Hatchard, 1847.

Anonymous. *Paddy's Leisure Hours in the Poor House; or, Priests, Parsons, Potatoes, and Poor-Rates.* London: John W. Parker, 1849.

Anonymous. *Plan of the Priests for the Management of Ireland.* London: Thomas Bosworth, 1852.

Anonymous. *Popery in Ireland as Exemplified in the Experience of a Ragged School Teacher.* London: T. Hatchard, 1857.

Anonymous. *Some Effects of the Irish Poor-Law; with a Plan for Emigration from Ireland.* London: Saunders and Otley, 1849.

Anonymous. *The South of Ireland and Her Poor.* London: Saunders and Otley, 1843.

Anonymous. *Thoughts and Suggestions on our Relations with Ireland.* London: James Ridgway, 1847.

Anonymous. *Thoughts on Ireland.* London: James Ridgway, 1847.

Anonymous. *Thoughts on National Education, as an Instrument of National Prosperity; and as a Mode of Diffusing amongst the Labouring Classes in Ireland Habits of Industry, Frugality, and Forethought; with an Introductory Chapter.* London: Thomas Cautley Newby, 1847.

Ashworth, John Henry. *The Saxon in Ireland: or, the Rambles of an Englishman in Search of a Settlement in the West of Ireland.* London: John Murray, 1851.

Asplen, George W. *A Lively Sketch of a Trip to Killarney and the South of Ireland.* London: A.W. Bennett, 1858.

Bennett, William. *Narrative of a Recent Journey of Six Weeks in Ireland, in Connexion with the Subject of Supplying Small Seed to Some of the Remoter Districts: with Current Observations on the Depressed Circumstances of the People, and the Means Presented for the Permanent Improvement of Their Social Condition.* London: Charles Gilpin, 1847.

Black's Picturesque Tourist of Ireland. Edinburgh: Adam and Charles Black, 1854.

Bright, John. *The Diaries of John Bright.* Edited by R.A.J. Walling. London: Cassell, 1930.

Broughton, Lord. *Recollections of a Long Life.* Edited by Lady Dorchester. Vol. 6, *1841–1852.* London: John Murray, 1911.

Burritt, Elihu. *A Journal of a Visit of Three Days to Skibbereen, and Its Neighbourhood.* London: Charles Gilpin, 1847.

Carleton, William. *The Black Prophet: A Tale of Irish Famine.* London: Simms and M'Intyre, 1847.

———. *The Emigrants of Ahadarra: A Tale of Irish Life.* London: Simms and M'Intyre, 1848.

———. *Traits and Stories of the Irish Peasantry.* 2 vols. London: William S. Orr, 1843–1844.

Carlyle, Thomas. *Reminiscences of My Irish Journey in 1849.* New York: Harper & Brothers, 1882.

Carlyle, Thomas and Jane Welsh Carlyle. *The Collected Letters of Thomas and Jane Welsh Carlyle.* Edited by Clyde De L. Ryals and Kenneth J. Fielding. 24 vols. Durham: Duke University Press, 1970–1995.

Corner, Julia. *The History of Ireland: From the Earliest Period to the Present Time, Adapted for Youth, Schools, and Families.* New edition. London: Dean and Son, 1855.

Croker, John Wilson. *The Croker Papers*. Edited by Louis J. Jennings. 3 vols. 2nd ed., London: John Murray, 1885.

Devon, Lord. *Letter from an Irish Proprieter to the Ministers of Religion of the District.* London: J. Bigg and Son, 1847.

Disraeli, Benjamin. *Benjamin Disraeli's Letters*. Edited by M.G. Wiebe. Vols. 4, 5. Toronto: University of Toronto Press, 1989–1993.

Doudney, David Alfred. *A Run through Connemara*. London: W.H. Collingridge, 1856.

Dufferin, Lord, and Hon. G.F. Boyle. *Narrative of a Journey from Oxford to Skibbereen during the Year of the Famine*. Oxford: John Henry Parker, 1847.

Duffy, Sir Charles Gavan. *Conversations with Carlyle*. New York: Charles Scribner's Sons, 1892.

"Editor and Sole Proprietor of the *Hull Advertiser*." *Brief Notes of a Short Excursion in Ireland, in the Autumn of 1852*. London: Whittaker & Co., 1853.

Ellis, George. *Irish Ethnology Socially and Politically Considered; Embracing a General Outline of the Celtic and Saxon Races; with Practical Inferences*. London: Hamilton, Adams and Co., 1852.

"Englishman." *An Earnest Plea for Ireland*. London: John Ollivier, 1848.

"Ex-Member of the British Parliament." *Irish Improvidence Encouraged by English Bounty; Being a Remonstrance against the Government Projects for Irish Relief, and Suggestions of Measures by Which the Irish Poor Can Be Speedily and Effectually Fed, Relieved, Employed, and Elevated above Their Present Degraded Position, without Taxing English Industry for This Purpose*. London: James Ridgway, 1847?.

"Fellow of the Dublin Law Institute." *Ireland and Irish Questions Considered*. London: J. Hatchard and Son, 1842.

Forbes, John. *Memorandums made in Ireland in the Autumn of 1852*. 2 vols. London: Smith, Elder, and Co., 1853.

Foster, Thomas Campbell. *Letters on the Condition of the People of Ireland*. London: Chapman and Hall, 1846.

Gale, Frederick. *Paddy Land and the Lakes of Killarney*. London: John Chapman, 1853.

Garwood, John. *The Million-Peopled City*. New York: Garland, 1985. [Originally published 1853]

Gaskell, Elizabeth. *North and South*. London: Oxford University Press, 1973. [Originally published 1855 in 2 vols.]

Gaye, C.H. *Irish Famine: A Special Occasion for Keeping Lent in England*. 2nd ed. London: Francis & John Rivington, 1847.

Gilly, W.S. ed. *Christmas 1846 and the New Year 1847, in Ireland. Letters from a Lady*. Durham: G. Andrews, 1847.

Gladstone, William H. *The Gladstone Diaries*. Edited by M.R.D. Foot and H.C.G. Matthew. 14 vols. Oxford: Clarendon Press, 1968–1994.

Gore, Montague. *Suggestions for the Amelioration of the Present Condition of Ireland*. 3rd ed. London: James Ridgway, 1848. [Originally published 1847]

Grant, Henry. *Ireland's Hour.* London: Thomas Hatchard, 1850.

Grant, James. *Impressions of Ireland and the Irish.* 2 vols. London: Hugh Cunningham, 1844.

Greville, Charles C.F. *A Journal of the Reign of Queen Victoria from 1837 to 1852.* Edited by Henry Reeve. 2 vols. New York: D. Appleton & Co., 1885.

———. *Past and Present Policy of England towards Ireland.* London: Edward Moxon, 1845.

Hall, Mrs. S.C. *Sketches of Irish Character.* Illustrated edition. London: Howard Parsons, 1842.

———. *Stories of the Irish Peasantry.* Edinburgh: William and Robert Chambers, 1850.

Hall, Mr. & Mrs. S.C. *Ireland: Its Scenery, Character, etc.* 3 vols. London: How and Parsons, 1841–1843.

Head, Sir Francis B. *A Fortnight in Ireland.* 2nd ed. London: John Murray, 1852.

Hearn, William Edward. *The Cassell Prize Essay on the Condition of Ireland.* London: John Cassell, 1851.

Hill, Lord George. *Facts from Gweedore: With Useful Hints to Donegal Tourists.* Dublin: Philip Dixon Hardy and Sons, 1846.

Hole, S.R. *A Little Tour in Ireland.* London: Bradbury and Evans, 1859.

The Irish Tourist's Illustrated Handbook for Visitors to Ireland in 1852. 2nd ed. London: Office of the National Illustrated Library, 1852.

"Irishman." *The Irish Widow; or, a Picture from Life of Erin and Her Children.* London: Wertheim and MacIntosh, 1855.

———. *Poor Paddy's Cabin; or, Slavery in Ireland.* London: Wertheim and MacIntosh, 1853.

Johnson, James. *A Tour in Ireland; with Meditations and Reflections.* London: S. Highley, 1844.

Kingsley, Frances Eliza, ed. *Charles Kingsley: His Letters and Memories of His Life.* 2 vols. London: Henry S. King, 1877.

Knox, Robert. *The Races of Men: A Philosophical Inquiry into the Influence of Race over the Destinies of Nations.* 2nd ed. London: Henry Renshaw, 1862.

Lambert, Henry. *A Memoir of Ireland in 1850.* Dublin: James McGlashan, 1851.

Latham, R.G. *The Ethnology of the British Islands.* London: John Van Voorst, 1852.

Laughton, John Knox. *Memoirs of the Life and Correspondence of Henry Reeve.* 2 vols. London: Longmans, Green, and Co., 1898.

Lever, Charles James. *The Confessions of Harry Lorrequer.* New York: Home Book Company, 1900. [Originally published 1839]

Lover, Samuel. *Handy Andy: A Tale of Irish Life.* London: J.M. Dent & Sons, 1907. [Originally published 1842]

Lyons, J.C. *The Science of Phrenology, as Applicable to Education, Friendship, Love, Courtship, and Matrimony, Etc.* London: Aylott and Jones, 1846.

Maberly, Mrs. K.C. *The Present State of Ireland and Its Remedy.* London: James Ridgway, 1847.

MacDonnell, Eneas. *Irish Sufferers and Anti-Irish Philosophers, Their Pledges and Performances*. London: John Ollivier, 1847.

MacElheran, John. *Celt and Saxon: Address to the British Association, on the Ethnology of England; Letters to "The Times" and other Journals, on the Races of Celt and Saxon*. Belfast: R.D. Read, 1852.

Madden, Daniel Owen. *Ireland and Its Rulers, since 1829*. 3 vols. London: T.C. Newby, 1843–1844.

———. *Revelations of Ireland in the Past Generation*. Dublin: James McGlashan, 1848.

Maguire, John Francis, MP. *Removal of the Irish Poor from England and Scotland, Shewing the Nature of the Law of Removal, the Mode in Which It Is Administered, the Hardships Which It Inflicts, and the Necessity for Its Absolute and Unconditional Repeal*. London: W. & F.G. Cash, 1854.

Manners, Lord John. *Notes of an Irish Tour*. London: J. Ollivier, 1849.

Martineau, Harriet. *Letters from Ireland*. London: John Chapman, 1852.

Massy, Richard Tuthill. *Analytical Ethnology: The Mixed Tribes in Great Britain and Ireland Examined, and the Political, Physical, and Metaphysical Blunderings on the Celt and Saxon Exposed*. London: H. Bailliere, 1855.

Maxwell, Herbert. *The Life and Letters of George William Frederick Fourth Earl of Clarendon*. Vol. 1. London: Edward Arnold, 1913.

Maxwell, W.H. *History of the Irish Rebellion in 1798; with Memoirs of the Union, and Emmett's Insurrection in 1803*. 3rd ed. London: H.G. Bohn, 1852. [Originally published 1845]

———. *The Irish Movements: Their Rise, Progress, and Certain Termination; with a Few Broad Hints to Patriots and Pikemen*. London: Baily Brothers, 1848.

Mill, John Stuart. *John Stuart Mill on Ireland, with an Essay by Richard Ned Lebow*. Philadelphia: Institute for the Study of Human Issues, 1979.

"Minister of the Gospel." *The True Source and End of Ireland's Destitution; together with an Appeal, to British Christians, on Behalf of Ireland*. London: John Snow, 1849.

Muggeridge, Richard M. *Notes on the Irish "Difficulty"; with Remedial Suggestions*. Dublin: James McGlashan, 1849.

"Native." *Remarks on Ireland; as It Is;—As It Ought to Be;—and as It Might Be: Sir Robert Peel's Plantation Scheme & c. Suggested by a Recent Article in "The Times"; and Addressed to the Capitalists of England*. London: C.H. Law, 1849.

Nicholls, Sir George. *A History of the Irish Poor Law, in Connexion with the Condition of the People*. London: John Murray, 1856.

Nolan, Rev. Thomas. *Motives for Missions. A Series of Six Lectures Delivered before the Church of England Young Men's Society*. London: Sampson Low and Son, 1853.

O'Connell, Catherine M. *Excursions in Ireland during 1844 and 1850*. London: R. Bentley, 1852.

O'Connell, Daniel. *The Correspondence of Daniel O'Connell*. Edited by Maurice R. O'Connell. 8 vols. Dublin: Blackwater Press, 1972–1981.

Osborne, Rev. S. Godolphin. *Gleanings in the West of Ireland.* London: T. & W. Boone, 1850.

Otway, Rev. Caesar. *A Tour in Connaught: Comprising Sketches of Clanmacnoise, Joyce Country, and Achill.* Dublin: William Curry, Junior and Company, 1839.

Parker, Charles Stuart, ed. *The Life and Letters of Sir James Graham, 1792–1861.* Vol. 2. London: John Murray, 1907.

———. *Sir Robert Peel from His Private Papers.* Vol. 3. London: John Murray, 1899.

Peel, Sir Robert. *Memoirs.* Edited by Lord Mahon and Edward Cardwell. 2 vols. London: John Murray, 1856. Reprint, New York: Kraus Reprint Co., 1969.

Perceval, Rev. M.P. *The Amelioration of Ireland Contemplated, in a Series of Papers.* London: W.J. Cleaver, 1844.

"Pistis." *A Trip to Ireland, with Observations on Killarney and Its Neighbourhood.* London: C. Mitchell, 1850.

Prichard, James Cowles. *The Eastern Origin of the Celtic Nations Proved by a Comparison of Their Dialects with the Sanskrit, Greek, Latin, and Teutonic Languages: Forming a Supplement to the Researches into the Physical History of Mankind.* 2nd ed.: Edited by R.G. Latham. London: Houlston and Wright, 1857.

Reid, Wemyss, ed. *Memoirs and Correspondence of Lyon Playfair.* New York: Harper & Brothers, 1899.

Rogers, Jasper W. *Facts for the Kind-Hearted of England! As to the Wretchedness of the Irish Peasantry, and the Means for Their Regeneration.* London: James Ridgway, 1847.

Russell, John Earl. *The Later Correspondence of Lord John Russell, 1840–1878.* Edited by G.P. Gooch. London: Longmans, Green & Co., 1925.

———. *Recollections and Suggestions, 1813–1873.* Boston: Roberts Brothers, 1875.

Scott, Thomas. *Ireland Estimated as a Field for Investment.* London: Thomas Harrison, 1854.

Scrope, George Poulett. *How to Make Ireland Self-Supporting; or, Irish Clearances, and Improvement of Waste Lands.* London: James Ridgway, 1848.

———. *The Irish Relief Measures, Past and Future.* London: James Ridgway, 1848.

———. *Letters to Lord John Russell, M.P. on the Further Measures Required for the Social Amelioration of Ireland.* London: James Ridgway, 1847.

Senior, Nassau. *Journals, Conversations and Essays Relating to Ireland.* 2 vols. London: Longmans, Green, and Co., 1868.

———. "Relief of Irish Distress in 1847 and 1848." *Edinburgh Review* 89 (January 1849): 116–140.

Smiles, Samuel. *History of Ireland and the Irish People, under the Government of England.* London: William Strange, 1844.

[Society of Friends]. *Distress in Ireland.* London: Edward Newman, 1846–1847.

Somerville, Alexander. *Letters from Ireland during the Famine of 1847.* Edited with an introduction by K.D.M. Snell. Dublin: Irish Academic Press, 1994.

St. G.S., A. *Sad Sounds from a Broken Harp; or A Faint Death Cry from Ireland.* London: Francis and John Rivington, 1847.

Stewart, Robert A.M. *New and Popular History of Ireland from the Beginning of the Christian Era to the Present Time.* 3 vols. London: John Cassell, 1851–1852.

Stoddart, Rev. George H. *The True Cure for Ireland, the Development of Her Industry: Being a Letter Addressed to the Rt. Honble. Lord John Russell, M.P.* 2nd ed. London: Trelawny W. Saunders, 1847.

Thackeray, William Makepeace. *The Irish Sketch Book, 1842.* Oxford: Oxford University Press, 1908. [Originally published 1843]

The Tourist's Illustrated Hand-Book for Ireland. London: John Cassell, 1853.

Trevelyan, Sir Charles. "The Irish Crisis." *Edinburgh Review* 87 (January 1848): 121–166.

Trollope, Anthony. *The Kellys and the O'Kellys.* Oxford: Oxford University Press, 1982. [Originally published 1848 in 3 vols.]

——— . *The MacDermots of Ballycloran.* Oxford: Oxford University Press, 1989. [Originally published 1847 in 3 vols.]

Tuke, James H. *A Visit to Connaught in the Autumn of 1847.* 2nd ed. London: Charles Gilpin, 1848.

U.K. Parliament. *Parliamentary Debates* (Commons), 3rd ser., vols. 83–96 (1846–1848).

——— . "Account of Public Monies Expended or Advanced by Way of Loan in the Years 1845–8, for the Relief of Distress in Ireland," *Sessional Papers* (Commons), *1847–8, Sources for Famine Expenditure*, 1 September 1848, vol. 54, p.16.

——— . "Expenditure of Ireland," *Sessional Papers* (Commons), *1849, Account of Net Public Income and Expenditure*, vol. 30, p. 181.

——— . "Public Income and Expenditure, from 1822 to 1849," *Sessional Papers* (Commons), *1850, Account of Net Public Income and Expenditure*, vol. 33, p. 158.

Walond, R.F. *Paddiana; or, Scraps and Sketches of Irish Life, Present and Past.* 2 vols. London: Richard Bentley, 1847.

Webb, C. Locock. *Suggestions on the Present Condition of Ireland, and on Government Aid for Carrying Out an Efficient Railway System.* London: Smith, Elder & Co., 1852.

Webster, William Bullock. *Ireland Considered as a Field for Investment or Residence.* Dublin: Hodges and Smith, 1852.

Weld, Charles Richard. *Vacations in Ireland.* London: Longman, Brown, Green, Longmans & Roberts, 1857.

West, Theresa Cornwallis I. Whitby. *A Summer Visit to Ireland in 1846.* London: R. Bentley, 1847.

White, George Preston. *A Tour in Connemara, with Remarks on its Great Physical Capabilities.* London: W.H. Smith and Son, 1849.

Wright, Thomas. *The Celt, the Roman, and the Saxon: a History of the Early Inhabitants of Britain, Down to the Conversion of the Anglo-Saxons to Christianity.* London: Arthur Hall, 1852.

SECONDARY SOURCES

Alatas, Syed Hussein. *The Myth of the Lazy Native: A Study of the Image of the Malays, Filipinos and Javanese from the 16th to the 20th Century and Its Function in the Ideology of Colonial Capitalism.* London: Frank Cass, 1977.

Banton, Michael. *Racial Theories.* Cambridge: Cambridge University Press, 1987.

Billington, Ray Allen. *Land of Savagery, Land of Promise: The European Image of the American Frontier in the Nineteenth Century.* New York: W.W. Norton, 1981.

Black, R.D. Collison. *Economic Thought and the Irish Question, 1817–1870.* Cambridge: Cambridge University Press, 1960.

Boylan, Thomas A., and Timothy P. Foley. *Political Economy and Colonial Ireland: the Propagation and Ideological Function of Economic Discourse in the Nineteenth Century.* London: Routledge, 1992.

Brooke, David. *The Railway Navvy: "That Despicable Race of Men."* London: David & Charles, 1983.

Cairns, David, and Shaun Richards. *Writing Ireland: Colonialism, Nationalism and Culture.* Manchester: Manchester University Press, 1988.

Cook, Sir Edward. *Delane of the Times.* London: Constable & Company, 1916.

Curtis, L.P. *Anglo-Saxons and Celts: A Study of Anti-Irish Prejudice in Victorian England.* Conference of British Studies at the University of Bridgeport, Connecticut, 1968.

————. *Apes and Angels: The Irishman in Victorian Caricature.* Washington: Smithsonian Institution Press, 1971.

Curtis, Liz. *Nothing but the Same Old Story: The Roots of Anti-Irish Racism.* London: Information on Ireland, 1984.

Daly, Mary E. *The Famine in Ireland.* Dundalk: Dundalgan Press, 1986.

Dasent, Arthur Irwin. *John Thadeus Delane: Editor of "The Times."* London: John Murray, 1908.

Davis, Graham. *The Irish in Britain 1815–1914.* Dublin: Gill and Macmillan, 1991.

Devine, T.M. *The Great Highland Famine.* Edinburgh: John Donald, 1988.

Disraeli, Benjamin. *Lord George Bentinck: A Political Biography.* London: Routledge, 1858.

Duggan, G.C. *The Stage Irishman: A History of the Irish Play and Stage Characters from the Earliest Times.* New York: Benjamin Blom, 1969.

Edwards, R. Dudley, and T. Desmond Williams, eds. *The Great Famine.* New York: Russell & Russell, 1956.

Finnegan, Frances. *Poverty and Prejudice: A Study of Irish Immigrants in York, 1840–1875.* Cork: Cork University Press, 1982.

Foster, R.F. *Paddy and Mr. Punch: Connections in Irish and English History.* London: Penguin, 1993.

Gash, Norman. *Sir Robert Peel: The Life of Sir Robert Peel after 1830.* London: Longman, 1972.

Gray, Peter. *Famine, Land and Politics: British Government and Irish Society, 1843–1850*. Dublin: Irish Academic Press, 1999.

Hadfield, Andrew, and John McVeagh, eds. *Strangers to that Land: British Perceptions of Ireland from the Reformation to the Famine*. Gerrards Cross, Buckinghamshire: Colin Smythe, 1994.

Harrington, John P., ed. *The English Traveller in Ireland: Accounts of Ireland and the Irish through Five Centuries*. Dublin: Wolfhound Press, 1991.

Hatton, Helen E. *The Largest Amount of Good: Quaker Relief in Ireland, 1654–1921*. Kingston & Montreal: McGill-Queen's University Press, 1993.

Hayley, Barbara. *Carleton's "Traits and Stories" and the 19th Century Anglo-Irish Tradition*. Totowa, N.J.: Barnes & Noble, 1983.

Hechter, Michael. *Internal Colonialism: The Celtic Fringe in British National Development, 1536–1966*. Berkeley: University of California Press, 1975.

Hilton, Boyd. *The Age of Atonement: The Influence of Evangelicalism on Social and Economic Thought, 1795–1865*. Oxford: Clarendon Press, 1988.

The History of the Times. Vol. II, *The Tradition Established 1841–1884*. London: The Times, 1939.

Jones, Wilbur Devereux, and Arvel B. Jackson. *The Peelites, 1846–1857*. Columbus: Ohio State University Press, 1972.

Kerr, Donal A. *"A Nation of Beggars"? Priests, People and Politics in Famine Ireland, 1846–1852*. Oxford: Clarendon Press, 1994.

———. *Peel, Priests and Politics: Sir Robert Peel's Administration and the Catholic Church in Ireland, 1841–1846*. Oxford: Clarendon Press, 1982.

Kinealy, Christine. *This Great Calamity: The Irish Famine 1845–52*. Dublin: Gill & Macmillan, 1994.

Koss, Stephen. *The Rise and Fall of the Political Press in Britain*. Vol. 1, *The Nineteenth Century*. Chapel Hill: University of North Carolina Press, 1981.

Lebow, Richard Ned. *White Britain and Black Ireland: The Influence of Stereotypes on Colonial Policy*. Philadelphia: Institute for the Study of Human Issues, 1976.

Lees, Lynn Hollen. *Exiles of Erin: Irish Migrants in Victorian London*. Manchester: Manchester University Press, 1979.

Lowe, W.J. *The Irish in Mid-Victorian Lancashire: The Shaping of a Working-Class Community*. New York: Peter Lang, 1989.

McClintock, Anne. *Imperial Leather: Race, Gender and Sexuality in the Colonial Contest*. New York: Routledge, 1995.

MacDougall, Hugh A. *Racial Myth in English History: Trojans, Teutons, and Anglo-Saxons*. Montreal: Harvest House, 1982.

MacIntyre, Angus. *The Liberator: Daniel O'Connell and the Irish Party 1830–1847*. London: Hamish Hamilton, 1965.

Mandler, Peter. *Aristocratic Government in the Age of Reform*. Oxford: Clarendon Press, 1990.

McDowell, R.B. *Public Opinion and Government Policy in Ireland, 1801–1846*. London: Faber & Faber, 1952.

Michie, Elsie B. *Outside the Pale: Cultural Exclusion, Gender Difference, and the Victorian Woman Writer.* Ithaca, NY: Cornell University Press, 1993.

Mokyr, Joel. *Why Ireland Starved: A Quantitative and Analytical History of the Irish Economy, 1800–1850.* London: George Allen & Unwin, 1983.

Morash, Christopher. *Writing the Irish Famine.* Oxford: Clarendon Press, 1995.

Morash, Christopher, and Richard Hayes, eds. *"Fearful Realities": New Perspectives on the Famine.* Dublin: Irish Academic Press, 1996.

Nead, Lynda. *Myths of Sexuality: Representations of Women in Victorian Britain.* Oxford: Basil Blackwell, 1988.

Nowlan, Kevin B. *The Politics of Repeal.* London: Routledge & Kegan Paul, 1965.

O'Connor, Barbara, and Michael Cronin, eds. *Tourism in Ireland: A Critical Analysis.* Cork: Cork University Press, 1993.

O'Farrell, Patrick. *England and Ireland since 1800.* London: Oxford University Press, 1975.

O'Gráda, Cormac. *Black '47 and Beyond: The Great Irish Famine in History, Economy, and Memory.* Princeton: Princeton University Press, 1999.

———. *The Great Irish Famine.* London: MacMillan, 1989.

Paz, D.G. *Popular Anti-Catholicism in Mid-Victorian England.* Stanford: Stanford University Press, 1992.

Prest, John. *Lord John Russell.* London: MacMillan, 1972.

Reid, Stuart J. *Lord John Russell.* New York: Harper & Brothers, 1895.

Said, Edward. *Culture and Imperialism.* London: Chatto & Windus, 1993.

Scherer, Paul. *Lord John Russell: A Biography.* Selinsgrove: Susquehanna University Press, 1999.

Shipkey, Robert Carl. *Robert Peel's Irish Policy: 1812–1846.* New York: Garland Publishing, 1987.

Sloan, Barry. *The Pioneers of Anglo-Irish Fiction 1800–1850.* Gerrards Cross, Buckinghamshire: Colin Smythe, 1986.

Stepan, Nancy. *The Idea of Race in Science: Great Britain 1800–1960.* Hamden, CT: Archon Books, 1982.

Stephen, Sir Leslie, and Sir Sidney Lee, eds. *The Dictionary of National Biography.* 21 vols. Oxford: Oxford University Press, 1917–.

Street, Brian. *The Savage in Literature: Representations of "Primitive" Society in English Fiction 1858–1920.* London: Routledge & Kegan Paul, 1975.

Sturgis, James L. *John Bright and the Empire.* London: Athlone Press, 1969.

Sullivan, Eileen A. *William Carleton.* Boston: Twayne, 1983.

Swift, Roger, and Sheridan Gilley, eds. *The Irish in Britain 1815–1939.* London: Pinter, 1989.

———. *The Irish in the Victorian City.* London: Croom Helm, 1985.

Waters, Maureen. *The Comic Irishman.* Albany: State University of New York Press, 1984.

Wolff, Robert Lee. *William Carleton, Irish Peasant Novelist: A Preface to His Fiction.* New York: Garland, 1980.

Woodham-Smith, Cecil. *The Great Hunger.* New York: Harper & Row, 1962.

Zach, Wolfgang, and Heinz Kosok, eds. *Literary Interrelations: Ireland, England and the World.* 3 vols. Gunter Narr Verlag Tübingen, 1987.

ARTICLES

Arnstein, Walter L. "Victorian Prejudice Reexamined." *Victorian Studies* 12 (June 1969): 452–457.

Brewer, Jr., Kenneth L. "Colonial Discourse and William Makepeace Thackeray's *Irish Sketch Book.*" *Papers on Language and Literature* 29 (Summer 1993): 259–283.

D'Arcy, Fergus. "The Irish in 19th Century Britain: Reflections on Their Rôle and Experience." *Irish History Workshop* (1981), 3–12.

Deane, Seamus. "Irish National Character 1790–1900," in *The Writer as Witness*, Tom Dunne, ed. (Cork: Cork University Press, 1987), 16: 90–113.

———. "The Production of Cultural Space in Irish Writing." *Boundary 2* 21 (Fall 1994): 117–144.

Ellis, John S. "Reconciling the Celt: Identity, Empire and the 1911 Investiture of the Prince of Wales." *Journal of British Studies* 37 (October 1998): 391–418.

Gibbons, Luke. "Race Against Time: Racial Discourse and Irish History." *Oxford Literary Review* 13 (1991): 95–117.

Gilley, Sheridan. "English Attitudes to the Irish in England, 1780–1900." In *Immigrants and Minorities in British Society*, Colin Holmes, ed. London: Allen & Unwin, 1978, 81–110.

Gray, Peter. "*Punch* and the Great Famine." *History-Ireland* 1 (Summer 1993): 26–33.

Hart, Jenifer. "Sir Charles Trevelyan at the Treasury." *English Historical Review* 75 (January 1960): 92–110.

Hernon, Joseph M. "A Victorian Cromwell: Sir Charles Trevelyan, the Famine, and the Age of Improvement." *Eire-Ireland* 22 (1987): 15–29.

Large, David. "The House of Lords and Ireland in the Age of Peel, 1832–50." *Irish Historical Studies* 9 (September 1955): 367– 399.

Lebow, Richard N. "British Images of Poverty in Pre-Famine Ireland." In *Views of the Irish Peasantry 1800–1916*, Daniel J. Casey and Robert E. Rhodes, eds. Hamden, Conn.: Archon Books, 1977, 57–85.

Morley, Tom. "'The Arcana of that Great Machine': Politicians and *The Times* in the Late 1840s." *History* 73 (February 1988): 38–54.

Neal, Frank. "Liverpool, the Irish Steamship Companies and the Famine Irish." *Immigrants & Minorities* 5 (March 1986): 28–61.

Nelson, James Malcolm. "From Rory and Paddy to Boucicault's Myles, Shaun and Conn: The Irishman on the London Stage, 1830–1860." *Eire-Ireland* 13 (Fall 1978): 79–105.

O'Neill, Thomas P. "Food Problems during the Great Irish Famine." *Journal of the Royal Society of Antiquaries of Ireland* 82 (1952): 99–108.

Ò Tuathaigh, M.A.G. "The Irish in Nineteenth Century Britain: Problems of Integration." *Transactions of the Royal Historical Society* 31 (1981): 149–174.

Swift, Roger. "The Outcast Irish in the Victorian City: Problems and Perspectives." *Irish Historical Studies* 25 (1987).

Touhill, Blanche M. "*The Times versus* William Smith O'Brien." *Victorian Periodicals Review* 15 (Summer 1982): 52–63.

Werly, John. "The Irish in Manchester 1832–49." *Irish Historical Studies* 18 (March 1973): 345–358.

Woods, C.J. "Irish Travel Writings as Source Material." *Irish Historical Studies* 28 (November 1992): 171–183.

PERIODICALS

Dictionary of National Biography
The Anglo-Saxon (1849)
Journal of the Ethnological Society of London (1848–1856)
Manchester Guardian (1840–1860)
Times (London; 1840–1860)

UNPUBLISHED MATERIALS

Bernt, Phyllis Weinroth. "William Makepeace Thackeray and the Irish: A Study in Victorian Prejudice." University of Nebraska Ph.D. 1979.

MANUSCRIPT SOURCES

British Library (London)

Bright MSS (Additional Manuscripts 43383–43389)
Croker MSS (Additional Manuscript 41129)
Gladstone MSS (Additional Manuscripts 44088–44565)
Peel MSS (Additional Manuscripts 40440–40594)

News International Archives (London)

Delane MSS (Vols. 2–3, 1845–1850)

Public Record Office (London)

Russell MSS (PRO 30/22): 1846–1852
Home Office files (HO 45), relating to Ireland & Irish: 1840–1860

West Sussex Record Office (Chichester)

Labouchere MSS (files 336–341)

Index

Carthage, Irish origins in, 38
Cassell, John, 132
Chambers, Robert, views on race,
  118–19
Chambers, William, views on Ireland,
  27
Charlton, J., views on Ireland, 65
Chartists, 59, 84, 111, 113–14, 163;
  Irish Chartists, 145
Clanricarde, Lord: and famine policy,
  69; views on Ireland, 66
Clarendon, George Villiers, Earl of:
  and coercion, 66, 83–84; and fam-
  ine policy, 68, 83–85; and *Times*,
  77, 94 n.160
Class: role in English view of Irish, 3,
  5–6, 142–48. *See also* England: Irish
  immigration to, workers of; Land-
  lords, Irish
Cobden, Richard, 58, 146
Coercion acts, 59, 63–64, 66–67,
  83–84, 94 n.156, 113
Cork, harbor and arsenal at, 75
Corn Law repeal, 63–64, 98, 101
Corner, Julia, view of Irish history,
  151–52
Cottenham, Lord, and famine policy,
  69
Cromwell, Oliver, 2, 69, 90 n.54, 120
Cruikshank, George, 28
Curtis, Lewis Perry, Jr., 3–4, 16 n.9,
  29, 45, 119, 162, 166 n.2
Cuvier, Georges, 120

Dangerfield, George, 19
Davies, John, view of Irish, 8
Deane, Seamus, 148
De Grey, Thomas Philip, second earl,
  56, 59
Delane, John Thadeus, 12, 46, 109;
  and Daniel O'Connell, 99; relations
  with government, 77, 94 n.160
Devon Commission, 20, 46, 58

Disraeli, Benjamin, 80; and Ireland,
  57, 63
Dublin, Industrial Exhibition in, 141
Dublin Evening Post, 149
Dufferin, Lord, views on Ireland, 85
Duffy, Charles Gavan, 112

Edgeworth, Maria, 36, 40, 43; *Castle
  Rackrent*, 35; *Essay on Irish Bulls*,
  44–45
Edinburgh Review, 82
Ellis, George, theories on race, 131–32
Encumbered Estates Act (1849), 85
England: characteristics of people, 11,
  13, 23–24, 29–30, 37–38, 74, 109,
  119, 132, 134, 137, 149–51, 153
  n.10, 154 n.23; fear of food shortages in, 76, 112; financial crisis in,
  81, 83, 112; Irish immigration to,
  10, 13–14, 31, 101, 104–5,
  112–13, 130, 142–48, 163–64;
  workers of, 76, 85, 88 n.20, 107,
  112–13, 130, 142–48, 152, 164
Ensor, Thomas, views on Ireland,
  65–66

Famine of 1846–1852, 2, 14; charitable response to, 106–8, 114, 124
  n.44; effect on English views of
  Irish, 5–6, 9–12, 97–121, 129–30,
  152, 163–64; effect on Irish opinion, 114–15, 136, 140, 149; encourages settlement, 135; historical
  studies of, 4, 9–10, 151–52; potato
  blight, 61–66; response of British
  government to, 70–87
Fenianism, 162
Foley, Timothy, 29, 149
Forbes, John, views on Ireland, 135
Fortescue, Lord, views on Ireland, 85
Foster, Roy, 45, 60, 86, 111
Foster, Thomas Campbell, "Irish Commissioner," 46–48, 76, 78, 99–100,
  104, 121

O'Connell, Daniel, 10, 20, 56, 79; and
Chartism, 145; criticism of, 46, 99,
123 n.36; death of, 113; and famine, 70–71, 106; and Repeal Association, 23–24, 59; and Lord John
Russell, 67; trial and imprisonment
of, 60–61, 88 n.12
O'Connor, Feargus, 145
Otway, Rev. Caesar, views on Ireland,
34
Owen-Madden, Daniel, views on Ireland, 22–23, 25, 30–31, 39

Palmerston, Lady Emily Lamb Cowper,
82
Palmerston, Lord Henry John Temple,
14, 161; and coercion, 84, 139–40;
and famine policy, 69, 72, 82
Peel, Sir Robert, 55; and famine policy,
72, 79, 106; Irish policies of, 56–67,
70, 161–62; response to potato
blight, 61–66, 70–72, 80, 86–87,
104; view of Irish, 64
Perceval, M.P., views on Ireland, 24
Pius IX, Pope, 69
Playfair, Lyon, and potato blight,
65–66, 90 n.40
Poor Law, application to Ireland, 11,
21–22, 37, 65, 67, 78–83, 85,
102–3
Poor Removal Act (1847), 145
Prichard, James Cowles, views on race,
30, 118, 120–21, 132
Priests, Irish: criticized, 40, 105–6,
117, 139, 151; and potato blight,
65; state support of, 57. See also Religion
Punch, portrayals of Irish in, 45, 111

Quakers, charitable activities of,
107–8, 114

Race: famine and, 9–10, 12, 76–78,
99–100; gender and, 4–5; historical

studies of, 2–5, 14, 16 n.9, 16 n.13,
29; imperialism and, 6–9; Irish
views of, 29, 148–50; liberal view
of, 10–13, 22, 29–31, 33, 46, 68,
104, 106, 108, 132–33; racialism,
2–10, 12–13, 31, 46–48, 68, 73,
76–78, 98–100, 104, 109–11,
115–21, 129–38, 144–45, 148,
150–52, 162–66; scientific theories
of, 12, 30–31, 48, 90 n.40, 98–99,
118–21, 130–33, 150, 164
Radnor, Lord William
Pleydell-Bouverie, and famine relief,
81
Railroads: and famine, 79–81, 112;
and tourism, 141
Rate-in-Aid Act (1849), 85
Relief Destitute Persons (Ireland) Act
(1847), 78–79
Religion, 33; anti-Catholicism, 28,
39–40, 69, 105–6, 116–18, 123
n.36, 135, 139–40, 143–44; evangelicalism in government, 9–10,
86–87, 95 nn.173–74, 122 n.10;
and famine, 13, 86–87, 100, 105,
139–40; fanaticism decried, 40,
102, 105, 140; and Irish immigration, 143–44, 148; role in English
view of Irish, 3, 39–40, 133,
139–40
Repeal Association, 10, 20, 23–25, 27,
32, 59–60, 64, 88 n.12, 106, 114,
162; collapse of, 113
Ricardo, David, views on Ireland, 103
Rogers, Jasper, views on Irish, 149–50
Russell, Lady Frances Elliot, 74
Russell, Lord John, 14, 55; attitudes
toward Irish, 4, 68, 74; and coercion, 66–67, 70, 73, 83–84, 94
n.156; Irish policies, 9, 11–12,
60–63, 67–68, 102–3, 161–62; and
Daniel O'Connell, 67; personal
flaws, 68, 86; response to blight and

About the Author

EDWARD G. LENGEL is an assistant editor with the Papers of George Washington documentary editing project in Charlottesville, Virginia.